SONG *of* DEWEY BEARD

LAST SURVIVOR OF THE LITTLE BIGHORN

PHILIP BURNHAM

University of Nebraska Press
Lincoln and London

Publication of this volume was
assisted by a grant from the
Friends of the University
of Nebraska Press.

Library of Congress
Cataloging-in-Publication Data
Burnham, Philip
Song of Dewey Beard:
last survivor of the Little Bighorn
/ Philip Burnham.
pages   cm
Includes bibliographical
references and index.
ISBN 978-0-8032-6936-1 (cloth: alk. paper)
ISBN 978-0-8032-6941-5 (epub)
ISBN 978-0-8032-6942-2 (mobi)
ISBN 978-0-8032-6940-8 (pdf)
1. Dakota Indians—South
Dakota—Biography. 2. Little
Bighorn, Battle of the, Mont.,
1876—Biography. 3. Dakota
Indians—Wars, 1876.
4. Wounded Knee Massacre,
S.D., 1890—Biography. 5. Dakota
Indians—Wars, 1890–1891.
6. South Dakota—Biography.
I. Beard, Dewey. II. Title.
E99.D1B93 2014   973.8'2092—dc23
[B]
2014017332

Set in Scala by Renni Johnson.
Designed by N. Putens.

For Michele

CONTENTS

ILLUSTRATIONS

PREFACE

Most biographies are written about people who are already famous: generals and actors, outlaws and artists, presidents and popes. But Dewey Beard's achievement is different. You'd be hard pressed to find an essay about him, much less a movie or a book. That's because his life was both epic and quiet, a man better remembered for what he endured than what he wrote, for what he saw than what he said. He was a warrior turned peacemaker, a survivor turned showman, an old man who outlived all of his children. In some ways his story is a representative one for a century of Plains Indian life. But his personal journey was an extraordinary saga by any measure.

When I found Dewey Beard, he was buried in an unmarked grave. There were no books about him. He didn't leave any letters to speak of, and most of the elders who knew him were gone. One day a local church official, in response to my questions about the old man, said sadly, "You're ten years too late."

I didn't believe him. I had taught years before in Lakota country, and I knew something about the people who lived there and how they respect the ancestors. Though not Lakota, or even Indian, I started going back to South Dakota every summer to piece together the story of Beard's life.

I soon came to realize it was more complicated than one life. I met some people who helped me along the way, and they became part of the story too, the story of a warrior and his people.

ACKNOWLEDGMENTS

This book would not have been possible without the many voices that appear in it. I am profoundly grateful to the late Marie Fox Belly, Leonard Little Finger, the late Francis Apple Sr., Evelyn Beard Yankton, Corliss Besselievre, Ernie and Sonja LaPointe, Mario Gonzalez, Geneva Wilcox, Rex Herman, Paul Herman, Birgil Kills Straight, Dave Kadlecek, Bill Groethe, Bob Lee, Putt Thompson, James Aplan, James Tidball, Lili Mae One Feather, Frosty Garnett, and the late Albert White Hat Sr. Many of them talked with me year after year, and they did so with all the compassion and good humor that made my effort a labor of love. Any mistakes or confusion in this book are of my doing, not theirs.

Many others who don't appear in the book were essential allies in completing the project. Among these are Harold Compton of the Bureau of Indian Affairs, Bernie Hunhoff of *South Dakota Magazine*, Joe Whiting, Michelle May of Oglala Lakota College, Pete and Kathy Newman, Charles Rambow, Doug Johns, Charles Trimble, and Richmond Clow at the University of Montana.

Much of my research was aided by the guiding hand of archivists and librarians across the country. These include LaVera Rose, Marty Frog, and Joel Minor at Oglala Lakota College; Nichole Ray at the University of Wisconsin–Eau Claire; Danelle Orange at Dakota Wesleyan University; Rod Ross, Mary Frances Ronan, and George Briscoe of the National Archives in Washington, DC; Ken Stewart and Matthew Reitzel at the South Dakota State Archives; Mark Thiel at Marquette University; Peter Strong at the Red Cloud Heritage Center and Jamie Behan at Red Cloud Indian School; Mary Robinson at the McCracken Library of the Buffalo Bill Center for the West; Elizabeth Thrond at the Center for Western Studies at Augustana College; Steve Friesen of the Buffalo Bill Museum; Hope Wallace of the Wassenberg

Art Center; Susan Kasten of *Beloit College Magazine*; Jean Gosebrink of the St. Louis Public Library; Sharon Smith of the Missouri Historical Society; Shannon Bowen of the American Heritage Center of the University of Wyoming; Carl Hallberg of the Wyoming State Archives; Jo Anna Scherer and Michelle Delaney of the Smithsonian Institution; Barbara Rotness of the Montana Historical Society; and Rev. Vincent Heier, David Grua, Donovin Sprague, and Martha Miller. I also would like to thank Sandi Solomon of the David Miller Estate. There are others who helped along the way, and I apologize for any oversight in neglecting to mention them.

My travels were long and sometimes exhausting. Along the way, many people gave me a place to rest and recover: Dennis and Sandy Gaspar, Mary McNally, Sharon Small, Brad Hamlett, the Pucketts at Lakota Prairie Ranch, and all of my family near Chicago.

Those who had a direct hand in producing the book gave exceptional support as well: Erin Greb for cartography; Heather Stauffer for editorial assistance; my anonymous readers at University of Nebraska Press for suggesting key improvements to the manuscript; my copy editor, Jonathan Lawrence, whose judgment was tactful and unerring; Sabrina Stellrecht, who efficiently guided the book during the production process; and especially my acquiring editor, Matt Bokovoy, who was knowledgeable, discerning, and supportive from start to finish.

Page Miller, Brian Brown, and Robbi Scharfe were with me the night I got the idea for the book and offered early encouragement. My family in Illinois and Washington State provided comfort and support, as they always have, when the road became a long one. Michele McDonagh, Greg Burnham, and Rod Ross read the manuscript when it was still rough and offered valuable advice for improvement.

I also owe a special debt to my long-ago friends and colleagues, living and passed, whom I knew at Sinte Gleska. They set in motion the long arc of this book years before I ever started it.

Finally, Michele did everything within her power to see the book through to the end. She is compassionate, strong, and wise. Her devotion made a long labor doable. And I'm thankful for Mallory, who has found many others who also appreciate her talents.

INTRODUCTION

It was a June day in 1955 when Dewey Beard sang his family's death song in a room of the Hotel Alex Johnson in downtown Rapid City, South Dakota. It was the last weekend of spring. I was three and a half years old. President Eisenhower had just announced that he was extending the military draft, while medical experts were recommending the Salk polio vaccine be continued through the summer. In Rapid City, *The Far Country*, a Western starring James Stewart and Walter Brennan, was opening at the State Theater.

Beard, who was living in a shack in a nearby Indian shantytown, had been summoned to the hotel for an interview. The eleven-story building still looms large in Rapid City, a blocky, gabled Tudor fort that went up in the 1920s. From the street, the half-timber and brick speaks of a Black Forest pedigree, while inside, entered from Sixth Street, it looks more like a lobby out of the heyday of national park lodges.

The interior must have impressed the old man, by then over ninety years old. From the high arched ceiling hung a chandelier of Indian war lances, the room decorated then much as it is now. The wooden columns are set on sculpted busts of Native warriors. The fireplace is cut from Black Hills stone. On the mantel sits a photo of founder Alex Johnson garbed in Native dress, a vice president of the Chicago and Northwestern Railroad who couldn't get enough of Indians and went by the local honorific Chief Red Star.

Johnson's hotel was the classiest watering hole for miles. It had its own radio studio and a bar with a merry-go-round platform. Franklin Roosevelt spent the night in 1936 when he came to dedicate the Lincoln face on Mount Rushmore—come to think of it, Gutzum Borglum, the Rushmore sculptor, did too. Over the years many a Hollywood cast for B Western movies has tasted the medicinal waters of the celebrated inn.[1]

On June 18 Dewey walked through the lobby with his wife, Alice, and a pair of friends from Sturgis. He was dressed in full Lakota regalia—beaded buckskins, moccasins, an eagle feather headdress, ermine skin tassels. The foursome boarded an elevator and ascended to their rendezvous. I often wonder what Beard, a man who probably didn't walk up a staircase until he was an adult, would have thought of a cage that glided up and down the interior shaft of a building with the push of a button.

They were supposed to come with John Sitting Bull, stepson of the famous Lakota warrior and medicine man of the same name. John was going to be interviewed by *National Geographic* for a feature on South Dakota. Since he was a deaf-mute he needed a translator, and his friend Dewey Beard, fluent in Indian sign language, volunteered. But Beard couldn't speak English. So, as he converted John's signs into Lakota, the editors planned, another translator would put it in the American vernacular. It was a rather elaborate game of telephone for a group of old Indian men to be playing.

But John died a few days before the interview. And that made Dewey Beard something of a novelty. He was now the last man standing from the Battle of the Little Bighorn, he claimed, the last to draw breath who had fought in the encounter that shocked America seventy-nine years before. There he sat, facing a spectacled white man in a sport coat and bow tie with a reel-to-reel tape recorder planted before him. The reporter greeted Dewey and Alice and thrust out his microphone, hungry for stories of how the Indians rubbed out Custer. He clicked the knob, and the spindles began to turn.

Fifty years later, I stumbled across that tape in the Library of Congress in Washington. It was only an accident I came on it at all, just a vaguely familiar name in a catalog. I called up the recording, settled into a sound-proof room, and told the technician to roll it. As I sat back and listened, the crackling and popping tape started to turn. What I heard first was an old man, raspy-voiced and confident, who crowed, "Wasu Maza emaciyapilo." "My name is Iron Hail."

Then he did something strange. He sang a song, a cappella. The pitch started high at the crest and plunged like a rapid shooting star, a descending

Plains chant from long ago. There were just a few words, which I had to translate later:

Oglala people,
Tell about me in a good way.
I am a warrior.

He ended with two loud yips.

An hour later, at the end of the interview, he sang the death song he had long ago chanted for his family. And Dewey Beard was dead before the year was out.[2]

For me, his story had just begun.

1

ORIGINS AND FAMILY

When Dewey Beard died, nobody could say for sure how old he was. The Indian Office, the bureaucratic czar of Native America, recorded his birth as 1862 in the yearly censuses. One direct descendant claims 1856. By 1907, when Beard told an interviewer he was forty-three, he seems to have shed a couple years. And by midcentury he had become ninety-three, or ninety-eight, or ninety-nine, picking up a little time here and there over the course of what had been a rich and adventurous life. The longer he lived, the harder his years were to measure. In a world where birth certificates were unknown and dates imprecise, Indian ages often shifted with the season. Dewey Beard eludes all those vital statistics that biographies usually rely on.[1]

What Beard saw in a lifetime was as big and bold and astonishing as a Dakota sky in full summer. As an adolescent he rode his buckskin pony up Deep Coulee and shot a U.S. trooper at the Little Bighorn. In his thirties he took at least two bullets at Wounded Knee and watched as half his family was killed. A half century later he was wrangling with the U.S. Army over ownership of his homestead. He was a nephew of Crazy Horse, a companion of Sitting Bull, a follower of Big Foot, an employee of Buffalo Bill Cody, and an acquaintance of bigwigs from matinee heartthrob Robert Taylor to the intrepid General Nelson Miles. Beard homesteaded, horse wrangled, buffalo hunted, movie acted, Ghost Danced, counted coup, killed in battle, and tasted the body of Christ in holy communion. "He's ranked up there with Dale Carnegie," laughs great-nephew Leonard Little Finger, who remembers that their obituaries appeared on the same page in *Time* magazine. Dewey Beard was an American original.[2]

His life spanned from the blood-soaked years of Gettysburg and Cold Harbor to the button-down decade of the 1950s. When he was born, Abraham Lincoln was probably still alive; when he died, Disneyland had just opened its doors. As Beard boasted to a visiting congressional committee in 1955, "I am 97 years old, but I am going to live to be 140." Given the spectacle of a wrinkled old Lakota warrior waving his fist at them, they must have been worried he was dead serious. Dewey Beard was as fearless talking to the Committee on Interior and Insular Affairs as he had been the day he saw Major Marcus Reno and the U.S. Seventh Cavalry riding toward the Indian camp on the Little Bighorn River some eighty summers before. He didn't flinch either time. But he didn't quite make it to 140 either. Two months after testifying, Beard was dead. It was one of the rare occasions the old man didn't keep his word.[3]

I can't tell his story in the conventional way. Dewey Beard's life can't be fixed on a typeset page, or stuffed in a photo album, or written with a briefcase full of facts. To do that, I would have to start with where he was born. It was on a bend of the Niobrara River in Nebraska, Leonard Little Finger tells me. But it wasn't in any place you could point to. And the year is open to question. So how do you begin the life of a man if you don't know where or when he was born? Or don't have any letters? Or aren't even sure who his mother was?

You write a different kind of story.

So let me start again: Dewey Beard was born about 1862. The president would have been Lincoln—or, if earlier, James Buchanan—sitting astride the bloodiest war in American history. Beard wasn't born in the States exactly, since the Niobrara would have been in Nebraska Territory, not incorporated as a state until 1867. And the Minneconjou Lakotas, a subtribe of the Western Sioux he was born in, were spread across what became the Dakota Territory in 1861, later divided into North and South Dakota. His people were an expansive and nomadic group that lived well beyond the battle lines of the Civil War. At the time of the faraway Confederate surrender in 1865, Beard was a young boy, perhaps an infant, too young to grasp its significance or even to have heard of it. By the time he was thirty, however, Dewey Beard would know what complete military defeat meant in depressing detail, and would never be allowed to relinquish the lesson.

He was a man of many names. He was called Many Wounded Holes, it seems, as early as 1880, suggesting some serious adventures in battle as a youth, though Indian names are easily misinterpreted. Rather mysteriously, his named turned to Whiskers by 1886, and soon after to Putinhin, a Lakota word meaning "hair on the upper lip." Indian names can be slippery, and their translations into English are often careless. But it was a small step from Putinhin to Beard, the name that stuck with him for the better part of a life. In fact, he may have been dubbed so because he had stirrings of facial hair, an unusual trait for a full-blood Indian. Whatever the reason, he went by "Beard" on the early ration rolls, and the name stuck. It was good enough until, about the turn of the century, the authorities decided Indians needed a second name. And so Many Wounded Holes, aka Whiskers, or Putinhin, the man officially known as Beard, was at last christened Dewey and ever after bore a full Christian name that might have been proudly worn to Sunday church by the most pious Presbyterian.[4]

Beard formally referred to himself through his adult life as Wasu Maza (in English, Iron Hail), a name taken from of one of his uncles and perhaps given for a battle episode in which Whiskers proved his mettle. As they grew older, it was common for Lakota males to earn names based on a personal exploit, a vision, or a name borrowed from a relative. Wasu Maza was his tribal mark, not the public name of Beard he used in church and town, the white world of wooden pews and frame houses and barbed-wire fences. It was as if Beard had two selves, each with its own name, its own language, and its own rules, reflecting the long track his life would take after a quiet birth in a buffalo tipi on the Niobrara River.[5]

His genealogy is impressive but patchy. His brother Joe said their great-grandfather was Black Buffalo, the Lakota chief who confronted Lewis and Clark in 1804 and later signed the Portage des Sioux Treaty before being given a military funeral in 1815. Putinhin himself said Crazy

Horse was an uncle, it would seem on his mother's side. And Hump, the Minneconjou warrior and U.S. Army scout, was probably his uncle or cousin. Beard's father was Horned Cloud (later shortened to Horn Cloud), who was said to have scouted for General William Harney in the early 1850s, following Black Buffalo's example in befriending the government, at least until their way of life was threatened. Horn Cloud was a friend, perhaps a cousin, of Spotted Elk (Big Foot), whose name has been tied to a small creek named Wounded Knee ever since he made camp there on a cold day in December 1890.[6]

Horn Cloud had several wives, probably more than one at a time, a common practice among the Lakotas. But the identity of Dewey Beard's birth mother remains a mystery. Some think she was Nest, who followed Horn Cloud to an untimely grave. Others, like Marie Fox Belly, Beard's great-granddaughter, think his real mother was wounded at Little Bighorn and later died in Canada while a refugee, buried near Moose Jaw. Nest, says Marie, was probably no more than his stepmother, a later wife of Horn Cloud. Other mysteries abound: Was Beard related to Sitting Bull, as some in the family claim? How close was the connection to Crazy Horse? Was Lone Horn, a powerful and famous chief, an ancestor? Whenever a descendant sketches for me a Beard family tree, it looks more like a creeper than a cottonwood, a scrambled, improvisational bush that changes shape every time it comes into leaf.

According to his South Dakota death certificate, Beard was born in March 1858. Marie says it happened in summer, though, when the big green horseflies were biting. But documents and stories about Beard rarely agree. He never showed Marie where he was born on a map, she admitted one day, but "I always wondered."[7]

Marie is a rememberer. She's the unofficial keeper of Dewey Beard stories, culled from years of listening to her elders. Almost sixty years have passed since his death, and on a reservation where life expectancy is ten years less than the national average, stories can get lost along the way. Her mother, Celane, was raised by Beard and was one of the last of the elders who knew him well. She died in 1998. Marie refers to Beard as *kaka*, grandfather. She speaks with a soothing and lilting cadence about

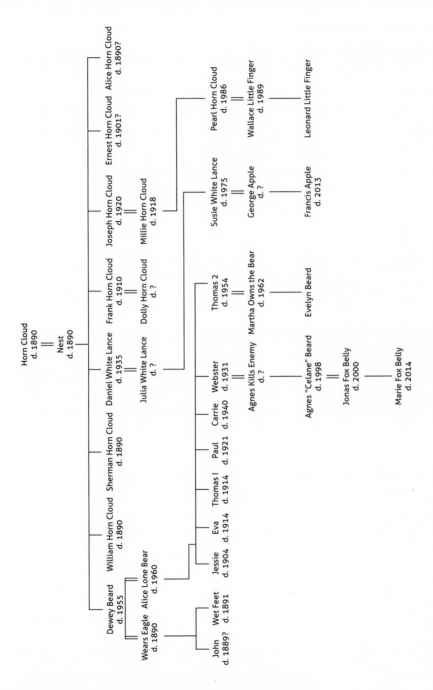

Horn Cloud's People: A Partial Family Tree (Erin Greb Cartography)

Kaka Beard, a man she recalls with surprising familiarity considering she was only four years old when he died.[8]

"I remember growing up and being a little girl but being close to my grandfather," she says one day, sitting in a paper-strewn office in the old hospital on the Pine Ridge Reservation. The radio leaks a sad trail of country-and-western ballads in the background. "I trailed him, I sat by him. When I was smaller and growing up, I didn't quite have all my teeth, so he would chew my meat for me and set them on the table beside my bowl like little haystacks. I ate with him, chased horses with him."

The first stories she tells are endearing and girlish. Marie says people are often surprised she knows so much. "I heard it all from listening to Kaka Beard. I guess I take it for granted that everyone knows." Dewey and his wife, Alice, raised Celane, so Marie says they were more like grandparents to her than great-grandparents. "Every day I think about it, I thank my parents for allowing me to know them."

Marie's recounting is a feat of memory—but whose memory? She was barely four when her great-grandfather died. How much can a four-year-old remember? When I ask about the name Beard, she says his whole name was Hawk's Beard. So how did he get that name, I ask. "I'll have to remember," she says. I'm not sure what that means, exactly—whether she's going to burrow deeper into her memory, or talk to someone else about it, or buy some time to come up with something that sounds plausible. When I note that Beard's official age seems to shift with the wind, she stiffens. "He was born in 1856," she says curtly. "He told me that. He knew when he was born."

Marie's mother would have known Beard as well as anyone. Born on Christmas day in 1928, Celane was only two when her father, Webster Beard, died, officially of tuberculosis. Marie claims he was murdered, though she isn't sure why. It has the makings of a tall tale, but I learn not to discard her stories out of hand. This is a culture whose main form of entertainment and education for centuries was telling stories—and in many families still is. Grandpa Beard once told Celane that if she didn't remember the stories he told her, she would be lost. And she seems to have done the same with her daughter, telling Marie much about Dewey and Alice that a little girl couldn't possibly have observed, but which she recounts in middle age with all the easy confidence of an oracle.[9]

There seems to be no difference, where Grandpa Beard is concerned, between what Marie has heard and what she's seen. Whenever we talk, I realize I'm hearing the oral tradition in action.

Marie is a mystery. When I first met her she was going by her maiden name, Not Help Him, though she'd been married for years. Names have a literal meaning in many cultures, but tracing their origins in Indian country is hard. For many Indians, the census names were handed out as casually as a bag of coffee on ration day, and though some Lakota names were given systematically by the government, they were often based on an ancestor's feat, a truncated phrase, a bad translation: Short Bull, Forgets Nothing, Her Many Horses, Gunhammer, American Horse. Not Help Him was somehow earned by a family ancestor long ago and passed down as a surname. But it made me nervous. Whenever I wrote or typed Not Help Him on a page, I was a little worried it would uncork the genie of the name. When I found that Marie changed her surname to Fox Belly a few years later, I was relieved—at least until I found out that Fox Belly was well known to Dewey Beard and died in the U.S. penitentiary in Leavenworth.[10]

Beard's father was Horn Cloud, a man who met his end at "the place of the great killing," *owicakte tanka*, as the Lakotas call Wounded Knee. Horn Cloud's father, by one account, was Yellow Hawk II, and his grandfather was Yellow Hawk I, who married an *iyeska* (mixed-blood) woman of French and Lakota descent. So says Leonard Little Finger, a man old enough today to have spent time with Beard when he was in his teens.

Leonard has a quiet but forceful pride. He's a diabetic, a common malady on the reservation, and suffers from numbness in his hands. Now in his seventies, he uses a walker to get around, his gait halting but determined. Like Marie, he's a fluent Lakota speaker, a skill only people over fifty are likely to have anymore. And like his ancestors, he refers to male siblings of a male parent or grandparent as "father" or "grandfather." "In our value system, to have a grandfather is extended, too," he explains. Dewey—in white terms Leonard's great-uncle—is the only Horn Cloud brother from that generation that Leonard knew. His maternal grandfather, Joseph, died in 1920, almost twenty years before Leonard was born. "Dewey was the one who called me grandson."[11]

I first met Leonard the day a dozen junior high graduates gathered for a naming ceremony in a school gym near Oglala on Pine Ridge. They looked like urban punks, turned out in baggy shorts, T-shirts, and wild haircuts, jittery at being the center of so much adult attention. After a cleansing with ceremonial sweetgrass smoke, they knelt on a red cloth one by one while a relative came up to pin a feather in their hair and give them an Indian name. (One of the boys had a burr haircut, so his dad tied the feather around his forehead with a string.) After a public feed of buffalo stew, they had a Lakota "giveaway" in honor of the graduates, and Leonard, then a teacher at the school, went home with a Pendleton blanket. The Lakotas give things away, valuable things, at every public function—generosity has been one of their cardinal virtues as long as anyone can remember.

Leonard tells how his grandfather Joe was Dewey's younger brother, perhaps his half brother. Joe was one of the few in the family to have any schooling, and his English was good enough to translate for outsiders, including the visit, in the fall of 1913, of William "Buffalo Bill" Cody, an autumn the Horn Clouds would long remember. Joe often translated for Dewey, whose English was poor even at life's end. Leonard still collects lease money from part of Joe's land allotment, made by the government a century ago.

Leonard's father, Wallace, went to Haskell Indian School in Lawrence, Kansas. He studied office work and accounting, and after graduation he went back to Pine Ridge, where he worked for more than thirty years for the Bureau of Indian Affairs (BIA), the modern-day name of the Indian Office. He was a federal employee, which gave his family a rare middle-class income in a tough environment like Pine Ridge. Wallace's father, John, Leonard's other grandfather, ran horses and cattle on an allotment near Oglala. Young Leonard was pounding fencepost staples at age five for John, and driving teams of horses at ten, spending July of every summer putting up hay. "That was my foundation," he says proudly. Like grandfathers Joe Horn Cloud and Dewey Beard, John Little Finger was also a Wounded

Knee survivor. Leonard remembers John showing him his wounds when he was a young boy.

When he graduated eighth grade, Leonard went to boarding school in Pine Ridge. "I couldn't take it," he says. "It seemed like when they locked the doors behind us, it was like this huge brass door was banged shut, and it was locked, and I couldn't handle that. I probably had too much freedom before. So I ran away." Many elders on Pine Ridge have similar stories, the runaways called "incorrigibles" in official records. Leonard later reconciled himself to the classroom and became one of the first Indians to graduate from Chadron High School in northern Nebraska.[12]

Born in 1939, Leonard was in his teens when Grandpa Beard died. He remembers being at a powwow in Wyoming in the early 1950s when Beard asked him to come along to visit the Little Bighorn battlefield. So far as he knows, nobody else in the family had ever done that. But his father, who came from the other side of the family, insisted he stay and dance. The boy was crushed. "There's things in your life you regret," says Leonard softly. "In my life that was one of them."

It was only in the 1970s, when he read Alvin Toffler's *Future Shock*, that he could fathom what his grandfather had experienced. "Here's Grandpa Beard born in a tipi, born when there's still a territory that they have ownership to, that's their homeland," he says. "Then he's raised riding horseback, and learning how to survive and how to live. Then fast-forward, and in the later years he's living in that little shack in downtown Rapid City. Just in one generation."

Rev. Francis Apple Sr. is another great-nephew of Beard's. Father Apple's grandfather was Daniel White Lance, another of Beard's younger brothers, who was shot several times in the leg at Wounded Knee and lived until 1935. Like many on Pine Ridge, Francis has the blood of a Wounded Knee victim in his veins, a badge many Lakotas wear with pride. Francis is an ordained Episcopal minister. And a sun dancer. A former accounting student. And a demolitions expert. And a college professor. And . . . lots of other things, too, as it turns out.

When Francis talks, he's as hard to follow as a broken-field runner. He also has no teeth. You can lose the point of a story on a toothless syllable, I've learned. His tales, sprawling and funny, don't always have an ending. You have to sort out the digressions from the details, the punch lines from the asides. "Anyway, I've got a thousand things I want to tell you in two minutes," he gushes the first time we meet, over a plate of bacon and eggs at the only motel in town. Then his mouth gets the better of him.

"You want to hear about Dewey Beard, do you? He had all his teeth when he was ninety-seven and no gray hair, it was kind of gold looking. He didn't have no hearing aid—he was alert, he walked fine.

"He had over one hundred head of horses, they were so inbred nobody could ride them. They tried to break them, they were rodeo people, but they couldn't. You couldn't even fence them, they'd break right through the fence. Outlaw horses. If you show up on the hill where that herd is, they take off. They'd bunch up and the leader would take them. But Beard goes over there and brings them back into the corral. How he could do it, I don't know. He rides a whole team of horses, trying to bring that herd in, talks to them, corrals them." Francis wheezes a laugh and grins like a little kid.

He wants me to know he's writing a dictionary of Lakota phrases and proverbs, by the way. Francis recommends I buy the title, but when I ask the name, he pauses. "Words of Wisdom," he grumbles finally. He's writing four books at once, he explains. I ask him where I can buy this one. "Well, that's a long story, too." It turns out the book's not finished yet. "They don't want it at the college because they're jealous of it. I went on TV and said those guys are getting big money when they're sitting around computers and playing games all day long. But you don't tell the truth around here," he chuckles, or "you get in trouble."

Francis can sing the mass in Lakota. He went to seminary at Nashotah House near Milwaukee and was ordained at thirty-seven—they called him "the kid priest." He considers himself Catholic and Episcopalian both because, so far as he can figure, there's really not much difference. He talks about how the high cost of gas has made it hard for the Lakotas to go to church anymore. Which reminds him, he says, taking a sip of coffee: a Japanese tourist once asked him why Indians drive big cars and have rolls of fat on their belly if they're so poor. Francis told him they don't own the cars, for one, the finance companies do. And the food, he says, looking at me suspiciously between bites of bacon, "you guys are responsible for."

I yank him back to Dewey's horses. "Beard had a little bay horse he used to ride," Francis starts up again. "He never ran the horse, just trotted it. But he could round up his horses. They were like deer to anyone else. But he would talk to them, and he would bring them in. They just knew him." Francis sizes me up for a moment. He's wearing a madras shirt with a blue jean coat turned up at the collar. His thin, graying hair is combed over his head, a grizzled but gentle look on his face. He peers at me across the table through his tinted glasses. Then he launches into the time they misdiagnosed his diabetes as hepatitis B, and he went on drinking big liters of Squirt for a year before they figured out their mistake. He thinks that was funny.

His granddaughter totaled his Monte Carlo truck the other day, he says suddenly. And that reminds him how Dewey Beard's son Tommy used to drive his fancy Chevy around, and once they were doing a tour in the Black Hills and their windshield wipers went out in a storm. So they got a big string and tied it to both wipers and pulled it back and forth so they could see. "They improvised," he says with a toothless smile, a skill no doubt inherited from their ancestors.

Francis was in his mid-twenties when Beard died. He had to have known the old man better than Marie or Leonard. So I want to visit him again. He promises he'll take me out to the old Beard allotment next time. How far is that? I ask. "A hop and two skips." That reminds Francis of, well, . . . another story. In the old days when Indians used to have really bad tires on their cars, they were curious about distances. "How far is Wanbli?" someone would ask. "Uh, you have to pump up your tire twice before you get there." Francis doesn't go for long without a wink and a nudge.

A group of young people sitting in the next booth suddenly breaks out in a ceremonial song. Francis winces. They're only supposed to sing that during a sweat bath, he says. He learned how to sing some of the old Lakota songs, though he's been slow to pass them on. There were warrior songs, death songs, social songs, ceremonial songs. Some get passed on, he says, and some don't.

I feel lucky that Francis is still alive. That's when I tell him about the Dewey Beard tape I found back in Washington. As soon as I do, he looks at me for the first time like I'm serious.

"I know that song," he says. "It's a warrior song. Someday I'll sing it for you."

Years go by before he ever gets around to it.

2

GROWING UP

The boy who would be called Putinhin grew up on the vast inland sea of the northern plains. His people migrated across an enormous area that stretches from the Sand Hills of northern Nebraska to the draws and ravines of eastern Wyoming, then up across the frozen ocean of eastern Montana, and over and down the badlands and buttes, the washes and dry gullies and gulches of western South Dakota. They lived in what geologists call "mid-latitude steppe," a rather grim name for the rolling short-grass prairie of a Lakota boyhood in the mid-nineteenth entury. Putinhin's generation was the last that would come of age before that sea of grass was fenced.

The land was huge. But just as a child is surprised to learn that the majority of the earth's surface is water, the plains dweller soon finds that most of the world is sky. Weather is the central and unavoidable fact of life. Putinhin's people would have known the weather as a vital force, a living spirit of the world that carried in its power a deep and profound mystery. For the Lakotas, who lived in buffalo-hide tipis and couldn't move further in a day than a horse could ride, weather meant more than a dropping barometer, a convection current, or a stationary front. It was a massive, even divine, presence in daily life.[1]

Even now, 150 years after his birth, the plains are an unforgiving place. Heavy spring rains turn dirt roads to gumbo. In summer, tornados crumple houses and fling cars and tractors through the air like playthings. The wind pummels everything in its path until you can see the wall of a trailer house bend under the force. The flapping of a loose shutter or drain spout keeps you awake worrying at night, and if the wind is blowing hard enough the next morning you have to kick the front door open. When there's no rain, the dust is so thick you move through a ground storm of dirt and grit with your teeth clenched and your eyes closed and burning.

And then there is winter.

I don't know how to imagine winter for people who camped on the plains. They found sheltered and protected places close to water in the lower elevations. The tipis were insulated, and held the heat of inhabitants efficiently, the dwellings pitched sometimes for miles along a stream. It was a time for storytelling, game playing, and resting. But the cold months are bitter on the plains, even now, even for protected strangers. I've driven a car in Lakota country through a ground blizzard so thick I couldn't see ten feet in front of me. I've driven over a hill on a moonlit night and plunged a car into a snowdrift on the other side and needed hours to dig myself out and back up the way I came, lucky to even have a shovel. What would it have been like with no horsepower but a single mount, judging the dips and swells of the broken land, the snow falling from an endless gray sky without a light even visible? Better not to venture out at all, I imagine, knowing the season could be deadly in the Lakota Moon of the Popping Trees (December) or the Moon of the Sore Eyes (February), named for the snow blindness suffered by looking too long at a whitened earth.[2]

Beard would have known how to ride a horse in a freezing storm without gloves, or cut a hole in the ice in deep winter to go swimming, a habit he kept until late in life. He would have known what it was to get caught without shelter in a summer downpour, the rain running off him as easy as the wind. He would have learned to see a front approaching for miles, the way a storm begins on the plains far off and gives a sense of an unfolding story as it nears. He would have seen darting shadows sweep across the land, moving clouds backlit by the sun behind them, giving the illusion, even as one stands still, that the sky is racing far ahead of the earth. He would have seen the eeriness of summer dusk, the sun setting in the west, its light bent by a stack of black clouds, the refraction giving the hills below a milky white, unearthly glow. And displays of summer lightning that look like branches of a forking cottonwood spread out against the sky, as though he were seated at the bottom of a draw, the entire world crackling and alive with fury around him.

Beard's people of birth were the Minneconjou Lakotas, who made the center of their homeland west of the Missouri River and east of the Black Hills in today's South Dakota. The Minneconjous, or "planters by the water," were one of seven subtribes that made up the western, or Lakota, branch of what are commonly called the Sioux. Those subtribes, which probably didn't evolve into separate entities until early in the nineteenth century, made up the Lakota nation, or *oyate*. They were no less rooted to the land than residents anchored to a single dwelling, but they were forced by exposure to the elements to camp where they could hunt and gather, moving purposefully, as nomads do, to find a suitable home for the season.[3]

They inhabited an ordered and symbolic universe. The seven Lakota subtribes made up one branch of the Seven Council Fires, which included the entire Dakota (Sioux) nation. In other words, Lakotas grew up in one of seven subtribes of one of seven council fires, an idea that expressed the magical position of Beard's people in a universe where the number seven was mystical and portentous. The Lakotas, by their own reckoning, were at the center of creation.[4]

If Putinhin was born when Marie says, in 1856, it would have been The Year That Whittler Died, according to the Iron Shell winter count, a calendar that began among the Minneconjous. Often painted on deerskins, the winter counts assigned a picture to each passing year that unfolded in a spiral pattern from the center of the design. The pictures recalled the most significant event of the year, usually natural events and intertribal struggles. Whittler—probably a reference to a Yankee trader—may seem an unlikely man to remember, but for a people reliant on trade goods like guns and kettles, his presence would have been vital. The year 1861 was The Year Long Foot's Entire Camp Was Killed. The year 1872 was The Year Old Woman Horn Fell from a Bank and Died. And the big fight with Custer (1876) was remembered as The Year We Went to Make a Treaty— the battle didn't even merit top billing. The years were called "winters," and it's logical that Lakotas figured their age by the number of winters they'd seen. But Beard's ever-shifting age in later life makes me wonder whether a running tally even mattered.[5]

As nations go, the Lakotas (Teton) were a small one. In 1868 they counted some twenty thousand people—and the entire Sioux nation (Santee, Yankton, Teton) about thirty-five thousand. Putinhin's first language was Lakota, closely related to Dakota (Santee) and N/Dakota (Yankton), mutually intelligible Sioux dialects. So the people Putinhin could have spoken with or understood hardly numbered more than the population of Columbus, Ohio, at the time. Teeming cities like Philadelphia and New York would have swallowed the Lakotas in a single neighborhood, and the size of those settlements was meant to overwhelm Indian visitors when they went east to visit the home of the "Great Father," a trip Beard would make many times.[6]

As a boy he learned the sign language used by tribes from the Texas panhandle to the Saskatchewan prairie. Since Indians spoke tongues that could diverge as much as Spanish does from German or Vietnamese, they made sign talk the lingua franca of the plains. It was a concise and efficient use of gestures, a rapid code that could reveal hostility in the sweep of an arm, approval or friendship in the angle of a wrist. Speakers relied little on facial expressions, and a single gesture could convey a whole sentence. The sign for "white man" was to trace with the right hand the imaginary brim of a hat just above the eye line, a common gesture in Lakota country by the time Beard was born.

The sign for the Sioux wasn't so benign: the speaker held an outstretched index finger or flattened hand in front of his neck and drew it across his throat from left to right. It was an unmistakable gesture of slitting a throat. In fact, the Sioux were said to have cut off the heads of their enemies at one time, a practice that seems to have faded when scalping was adopted. A custom indulged by both whites and Indians, scalping was how the Lakotas denied their enemies entry into the spirit world—and how whites provided proof of Indian kills and collected bounties. Whether or not their ancestors practiced decapitation, to mutilate an enemy corpse was a sign of accomplishment among the Lakotas, an act Beard would have witnessed, if not practiced, while growing up.[7]

Even the most devoted warrior begins life as a child. And Putinhin grew up in a culture where children were the object of great tenderness. They were beloved and indulged by parents and extended family, and corporal punishment was unknown. But there were limits to a child's freedom all the same. A boy learned to avert his eyes or bow his head in the presence of elders. He was encouraged to be shy in social settings, probably an anchor to a childhood without formal discipline. Self-restraint was valued, and physical contact was largely forbidden except in game playing or war.[8]

As an eldest son, Putinhin held a position of honor. Lakota life, in fact, was structured around the relationships of siblings. The word for "older brother," for example, was different from the word for "younger brother," and the word chosen depended on whether the speaker was male or female. Beard's younger brothers would have called him *ciye*; his sister would have called him *tiblo*. Putinhin, too, would have addressed others by their kinship relation ("Little brother"), not by their given names. The obligations for each relationship differed. It was the elder's responsibility to teach and discipline his male siblings—in fact, Putinhin would eventually have as big a hand in raising many of his brothers as he did in raising his own children.[9]

And his brothers were many. Lakota people still use words like *cousin*, *grandfather*, and *brother* in what seems a metaphorical or careless way, especially to outsiders. But cultures differ in how they define kinship and family. Leonard Little Finger told me he had many grandfathers—a lucky man by any account. The extended family Beard grew up in was a central part of Lakota tradition into the middle of the 1900s, and in many families it still exists.[10]

"When I was small," recalls Birgil Kills Straight, another great-nephew of Beard's, "I had three mothers as far as I knew: my own mother, my aunt Susie Apple (Francis's mother), and another aunt. When we were kids we had three houses, three places to eat." Birgil, now in his seventies, says it was only in his early teens that he realized the other kids were cousins, not brothers, and that two of his mothers were not his biological parents. "I did not know at the time that [Beard] was not the biological father of my mother." His mother called Beard "father" because he was her paternal uncle, and a father's brothers are considered fathers in the Lakota way. Putinhin, one might say, was raised in a very large family.[11]

Beard traveled and camped with a small group of extended families, fifty to one hundred people related by blood, marriage, or adoption. This *tiyospaye*, as the Lakotas called it, was the basic social unit, and its members lived together by choice. People might marry out of the group or be adopted in, so membership was fluid. The family that hunted together prospered together—and suffered together, too. In large summer encampments, they set up their lodges in a careful and predetermined order. Putinhin noted that his family often camped next to the great warrior Crazy Horse, a clue to their close relation, probably one of blood. His people lived in round hide dwellings pitched in circles that echoed the roundness of sun, moon, and the turning seasons. So it was that the Lakotas came to regard their world as the *cangleska wakan* (sacred hoop), strong and impenetrable.[12]

Each *tiyospaye* governed itself through a council of respected men, usually warriors. These men chose *wakiconza* (executive officers) who managed the details of camp and picked others to enforce their will. Major decisions were made in a band council in which anyone of sufficient age could speak. There could be bitter division and loud disagreement in council, which might continue for days. Eventually the band reached accord by unanimous consensus, not majority vote, a process that utilized peer pressure and required substantial compromise. A dissident member might end up going to live with another group. The *cangleska wakan* required the unified voice of the people.[13]

The people camped where wood and water and grass were plentiful. But they were ever alert to danger. When Beard was a boy, a Lakota village could strike camp in a quarter of an hour. They could cover twenty-five miles in a day—first with dogs bearing their loads, later horses—more than twice that if pressed. They carried their communal hearth with them, burning coals that would light the council fire at the next camp. Lean and mobile, they packed and transported everything of value, the buffalo-hide tipis, the animal robes, the parfleche cases filled with needles and awls of buffalo bone, the children's toys, the weapons, medicine bundles, ropes and quillwork and clothing, all of it piled on angled travois poles, dragged at first by dogs, and later horses. Even as an old man, Beard would migrate from home to home according to season, a hard but cleansing habit instilled in him as a young boy.[14]

Life was precious but fragile. Death might come in the midst of battle. It might find one in the crossing of a bloated river in spring. Or exposure to extreme heat and cold. More often, as Putinhin grew up, death came quietly and without warning. Contagious germs arrived from Europe, passed from tribe to tribe before white people ever arrived in their territory. While epidemics could strike down anyone, they found fertile ground among Indian people, who had no biological immunity. The Lakotas suffered, although their nomadic ways and early inoculations from the government spared them the huge losses borne by more sedentary tribes. Still, the contagions began before the army ever came and continued long after doctors arrived on the reservation. The winter counts include many years remembered from a flash outbreak of measles or smallpox, the image of a man covered in spots all that remains to recall the passage of a deadly plague.[15]

By the time he reached puberty, Putinhin passed from the protection of his mother to that of his father. For males, the training for war began with a battery of games. Older boys would place a hot coal in the crook of a young boy's arm and see if he would cry out. After spring rains they would hurl packs of mud at each other, some stuffed with burning coals. In the swing-kicking game they would attack each other in teams, using buffalo robes as shields. (Boys were often bloodied, but bad feelings were buried.) They dove into ice-cold water in winter, played follow-the-leader in rough country, learned how to mount a galloping horse from a running start. Even as an older man Beard was said to be able to outrun a horse on foot in a hundred-yard dash, a not implausible feat given his early training.[16]

Boys didn't wait long to prove themselves in the hunt, and no pursuit was more important. The Lakotas have no generic word for *animal*, so every species represented a distinct and sacred source of food. Beaver, Deer, Antelope, Porcupine, and Buffalo agreed to give themselves up to the hunter for his people, if he acted in the correct manner. Prayers were said before the hunt, and the kill, if successful, had to be shared with others. Hunting small game prepared boys for the big kills that defined a life built on predator and prey.[17]

Leonard chuckles when he remembers a story Beard liked to tell him about the old days. "When he was a little boy, less than eight years old, his father had just made him a new bow and a quiver full of arrows. This was when buffalo were dwindling and food was getting scarce. They were down on the Niobrara, and they told him to go out and do something. So he went and followed a buffalo path.

"The buffalo had gone there so much they had worn the ground down into a rut. The boy heard a buffalo wallowing in the sand along the river, and he peeked to see what it was." Leonard explains that he had a choice to make. "He wanted to go back and tell his father, but he was far from home, and he thought he might lose the buffalo. The other choice was to kill it. And that's what he decided to do.

"He was so small he was hidden in the furrow of the trail. The boy crept up until he came very close to the buffalo. He said it looked like a huge mountain that was breathing in and out. He knew how to kill a buffalo by then, so he shot an arrow that landed where the ribs end, near the heart. He fired. The buffalo snorted, jumped up in the air and went crashing through the willows. The boy ran and chased him. Here and there he could see splotches of blood, and then all of a sudden he couldn't hear it anymore. When it finally came into view, it was lying there, dead."

I can tell this is one of Leonard's favorite stories, one he has told many times. "He ran as fast as he could back to the village and told his father. 'I shot a *tanka!*' But his father wouldn't believe him, 'Don't be joking. We need food,' he said. But the boy, who didn't know what else to do, started crying. Finally, his father said, 'I believe you.' The son took him back to the spot, and sure enough, the buffalo was there. There was great joy in the camp. They skinned the animal, everyone took a piece of meat and went back to the village, and they had a big feast of boiled soup and roasted ribs. That night his father sang an honoring song for him." A well-trained boy would have offered a prayer of thanks to the animal, no doubt. And if common practice was followed, it was Putinhin who ate the liver.[18]

Leonard's story has all the bluster of a Davy Crockett yarn. On the plains, though, such feats weren't uncommon. Boys were instructed in how to use a bow and arrow from the time they were toddlers. Lakota showman

Luther Standing Bear killed his first buffalo at about the same age and said his boyhood bow felt like an extension of his body. In a world where food was elusive, accuracy was urgent. An adult hunter who took more than one arrow to bring down a buffalo might be publicly shamed. Two things about Leonard's story stand out: Putinhin fired only one arrow, and his family shared the kill with everyone.[19]

To his younger children, who later trooped off to a small schoolhouse during the Great Depression, Beard's education would have seemed quaint. He probably didn't set foot in a room with four walls and a roof until he was an adolescent. He never learned how to read, write, or even sign his name. He said the Lakotas didn't count higher than a thousand when he was young, for the simple reason they didn't need to. A ledger book and pen would have been about as useful to Horn Cloud's son as a bow and arrow would be to a Cordon Bleu chef.[20]

A Lakota school had no windows or walls. A boy like Putinhin would have had his own mount as soon as he could sit upright and balance himself. He would have learned, with the help of others, how to break a pony in a day. He would have been able to pick up an injured man on the ground while riding at a gallop or guide his horse with only his knees. Boys learned to stand in cold water to keep their legs from chafing when in contact with a horse's back. They even learned to sleep in the saddle if necessary. Marie says Beard could ride a horse even into his nineties, "the way they do when they go to war," straddling the horse on the far side and gripping the mane, his moccasins peeking out from behind.[21]

Putinhin would have known how to measure, cut, notch, sand, shape, paint, feather, and point an arrow. He would have learned how to cut and fire a branch of ash for a bow, and cut the string from buffalo sinew. He could tell by watching a herd of mustangs whether they were walking to or away from a water source, whether a broken branch was the work of nature or man, whether animal scat was dropped at leisure or in a hurry. His education would have taught him to distinguish a creek from a water hole at a distance by the color of cottonwood leaves nearby. He would have walked in ravines and draws instead of on ridges, as white men did, careful to screen his movements. He learned how to start a fire with a bow drill and flint and how to walk across the prairie at night without the stars. For hunter-gatherers like the Lakotas, the idea of tilling and planting a field would have made no more sense than camping in a square formation or baiting a buffalo. What looked like instinct from the outside were learned skills as complex as anything a white man could do with a moldboard plow or the long division.[22]

Some people figured Indians had it in the blood. But they were wrong, sometimes dangerously so. When he fought in the Korean War, Francis Apple remembers being ordered by his superiors to "walk point," or lead a patrol into enemy country. An Indian was supposed to be able to smell out an ambush, his officers thought, and there was something *wakan* (holy) about Indians from the old days. He laughs at that story now, a tale other Indian veterans also tell, but he didn't have any more chance of surviving a patrol like that than a kid from Columbus or Hoboken.[23]

In fact, *wakan* spirits, a complex and diverse group of powers, ruled—and still rule—the Lakota world. A holy man could talk with animals or trees. Warriors kept amulets of power from the natural world. The spirit of an animal lingered in its body after death. Beard wore a bear-claw necklace given him by his grandfather, in fact, a powerful charm in a culture where "bear medicine" was a revered form of healing. The world he lived in was alive with spiritual force, edged with ceremony and sacrament, bound by elaborate and exacting protocol. Putinhin learned how to ride, run, dance, fight, shoot, and kill in full view of spirits good and bad, a universe bursting with energy, electric and animated, tactile and yet invisible to the untutored eye.[24]

Putinhin also learned from an early age how to pray with the pipe. In Lakota history, the pipe was given to the people by the White Buffalo Calf Woman as a symbol of peace and goodwill. Lakotas smoked pipes—and still do—in daily prayer, asking blessings and offering prayers to the *wakan* spirits. A man wasn't whole without a pipe. It was smoked to ward off hard times, or to honor key events like the sun dance, a personal vision quest, or the adoption ceremony known as *hunka*. The young boy would not have considered any major undertaking without smoking and communicating with the spirits first. The original sacred pipe, guarded closely during

Putinhin's lifetime, is held today on the Cheyenne River Reservation by an appointed keeper.[25]

The Lakotas were neither small-minded nor inflexible. As late immigrants to the plains, they adapted to a world where the horizon was long, the margin for error short. Putinhin became an expert horseman, though his people didn't domesticate the horse, *sunka wakan* (holy dog), until the early eighteenth century. He was a good shot with a rifle, though guns weren't a common possession of the tribe until about the time of Lewis and Clark. A Lakota from the early eighteenth century, if transported through time, would have barely recognized the technology of Dewey Beard's people, no more than Benjamin Franklin would have felt at home among the steel girders and factory grime of the Gilded Age. The Lakotas reinvented themselves on the plains several times.

When the railroad came, early in Beard's childhood, it split the buffalo herds and made a bridgehead for the invasion of Lakota country. The steel rails brought hunters with buffalo guns who sent hides back by the carload. The backbone of the buffalo economy was broken. But Beard and others learned to cope with that, too. One day he would ride the rails as a salaried showman, a connoisseur of survival, if not a wholesale convert, to the white world. But the "iron horse," as many times as he rode it, was a mount he never broke.[26]

Francis calls Beard a warrior, and the Lakotas were a warrior culture. Some men specialized as hunters or scouts, but many were trained from childhood to fight. A boy accompanied his first war party at about the age of twelve. When Beard went on his, perhaps as early as 1874, he was said to be tough enough to stand and fight even when tethered to the ground by a rawhide thong. But the active years of a warrior were not much longer than a career for today's professional athlete, from the mid-teens to mid-thirties. Francis says Beard became a member of the Kit Fox Society, a warrior fraternity that performed policing functions in the tribe. Membership required bravery in battle, an honor perhaps echoed in his early census name, Many Wounded Holes.[27]

Most Lakota men trained for battle. They carried shields painted with designs revealed in dreams. They raided enemy villages to capture horses and women. They took the scalps of enemies for honors. They were awarded a feather for each signal accomplishment, and the manner and color of their display was a language in itself. Killing an enemy was valued, but it was not the consummate act of bravery. The warrior's highest honor was to "count coup," or strike an enemy with a hand or weapon without killing him, an act that had to be witnessed and verified in public.[28]

The people of Sitting Bull and Crazy Horse and Red Cloud grew more powerful, sometimes pushed by forces beyond their control. The removal of eastern tribes across the Mississippi crowded the Lakotas and their neighbors. The great buffalo herds, dwindling as they moved toward the continental divide, drove the tribe further west in Beard's youth. On the back of the "holy dog," the Lakotas spread across the northern plains—but the horse would heighten class divisions within the tribe and increase the likelihood of warfare. By 1870 their prairie empire, contested by numerous enemies, cut a swath across several states, a grand perimeter that would take several tanks of gas to drive around even today. They boasted of their accomplishments and kills as they went. But warfare wasn't just glory; it was controlling land and resources, especially as the buffalo vanished.[29]

Enemies like the Crows and Arikaras beheld the Lakotas with dread. For forty years Putinhin's people waged war on the Pawnees, a tribe largely unarmed and agrarian after signing a treaty with Washington, and almost obliterated them. In 1873 a Lakota party surprised a Pawnee village and killed one hundred men, women, and children. Their skill as warriors made them so feared that neighbors like the Cheyennes eagerly sought to reach a peace when possible.

Lakota history didn't follow an inevitable arc. They made alliances and broke them. They banded with some tribes and brawled with others. They took land and gave it up. They traded pelts for iron kettles from Europe and horses from Mexico and were intimately tied to the international fur trade. They negotiated with Lewis and Clark, even as they threatened them. They welcomed whites who married into the tribe, and they harried others. They took heavy casualties at Blue Water Creek in 1855, but later chased the U.S. Army out of the Powder River Valley. They bartered with commissioners, bluffed and bullied and retreated on the battlefield, kept the peace when possible. In the end they ran headlong into an empire bigger, wealthier, and more ambitious than their own.[30]

The newcomers they knew as *wasicu*—white people. The word, in Lakota, may derive from "people with power," though other etymologies exist. The *wasicu* didn't respect the buffalo, and they didn't esteem the sacred Black Hills, except for the gold buried there. They seemed oblivious to Lakota deeds. They were ignorant and fat, bald and lumbering. They couldn't handle a bow, got lost in broad daylight on patrol, and rode horses with saddles so big they could barely stay astride. The white people who came by the wagonload were a mystery: strong in arms but weak of limb; full of gifts but greedy; few at first, but endless later on. They didn't know anything about war except how to march and kill.[31]

They were dangerous enemies, not respected ones. Luther Standing Bear said the old-time Lakotas disdained white men as pitiful fighters. Putinhin, of similar mind, told Francis that killing a white man was considered an indignity.[32]

He might have been exaggerating, of course. If not, it was an indignity he endured on many occasions by his own telling, the first time when he was barely in his teens, if that.

3

LITTLE BIGHORN

On Last Stand Hill, morning comes slowly. We gather near the Indian memorial, not a hundred yards from where George Custer and many of his men fell on a summer day in 1876. We sit cross-legged, facing east. At first, the only sound is the faint blare of a coal train leaving Hardin at 5:30 a.m. Then twilight lifts to the lone chant of a Cheyenne medicine man. The elders light a pipe and share a long smoke while the rest of us pass around a bowl of burning sage, smudging the smoke over our bodies. The tip of the sun breaks through a thick bank of morning clouds in the east.

A Lakota elder stands up. He gestures at the fields of sweet yellow clover barely visible in the light. "My people tell a story about Little Bighorn," he begins. His grandfather, Hollow Horn Bear, fought at the battle. After the fight was over, he tells us, the Indians took a lone surviving soldier and walked him around the battlefield, giving him a good look at the carnage. They did it to make him a "witness," the man says, and after that they let him go. Years later, when visitors ran across a strange, raving man being held in a cell at Fort Meade, South Dakota, the army would tell them he was just crazy. But he wasn't crazy, the elder reminds us. He had seen things too terrible to talk about.

The elder is Albert White Hat Sr., a man who taught me about Lakota medicine and prayer thirty years before when I lived in Lakota country. The sunrise service he led on June 25, World Peace Day, is held every year to remember what no one calls the "Custer Battle" anymore, except for old-timers and hardcore battle buffs. Later, I ask Albert why they said the soldier was crazy. They hid him in the jail to keep him a secret, he says. They didn't want anyone describing the awful defeat that had befallen the army.

The Witness is an Indian story. It holds an important truth, whether or not you take it literally. We're drawn to Little Bighorn because no one got away, at least no one in a few companies of the U.S. Seventh Cavalry. There's something that fascinates us about annihilation, a curiosity to know what happened when no one came back to tell about it. Just as we have creation myths, we have ones about extinction, too—stories about a lost colony, a wrecked ship, a doomed army, even a ruined world.

The bookshelf on the Little Bighorn is long. You could read a book every week for a decade and not come to the end. Still, the battle was a skirmish compared to Shiloh, a small clash next to Antietam. The battle must speak to something deeper than numbers. The Alamo is the closest story we have like it, a stubborn holdout of doomed "heroes"—but that siege didn't have thousands of painted Indians, the high mystery of Sitting Bull and Crazy Horse, or the legend of a Civil War hero who cut a more reckless and dashing figure than Davy Crockett. Survivors are the last link to a lost event or age, whether Wounded Knee or the sinking of the *Titanic*. When the last veteran of World War I passed on, in 2012, it was mourned as the end of an era.[1]

So there are scholars and enthusiasts who recall the troop movements of June 25, 1876, better than the itinerary of their own honeymoon. People unravel and replay the memory so we can understand what went wrong—or right—as if we might know exactly who or what was responsible if we had all the facts. Any artifact is a jewel, any shard a prize. In 2010, the only cavalry flag not lost during the battle sold at a Sotheby's auction for $2.2 million.[2]

Of course, there were many witnesses who survived that day. There were soldiers in the Reno command who attacked the Indian village but retreated and survived. There were hundreds of victorious Indian warriors. Many of their women and children saw the fringes, if not the center, of the battle.[3]

By general acclaim, and most certainly his own, the last combatant standing, almost eighty years later, was Dewey Beard. He wouldn't have gone by that name at the time. It's even hard to know how old he was when the sun rose on the morning of the battle. Marie figures he was near twenty, but most historians put him in his early to mid-teens. By his own reckoning he was an adolescent.

Last man standing, of course, was a status it took a lifetime to earn. Beard wasn't the last when he came to the battle's seventy-fifth anniversary in 1951, where the Hardin High School band played the Custer anthem "Garry Owen" for a crowd of ten thousand and closed a day of festivities with "The Star-Spangled Banner." He danced a round or two with his former enemies, the Crows, and was reported to be spry on his feet.[4]

The battlefield I've come to visit many times is a haunting place. This year the land is in high health. The fields between Busby and Crow Agency are carpeted in yellow clover. Thanks to heavy rain, the draws and swales are full of color, a welcome respite from many dry seasons. A lonely nostalgia reigns over the monument, carved out of gullies and draws that border the meandering river where the Indians were camped. In a sense, the whole monument is a graveyard. The soldiers are marked individually where they fell, a stark contrast with the collective Indian memorial dedicated in 2003.

The air is spooky and quiet. The gravestones look random, even accidental. A marker here. Two there. A cluster of five or six along the ridge. Another casts a long shadow across a walking trail. Unlike the national cemetery nearby, the scattered stones look to have been sown broadside across the coulees and ravines. A fiddler plays Ken Burns's Civil War anthem, "Ashokan Farewell," in a welcoming tent. A tour bus rolls along Last Stand Ridge, while in the monument amphitheater Cheyenne singers perform an honor song for the Suicide Boys who vowed they would fight to the death and indeed perished in the battle that day.

It all happened in a single afternoon in June of 1876—or, as the Lakotas might say, the Month When the Ponies Are Fat, in the Year They Went to Make a Treaty, in a battle called the Greasy Grass.

A mountain range that rises out of the South Dakota prairie, about two hundred miles from Little Bighorn, the Black Hills look from afar like a low-lying dark cloud. The Lakotas call the Hills sacred, the place where

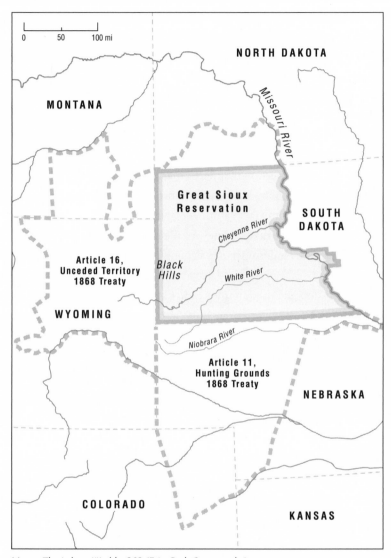

Map 1. The Lakota World, 1868 (Erin Greb Cartography)

they go to fast and pray and be close to the Great Spirit. The mountains, a place of spiritual and physical sustenance, were called the "meat pack" by the Lakotas for their plentiful supply of game. The winter counts suggest their ancestors didn't arrive in the Black Hills until the late eighteenth century, but they quickly made them their own. The area was part of the

Great Sioux Reservation established by the Fort Laramie Treaty of 1868, with strict guidelines for keeping the land in Lakota hands.

But the Hills were in the path of a great western migration, led by the railroad and the army and followed in their wake by speculators, miners, and homesteaders. In 1874 a U.S. Army expedition led by George Custer discovered gold in the middle of the "meat pack." Fearing it couldn't restrain the freebooters soon to converge on the area, Washington sought to bring the Lakotas in to the agencies and renegotiate their treaty.

In late 1875 the government ordered that all hunting bands should come in by the end of the following January. Horn Cloud and his family, including Putinhin, were probably camped for winter far from any of the forts, and it's dubious most Lakotas knew of the decree anyway. Besides, going to a fort meant surrendering their weapons and giving in to "civilization"— becoming farmers, eating white bread, sending their children to school. If the Horn Clouds did go in, they didn't stay very long. Soon, like many others, they were considered "hostiles" by default, in violation of the Interior Department decree.

The army rode after them in the spring of 1876, dividing its command to crush the Lakotas and Cheyennes in a pincer movement converging in eastern Montana. Led by Sitting Bull and Crazy Horse, the Lakotas tried to stay a step ahead of the soldiers and avoid an open fight. On June 17, General George "Three Stars" Crook caught up with them on Rosebud Creek, leading a force of over a thousand men. The Lakotas and Cheyennes, with perhaps half that number, tangled with the soldiers and their Crow scouts for the better part of a day. A battle of cut-and-dare chases, chaotic charges, and hard fighting left nine soldiers dead and twenty-three wounded. Putinhin was likely present, though it's hard to know what role he played. Seeing the soldiers volley and regroup, the confusion of noise and smoke in close fighting, and the death of two dozen or so of his own people would have given him an early and bracing taste of battle.[5]

Only eight days later, it was a different command that stumbled on the Lakotas and Cheyennes, fresh from celebrating what they considered a victory on the Rosebud. Camped along the Little Bighorn River, they were discovered by the Seventh Cavalry under Lieutenant Colonel George

Armstrong Custer, a Civil War star and Indian fighter practiced in the nasty prairie tactics of surprise-and-destroy. Putinhin's people were now outlaws by order, a tribe that had signed a treaty that was breaking down amid mutual distrust and suspicion. Most Americans would have regarded the Lakotas as a distant threat at best. But it wouldn't be long before they were the most hated people in America.

Millions of words have been written about that day, June 25. But the warrior doesn't see the whole battle. Somewhere in the epic story of Little Bighorn lies the deeply personal. This is what Dewey Beard remembered . . .

It was a hot day in early summer. Putinhin slept until late morning. He had been out hunting buffalo the night before and returned to camp with meat, as was expected even of an adolescent. It was a huge camp that snaked along the river, he said, the largest he would ever see before or after, filled with Lakotas, Cheyennes, Yanktonais, Santees, Assiniboines, Arapahos, and Gros Ventres. To his interviewer sixty years later, he refused to guess how many people were there. "In that long-ago time none of my people knew more than a thousand numbers. We believed no honest man needed to know more than that many."[6]

The women were gathering turnips when Puti got up. He took a dip in the Little Bighorn and went back to camp for a meal about midday. His uncle warned him to stay with the horses after he finished eating, because he had a feeling something bad was afoot. The boy had gone to join his brother herding horses on a nearby creek when he heard shouting in the village. People were calling out that soldiers were approaching the camp.

He clambered up Black Butte, along the river, to have a look. What he saw in the valley below, in the bright light of midafternoon, staggered him. A mounted troop of soldiers was riding toward the tipis of his Hunkpapa cousins to the south. The soldiers dismounted about a hundred yards from the camp and began to shoot from a skirmish line, and the women and children scattered with the gunfire. Realizing they had been ambushed, Puti ran back to the village. He found his fighting pony, a buckskin mustang, and prepared for battle by braiding the horse's tail and smearing hail spots with white paint on his own forehead. He was bristling to meet the soldiers, but his father, Horn Cloud, made him wait, giving the anxious boy advice before letting him ride into the melee.

The Lakotas and Cheyennes forced back the first assault, but soon soldiers were sighted across the river. The boy begged his father, and finally Horn Cloud let him go. If his son didn't get into the scrape soon, it might end before he had a hand in it, so the father slapped the pony on the rump, and it took off with the boy holding on for dear life. He saw an old woman about to cross their path. "Look out, grandma!" he yelled, but the horse dealt her a glancing blow, and she was knocked back into the river.7

The boy was armed with some steel-tipped arrows and a bow. He reined in the horse and followed some men riding out of the village. After he fell in with a group of four other Lakotas, three armed with rifles, one tumbled from his horse, and Puti moved forward to take his place. They heard the firing far away from the village and rode along the river. On the other side they could see clouds of dust and hear the loud popping of gunfire. With hundreds of others, they forded the Little Bighorn and galloped in full stride up the swells of the Greasy Grass.

By now it was late afternoon. Beard and his companions rode up the gullies on the east side, probably up Deep Coulee toward Last Stand Hill. Bullets whistled around them. The high sun blazed off the Indian knives and clubs. Arrows whizzed by, the Indians shooting them high in the sky to rain down on the dwindling clusters of soldiers. A group of *wasicu* tried to run. Beard took command of his party in spite of his age. "I led them in front as the soldiers were making a getaway . . . and we got them turned."8

He wanted them to know he wasn't afraid. The boy yelled out the Lakota war cry, "It's a good day to die!" A companion, Spotted Rabbit, dared him to help take the soldier leader alive on the hill. They rode toward a tall white man in buckskins, seated on a sorrel-colored mount, who was yelling at the soldiers. Walks Under the Ground, a Cheyenne, rode up and broadsided the man's mount, toppling horse and rider. Puti's own horse shied away. Thunder Hawk, a Minneconjou, came up from behind and shot the soldier leader with a gun. The soldier had short hair, Beard said, what seemed strange for a man he later heard described as "Long Hair." If, indeed, it was Long Hair at all.9

They had tried to capture him at first, not kill him. But the time for killing was at hand. As he rode across the field in the smoke and dust, the boy saw a soldier raise a pistol. The man emerged from the mist like a phantom and pointed his gun straight at him. Puti notched an arrow to his bow and fired before the trooper could pull the trigger. His aim was true: the man crumpled in front of him like a felled deer. "I hit him on the head with my bow," said the young Minneconjou, the first to count coup on the fallen soldier.[10]

By this time, the battle was nearly done. Brave warriors turned scavengers in the early evening light. Horn Cloud's eldest son found a bag with some hardtack and bacon in it that smelled good. "Even while they were fighting," he said, "I thought I'd have a snack." He came back and picked up an army bugle, a hard and shiny treasure even if he could hardly get it to make a sound. He told a friend later he took a horse—and a big cavalry mount would have been a major prize.[11]

The boy rode up to see a dying soldier on the ground surrounded by a group of Indians. They made gestures to strike him, and he was almost crazy waiting for the death blow. Women in the crowd were laughing. Then an Indian rode up with his son draped over his horse. He was singing a death song in his honor. When he saw the soldier he pulled up sharply, threw his leg over his mount, and jumped to the ground with a pistol in hand. He walked up to the bluecoat and shot him without a word. Leonard says Putinhin still remembered that event when he was an old man.

The field was littered with hundreds of bodies, a sight Beard would see only one other time in his life. Women wandered about crying for lost ones, and the bitter ones brought axes to crush the heads of wounded soldiers, the Yanktonai Thunder Bear remembered. Others picked over the corpses lying on the hills and in the draws. The young boys moved from body to body, said Eagle Bear, an Oglala, shooting them with arrows and rifles and lifting scalps. Many of the corpses were dismembered. The bodies of Lakotas and Cheyennes were bloated in the hot sun with maggots before the firing even ended, said Cheyenne eyewitnesses, and Indian dogs gnawed at the corpses and littered the camp with human bones. Many Lakotas and Cheyennes took revenge for what had been done to their relatives at Blue

Water Creek (1855), at Sand Creek (1864), at Washita (1868). In the years to come there was much the boy would remember and reflect on from that day, a day unlike any other his people had known.[12]

The hardtack and bacon he devoured. The bugle he kept and passed on to his family. The horse he later rode to Canada. And within the time it takes to eat a leisurely meal, the Battle of the Greasy Grass was over.

Beard's first detailed account of the battle, so far as we know, didn't appear in print until long after he died. His "as told to" version was interesting not only for the warrior who told the story but for the man who wrote it down. The scribe was David Humphreys Miller, a minor Hollywood luminary who would forge a reputation painting and writing about Plains Indians and become Beard's adopted son along the way, Putinhin's most important link to the white world.

The son and great-nephew of artists, Miller, who was said to have held a paintbrush before he used a pencil, started drawing at the tender age of three, about the age Putinhin learned to ride a horse. It was the accounts of Little Bighorn that fascinated him as a child and stirred his curiosity about the survivors. Sixteen years old, with one hundred dollars in his pocket and the blessings of his parents, Miller drove the old family Plymouth from his home in Van Wert, Ohio, to Pine Ridge, South Dakota, in 1935. There he interviewed and painted dozens of Indian veterans of the Custer battle, a project that would stretch over many summers.

Miller didn't know anyone on Pine Ridge. He went armed only with a letter of introduction from the Presbyterian Church. The missionaries in South Dakota took him for older than his age, and they gave him a parolee, Silas Afraid of Enemy, as a translator. It was Silas who scolded the boy one night when they were bedding down in the Badlands and he saw Miller trying to hide some money in a bedroll: "Hell, kid. You don't have to do that. Ain't another white man around within fifty miles."[13]

Afraid of Enemy must have done something right. Over time, Miller became adept in Plains Indian sign and Lakota, the two languages, it turned out, Beard was fluent in. He would drive as many as four hundred miles to interview and paint a warrior, he said, sometimes sketching at night by the headlights of the old Plymouth. Over the years, he claimed to learn fourteen different Indian languages. They called him, in Lakota, Wasicu Maza, Iron White Man.

Wasicu Maza served in China during World War II with the Flying Tigers, using his artful hand to draw bombing maps for the Fourteenth Air Corps. He later did illustrations of the Pacific Proving Grounds for the Atomic Energy Commission in the early 1950s, but government work didn't suit him. It was cowboys and Indians who drew the young Ohio artist westward and kept him there for the balance of his life.

In the 1950s he found good work as an Indian consultant in Hollywood. Miller arrived in Tinseltown when Westerns were the main course of American film and television. He scripted episodes for *Rawhide* and acted as technical adviser for *Yancy Derringer* and *Desilu Playhouse*. He was dialogue and technical consultant for dozens of films, including *How the West Was Won*, *Chief Crazy Horse*, *Stagecoach* (the remake), and *Cheyenne Autumn*. (As a dialogue coach he ended up teaching Native actors words in their own language.) His repertoire wasn't just shoot-'em-up stuff, either: he penned a *This Is Your Life* episode in 1960, for example, that honored Indian artist Oscar Howe. Miller is listed as technical adviser on many small-screen Westerns through the 1960s that depict Native people with considerable compassion—and sometimes sappy sentimentality.[14]

By Hollywood standards, Miller knew his trade. He'd spent time on reservations. He claimed to have chased down some seventy survivors of Little Bighorn to hear their account of the battle. He found time to write two books along the way, on Little Bighorn (*Custer's Fall*, 1957) and Wounded Knee (*Ghost Dance*, 1959)—both heavily based on Indian sources, a groundbreaking idea for its day. More important, he could talk the way full-blood Indians do, even if Hollywood—and its patrons—couldn't tell a swatch of Navajo from Swahili.

Miller was also given to bouts of exaggeration. His claim to speak fourteen Indian languages is impossible to test, of course, but unlikely. Marie Fox Belly, who knew him, says he spoke Lakota well. But other languages on his résumé—Crow, Navajo, Cheyenne, and Kiowa—come from different language families with different word stocks. Knowing Lakota and learning

Navajo is like knowing French and learning Mandarin—difficult to master in ten summers, let alone two or three. Not even field experts like George Bird Grinnell, who spent most of their professional lives among Indians, would have ventured such a claim. More likely is that Miller may have sounded in Cheyenne the way Tonto does in English—and not that good in some of the other tongues. But who in Hollywood would have known the difference?[15]

Miller probably knew a couple hundred words in most of those languages, no small feat in itself. His knowledge of Indian sign, which he claimed to be fluent in, would have helped his comprehension even more. But he was a better artist than historian, and one reason is that, in the realm of words at least, he was working from an incomplete grasp of what people told him. In 1950 he candidly admitted to one journalist that the only Indian language he knew was Lakota, and "I can understand quite a bit more than I can speak."[16]

He was unreliable with facts. Miller says Dewey was almost eighteen years old at Little Bighorn—but Beard, somewhat reckless with numbers himself, says he was much younger. Miller says that John Sitting Bull, Little Bighorn's next-to-the-last survivor, triggered the Wounded Knee incident in 1890—but John wasn't even there. Miller says Beard took the name Dewey after the turn of the century, but he adopted the name before that. Did Miller's Lakota serve him poorly? Did he fail to write the facts down and rely too much on his memory? Did his Indian sources have fun at his expense—or simply have foggy memories of their own? Many scholars today treat Miller's historical claims with extreme caution.[17]

The Lakotas like to tell stories, after all. A lot of good-natured ribbing can hide in the lining of a tale, something a listener would be mistaken to take literally. The game of elaborating on a detail or figure of speech is an old art. And a young man far from home would have been an easy mark for practiced raconteurs. Lacking a firm grasp of Lakota (or Cheyenne), the boy from Van Wert could have easily confused a deadpan jest or hazy recollection for a reliable point of fact.

Still, Miller made the early trips out to South Dakota, a gutsy adventure for a Depression-era teenager. And he got many of the Little Bighorn veterans to talk, even if the translations are murky. We have the warrior portraits still, an impressive gallery of bright pastels with a fine sense of line and color, exhibited over the years in places from the National Cowboy Hall of Fame to the Buffalo Bill Historical Center. Of his field notes, scribbled in pencil in small spiral notebooks, only a few apparently remain.[18]

He forged a close bond with Wasu Maza, Iron Hail, a man he deeply admired. It was Miller, in fact, who got Beard bit roles in movies like *Tomahawk* and *The Last Hunt* in the warrior's waning years. Beard "adopted" Miller in the early 1950s—though by the artist's own admission he was one of more than a dozen Indians to do so. Miller painted him repeatedly over the years, in both traditional regalia and faded street garb. "Whether dressed as an Indian or as a grotesque old scarecrow," Miller wrote, "he never failed to express a majestic benevolence that set him apart even among his own tribesmen."[19]

Miller married Jan Boehme in 1954 in Rapid City. The location crew for George Sherman's *Chief Crazy Horse*, a film Miller was consulting on at the time, took a break to attend the nuptials, and Sherman served as best man. Beard gave the new couple his red and green courting blanket, bordered in yellow with a band of beadwork across its width, and he posed with the newlyweds for society-page photos. In the awkward and enduring marriage between Hollywood and the American Indian, Miller seems to have been liked by plenty of people on both sides.[20]

Marie remembers Miller fondly. He would eat a boiled egg and drink a beer for a meal, she recalls. And he got Marie her Social Security number when she made a cameo appearance in one of Beard's films. Miller offered to take her from the reservation and raise her in a middle-class home in California—perhaps the least Beard's adopted son could do for the family in later years. But Marie's mother would have none of it, preferring that her child learn Indian ways on Pine Ridge. Before he died, he sent Celane a couple tents and a modern tipi, and together they made a special visit to the place where Beard's parents were buried. But he was already far along in his cancer by that time, Marie remembers, which finally took him in 1992.

Putt Thompson was there when friends and family paid Miller their last respects. Putt owns the sprawling Custer Battlefield Trading Post, a frontier-style general store crammed with postcards and souvenirs across the highway from the battlefield. He grew up on a Texas dairy farm, came one year to Crow Fair, the annual tribal rodeo and pageant, and never went back. He was a tour guide at Little Bighorn and met Miller in the 1980s, when the author gave him a battlefield tour in a fancy white Cadillac. It was Miller's book on the Custer battle that brought Putt to the area in the first place.

When Miller died, Putt went up to Mount Coolidge in the Black Hills to help scatter his ashes, at least half of them. (The other half are on Pine Ridge, says Marie, close to his adopted father.) Putt was the first of a big crowd to arrive that day, and got a little nervous waiting for the others. The Indian contingent, including Marie, didn't show up for a couple hours, so Putt and a friend split a bottle of gin while they waited.[21]

The Pine Ridge people finally drove up in a caravan of Suburbans, lugging several video cameras with them. They also took a ceremonial pipe on the peak and prayed to the four directions. Then one of the family told Putt to scatter the ashes. He sawed open the hermetically sealed can with a knife, and as he was rolling back the top, the bag ripped open. A gust of wind came up suddenly and blew the ashes back in his face. Celane screamed. But the remains were blown away before he could cram them back in the can. Putt shakes his head and looks up sheepishly from under the brim of a ten-gallon hat: "They got it all on videotape."

Putt eats, sleeps, and sells Little Bighorn. One day he showed me a postcard tintype of Crazy Horse that he vends at the trading post. People had warned me about the photo. It's said that Crazy Horse was never photographed, a claim that's only burnished his reputation as a romantic figure. But Putt Thompson doesn't accept that part of the legend. Partly from his efforts, the Lost Photo of Crazy Horse hangs over Lakota country still. Putt owns the tintype of a young Indian man standing on a parquet floor, his chest covered with a breastplate, a blanket draped over his arm, a single white feather pinned to his hair. This is Crazy Horse, he says. The image is displayed and sold at the Custer Battlefield Museum near Garry Owen.

The image resonates, because beyond Putt Thompson's store, or Dave Miller's drawings, or Dewey Beard's stories, or even the seventy-six-acre monument itself, rests the spirit of Crazy Horse. He was the archetypal Plains warrior, a master tactician of feint and charge. A quiet and brooding man, light-skinned and light-haired, his exploits in battle were legendary long before Custer came, notably his leadership in annihilating Captain William Fetterman and eighty soldiers in 1866. In his mid-thirties by the time of Little Bighorn, he is credited by many with leading the charge that broke Custer's command in the final phase of the battle.[22]

Beard was close to Crazy Horse—Tasunka Witko—a name inherited from his father and a bad translation (as so many are), probably meaning something like Man Whose Horse Is Sacred. Beard called him "uncle," but what that means isn't entirely clear. He recalled at Little Bighorn that Crazy Horse had a rope bridle that passed underneath the lower jaw of his horse and around the ears, and he tied his medicine on the rope before he rode across the river to fame and glory.

Until his dying day, Beard believed in the magic of the Lakota leader. "These are sacred men," he said of Crazy Horse and Sitting Bull. "They're holy, they're special, and the bullets cannot touch them." He was right about the last point, at least for Crazy Horse. Tasunka Witko had been facially scarred by a bullet in a dispute over a woman when he was a young man. But he was said to believe he was impervious to gunfire in battle. A man of mystic visions and trances, Crazy Horse was the hero of the Lakotas' greatest day against the *wasicu*. And no bullet touched him in the melee.[23]

Beard once looked at the tintype that Putt now owns—looked at it a long time, said friend Jake Herman—and agreed it bore a likeness to the great man. But in the interview at the Hotel Alex Johnson, not long before he died, Beard never suggested he'd seen a real photo of the warrior. By the mid-1950s, only one living person was said to be alive who could verify the original tintype: Grandma Dirt Kettle, reputedly 101 years old, who had been in camp at Little Bighorn and knew Crazy Horse personally. There was just one problem—by the time the photo got around to her in 1956, Dirt Kettle was deaf and blind.[24]

Dave Miller didn't get to paint Crazy Horse, who died too young to wear the dubious badge of "survivor." Putt Thompson still sells his postcard like penny candy, and the battlefield cultivates him as a great hero. As for Beard, he would only say on the record that the best likeness of his uncle was a man he once knew, Comes Out Holy, whose resemblance was uncanny. Comes Out Holy's children had a photo of their father, he said, but would never show it. They offered to sell it to him once. "I wanted that picture," he said, "so I could show it to whoever wanted to see what Crazy Horse looked like." But Dewey Beard never had much money. And the picture of Crazy Horse had to stay in his memory, which it did for a very long time.[25]

A big thing happened to Putinhin at Little Bighorn—he shot a man. He doesn't say he killed him, because that would have been difficult to know. But he doesn't appear to have said anything about the incident to Dave Miller. In fact, he seems to have barely mentioned it in any interview until the one, almost eighty years after the fact, that's buried in the Library of Congress. Maybe he was lost in a fog of old age. Maybe he gave *National Geographic* a bloody tale he was tired of hiding. Or maybe he just made it up.[26]

Old men tell whoppers, especially about war. Jim Aplan, an antiques dealer near Rapid City, met Beard when Jim was a boy and has heard tales about him ever since. "Dewey did everything from ride for the Pony Express to patch the crack in the Liberty Bell," he quips. Which means he's heard a lot of hogwash about him. A tale is a give-and-take thing, Aplan explains. "There's two parts to a story—there's the teller, and there's the audience. If the audience wants a certain kind of story, the teller will comply."

Will Robinson, director of the South Dakota Historical Society for many years, voiced similar doubts. He met Beard once and confessed to being unimpressed. He didn't understand how the old Lakota's age seemed to change from census to census. He figured the old man was no more than thirteen when the battle took place, and if he was there at all, he would have hidden in safety with the women and children. "Frankly I have thought and still do that a lot of the 'OLD' Indians have told so many different stories so many different times that they actually didn't know the truth from romance," he wrote. A graduate of the Chicago University Law School, Robinson wasn't easily impressed by tales of derring-do. "[Indians] are not very different from white men in that regard," he wrote to a friend of Beard's. "But because of the language barrier—it involves a bit more mystery. I have regarded Dewey Beard's capitalization on the Little Big Horn as a sound financial venture for which I had no quarrel."[27]

Was Beard truthful? He was known for decades on Pine Ridge as a Little Bighorn veteran, an honorific hard to maintain among other survivors if untrue. No one in the Indian community called him out for being a liar, at least according to the record, even when he became celebrated and well known. Old Grandma Dirt Kettle herself said she saw Beard at the battle, which may not mean much considering her advanced age when she recalled it.

Indians were careful about what they said on the subject of Greasy Grass. In fact, veterans of the clash long feared being punished for the "Custer massacre," as the event was called in official circles until well into the twentieth century. It was no surprise that many were quiet about their kills. Though defending their families, the Lakotas and Cheyennes had committed an unpardonable crime in the eyes of most Americans. Rather than make up a story, it's just as plausible that Beard, tired of not telling the whole truth about what he did, finally spoke for the record.[28]

Beard's account of Custer's death isn't surprising, on the other hand. Many Cheyennes and Lakotas claimed credit for having killed the famous leader, if only to burnish their own fame. Witnessing the event, as Putin-hin said he did, was a degree of celebrity only once removed. But vying for honors in toppling a chief was different from admitting a nameless kill in the tall grass coulees of Little Bighorn. There was no glory and no romance in that for a vengeful American public.

There's another possibility: Beard may have witnessed the battle from a distance, heard accounts later from those who fought, and merged their memories with his own. The stories, in the oral tradition, would have become his to retell as he heard them, perhaps with a bit of playful mischief in mind. The Lakotas have a long tradition of Trickster tales in which Iktomi the Spider teases his audience and invariably tricks them, usually in a buffoonish vein with slapstick violence and a heavy-handed moral. (We have Beard on tape telling classic Iktomi tales, even making sound effects with his hands and laughing.) It's possible he recounted to reporters a homegrown stew of all he had seen and heard, first- and secondhand, that day, much as Marie does in remembering her great-grandfather. It would have gotten an old man a lot of attention, and it would have been a personally satisfying way to recall a time when the Lakotas carried the day.[29]

The attention was pretty bloodthirsty for all that. In truth, his interrogator at the Alex Johnson was more curious to know if he'd lifted someone's scalp than if he'd dropped a trooper. Scalping had to be spine-tingling fare to the readers of *National Geographic*. Putinhin grew impatient with the lurid questions. "I didn't see anyone taking a scalp," he grumbled, "but I did see some bodies that had been scalped." He referred to it in Lakota as *wawicaspapi*—the act of removing fat from a cut of meat—a colorful, if bleak, metaphor that ended up, like so much else, on the cutting-room floor.

The translator was Johnny Bruguier, a mixed-blood of Lakota and white parents said to be descended from the first settler of Sioux City, Iowa. Bruguier was kind to offer his services, but he was no more a translator than Dave Miller was a scholar. Johnny scouted for the government during the Wounded Knee campaign, a fact that couldn't have endeared him to Putinhin. Though eighty-seven years old when they gathered in Rapid City that day, Bruguier was still Beard's junior, and the old man referred to him, a little disdainfully, as "boy." To a full-blood Lakota, a man like Bruguier couldn't be trusted. "I ain't got no name in Sioux," he blurted at the outset of the hour-long chat.

Some of Beard's words crumbled away as fast as Johnny could sweep them up. Full of missed nuance and botched details, the conversation must rival what happened to many a Native speaker over the years, whether in government parley or in front of a media microphone. The words are mangled and broken and patched carelessly back together. Bruguier confused the words for *drink* and *do*—and asks Beard what he drank at the battle instead of what he did. Beard tells the story of how Crazy Horse was shot in the face in a fight over a woman, and Bruguier misses most of it. "All of my brothers grabbed their bows and arrows and attacked," he says of the battle. "And as they attacked, they fought them and they killed them." All of that becomes, in Bruguier's idiom, "They cleaned them up." They ask Putinhin at one point whether he knew the name of the man he shot and perhaps killed. Even Johnny had to laugh at that one.

"I'm the only one left alive," Putinhin finally says, and indeed, Bruguier gets that one right. But it was, in the original Lakota, more an admission than a boast, a humble recognition of fate instead of a fact swelled with pride. However dim that day may have seemed to a very old man, it was the singular achievement many strangers would know him by, at least among those who knew him at all and believed his story. "I was only a boy," he says to Bruguier, almost apologizing for his inexperience. But Johnny doesn't say it.

The sad thing was that none of it had to happen at all, Beard concluded. If the soldiers hadn't attacked the camp, his people wouldn't have bothered them. But the troopers were after something more than just an Indian village, he explained. It was the gold under the ground of the Black Hills they wanted.

"They got the Hills anyway," he groused, his voice fatigued after more than an hour of chatter. "So what's the difference?"[30]

Before I left Little Bighorn, I had a chance to see a rerun of the battle, performed every year around the anniversary. There are competing versions, Indian and white, which seems only fair. At the Indian-run reenactment we pay fifteen dollars for a grandstand view of a bloody pageant held where the Cheyenne camp would have been on the west side of the river, downstream from where Putinhin camped with his family. The master of ceremonies is cowboy poet Henry Real Bird, who announces over the public-address system the imminent arrival of "the centaurs of the plains." Medicine Tail Coulee, where many Indians forded the water in hot pursuit of the Seventh Cavalry that day, is just across the river. "You are now all Indians," chirps Real Bird. "We should protect the water, and we should protect the ground, and we should protect the wind." And then, in the distance, you hear the sound of yipping riders.

The Crow Indian centaurs gallop onto the field, their bare skin smeared with blue, red, and yellow war paint, more than a hundred of them. The youngest are barely seven or eight years old. Most have twenty-first-century bodies, victims of too much sugar and too many carbs, and there's no hiding a belly when you're dressed down for a hot summer day like this one.

A few take unscripted falls that hurt a lot more than any blast from a cap gun in the battle that follows. The river is fast and high, and watching the warriors cross the ford is lovely, the water lined with cottonwoods and box elders, their leaves trembling in the breeze.

They're Indians, all right, but not the right kind—these are Crows, not Lakotas or Cheyennes. Since the Crows scouted for the cavalry, they hardly seem the right stand-in for Crazy Horse's people. I don't think Dewey Beard would have approved. It would be a little like reenacting the Alamo with Davy Crockett and Jim Bowie played by illegal immigrants. But the real victors of the battle, or their descendants, don't have much to do with Real Bird's upbeat pageant. For them, the day of the Greasy Grass is bittersweet. It's like a tape loop that offers a faint reminder of what a herd of tumbling horses looked like at full tilt back in the days when they burned buffalo dung and a warrior could launch a half dozen arrows in the air before the first one struck the ground. And from what everybody tells me, the Lakotas and the Crows still can't stand each other.[31]

Instead, the Cheyennes and Lakotas remember in their own way. Several dozen of them make a sixty-mile ride on horseback from Ashland to the battlefield. The Morning Star riders appear on a ridge above the monument, then descend the green and yellow swells toward the main road and end their trek by hoisting the Cheyenne tribal flag and Old Glory. A group of runners comes forty-five miles from Medicine Deer Rock. It's a tribute, not a celebration, a subdued ceremony not at all like the scalp dance their ancestors were said to have celebrated the evening after the battle.[32]

It was here that Beard offered to take Leonard in the early 1950s. It may have been the only time he went back. Little Bighorn is the event he is remembered for, if remembered at all, though he could never have guessed it at the time. He's an appendage of the battle, tethered like a supplicant tied with a leather thong to a sun dance tree. He lacked the stature of Crazy Horse or Sitting Bull, but his life, unlike theirs, would encompass the long-term victories and hardships of a whole tribe. He narrowly avoided being murdered, as they were, and he survived long enough to see a people transformed. Putinhin, in many ways, is the Lakota Witness.

Dewey Beard never escaped from Little Bighorn. As he grew older and his contemporaries fell away, he became something of a ghost. He was the witness of what had happened on the day that everything went right for the Lakotas, in a story where so much would later go wrong. He was a survivor not only of the battle, as he would have it, but of a way of life his children would barely know and his grandchildren would struggle to remember. The lifeline back to that place and that day must have haunted him.

It was the last day he was ever a boy.

4

CANADA

Dewey Beard didn't talk much about Canada, at least not to reporters interested in stories of mayhem and massacres. He may not have wanted to remember it. He was only a teenager at the time, and his years in the north would have seemed a strange interval—the aftermath of the Custer fight and the prelude to a crushing defeat that would break his life, not to mention his family, in two. The passage from one to the other was uncertain and treacherous, a period in which Putinhin's family learned the harsh lessons of exile and hunger after being chased from the land of their birth by a vengeful enemy. As time passed, there were only a few Lakotas who could remember those years.

A few days before Dewey Beard and his friend John Sitting Bull were expected at the Hotel Alex Johnson in June 1955, the next-to-the-last survivor of the Little Bighorn, and a veteran of Canada, bit the dust.

Ernie LaPointe remembers that day. Ernie's mother, Angelique, was Sitting Bull's granddaughter. John was Sitting Bull's stepson, and he boarded with Angelique and her family on the Pine Ridge Reservation west of Oglala during his last years.

John kept to himself, recalls Ernie, who was only a boy at the time. The old man had his own space in the home, his long headdress hung on the wall and a stack of regalia in the corner. Some of those objects he had at

Little Bighorn, and Angelique used to say he could tell how and when he earned every feather on the headdress. "He was a courageous guy in his own way," Ernie says, a mild way to put it for a man who survived imprisonment, war, starvation, exile, poverty, and even, as an old man, the burning-hot klieg lights of Hollywood.

Like many Oglalas, Ernie is a veteran. He enlisted in the U.S. Army in 1966 because "I was one of those guys who had to know what war was." He found himself in the DMZ in Korea on the searchlight team watching for infiltrators when the North Koreans captured the Pueblo. He was in the 101st Airborne, even though they weren't "airborne" at the time, he explains, but air mobile, as in helicopters. Ernie, in Uncle Sam's hire, was a Spec 4 private, a radio operator for the same army that had driven his great-grandfather into exile a century before.

Ernie did one tour in Vietnam that finished in 1971. "You'd fight over a plot of ground the size of my front yard," he says. (His house, a small bungalow, is tucked away in the Black Hills town of Lead.) "You'd fight for it for several days, take it from the VC, then the choppers would come and take you out. So you'd ask yourself, 'What's this all for?'" Ernie grew disenchanted with the war and was later discharged. But Sitting Bull's great-grandson came back wounded in spirit. Diagnosed with post-traumatic stress disorder, he now receives disability payments but doesn't talk much about the war. "I saw stuff over there," he says bluntly, but without elaboration. Once he told me, with a flash of pain and pride, "I graduated from the University of South Vietnam."

For a long time, Ernie didn't talk about his lineage, either. His mother taught him to be humble about his origins, but his family tree was anything but modest. He watched as others pretended to be close relatives of his great-grandfather. "I came out in 1992," he says. That year, a bust of Sitting Bull was unveiled in Oklahoma, and some wannabe relatives went down for the dedication. Ernie and his sisters decided to crash the reception. "We busted in on them people down there. They were all shocked. They didn't know who in the hell we were. That's when I started my trek toward straightening up our lineage."

Ernie had the look, all right—a husky Lakota guy with long braids, a generous nose, and prominent high cheekbones. But the last name was all wrong. Angelique divorced her first husband, Little Spotted Horse, and remarried Claude LaPointe, with whom she had Ernie. "People see me," says Ernie, and "they say 'you don't look like a LaPointe.'" For years he and his wife, Sonja, vied with others for the repatriation of a lock of hair taken from Sitting Bull soon after he was killed in 1890. The hair sat in an envelope in a musty Smithsonian Institution drawer in Washington for over a century. When, in 2008, the Smithsonian confirmed Ernie and his sisters as the closest direct descendants, the hair was returned to the family. It was a link to his ancestor that Ernie would savor until the spirits later told him how to dispose of it.[1]

Sitting Bull's stepson was John Sitting Bull, whose name, like Dewey Beard's, was something of a fiction, a label invented to make a mark in the white world. It was a stage persona for a bit Hollywood career that John, like Dewey, took up late in life. The movie people would send a limousine to fetch him on Pine Ridge, and guys in suits would help him into the car, Ernie remembers. In fact, Ernie reasons, the old man didn't even know that he was called John Sitting Bull, because he couldn't hear in the first place, and he couldn't read either. His real Lakota name, Wanakiksin, in English, was Refuses Them, probably because John would shake his head when someone started to talk to him. At home the LaPointes simply called him Kaka Eya Sni, Grandpa Who Doesn't Speak. Dave Miller communicated with him in Indian sign. He said John could sense drum vibrations in the ground at tribal dances and that when he flew in an airplane once his hearing was temporarily restored.[2]

Ernie scoffs at the Miller stories. Late in John's life some Hollywood pals bought him a hearing aid, he says. "They brought it to our house on the rez. He didn't want to put these things in his ears. But they did. The guy turned it on. He said 'Can you hear me?' and John went 'Yah!!' That's the only time I ever heard him say anything. And he just threw them away. He didn't want to get around them again." A local paper claimed it was actress Suzan Ball, performing in *Chief Crazy Horse*, whose husky singing voice brought a smile to the old man's face with the device in his ear. The public story doesn't jibe at all with the family one, and that happens all the time on Pine Ridge.³

Among John's favorite visitors were Henry Little Soldier, his half brother, and Dewey Beard. Dewey and Refuses Them had a lot in common. They were, by their own account, Little Bighorn veterans. They later rode in Wild West shows to earn some cash in a world of bank loans and tight credit. And they also came to play cameo roles in Hollywood, courtesy of Dave Miller. So they had a lot to gab about during the Moon of Ripening Chokecherries and the Moon of Ripe Plums, as the old Lakotas called the months of high summer.

"On a summer day like this, it would be hot," recalls Ernie. Beard and Little Soldier "would show up early in the morning, and they would spend a couple days at our house. They'd all sit around the corner of the house in the afternoon and light these little pipes and put *sincasa* [red willow bark] in it. They'd fire them up and get smoked up. They'd start laughing out loud, all three of them. You were listening, but all you could hear was puff, puff. All of a sudden one of them goes, 'That was a good one,' and they'd chuckle." Ernie would ask his mom later what they were laughing about. "They're communicating," she told him. "They speak with their mind."

Little Soldier was going blind, and Sitting Bull was deaf. So Beard was the only one with his full faculties. They must have "talked" by using a mix of sign and voice. One of them signed, another spoke, all would listen and watch, a garrulous but discreet round robin of old-timers. They would sit and tell each other funny stories, Ernie remembers. But the kids couldn't go around, because they weren't supposed to disturb the elders. At night during storytelling time, Ernie's mom would tell the kids what they'd said, usually about how a good sense of humor helped get them through the old days.

John died one summer, Ernie says. It was 1955, in fact. "He went to sleep one day and never woke up. They put this big curtain up. My mom and my aunts came in, and they went in there and changed his clothes after he died. They put him in what he wanted to go to the spirit world in. When they took the curtain off, it was like he was laying there sleeping. It was like he laid down for a nap.

"A lot of these old guys would come and see him. This one guy said he had traveled all day and all night to get there. They were waiting for the undertaker to come up in his car and take him to the funeral home, so in the meantime they had a wake. This guy came in, and he was holding John's hand. He didn't say nothing, he was just sitting there. Other guys and women were coming in, too. Later my mom went in there and she put up a little cot and says in Lakota, 'You can lay down here and rest.' He lay down in the cot on his back, and he went right to sleep." That guy was Dewey Beard.

Ernie was savoring the memory. "A few minutes later here comes another old guy. In them days they had these silver dollars, and they'd put them right on the eyes" of a corpse. "He come in there and he put them on the guy's eyes while he was sleeping." All of a sudden the sleeper awoke and sat upright.

Ernie laughed.

"I may look like I'm dead," Dewey huffed, "but I'm not."

"Aiiiiiiiiii!" the other guy cried.

"They say the spirits like humor," Ernie chuckled. "I thought he was going to have a heart attack."

In the end, Putinhin had lost another of his old friends. With Refuses Them gone, Dewey Beard was, according to the list, the last man standing from Little Bighorn.[4]

But that was a long time later. There was much for the two men, Refuses Them and Putinhin, to remember in the LaPointe yard on summer days over a smoke of red willow. They say memory clouds over the hard times. And the years they spent together in "Grandmother's Land," to the north, were as hard as times ever got.

The Little Bighorn made the Lakotas and Cheyennes the most public enemies in America. The press stomped and fumed about the "massacre" of Custer, and much was written about bringing the hostiles to justice. The Lakotas spent the fall and winter of 1876 outrunning the U.S. Army, which was determined to deliver a devastating blow and avenge the loss of Custer's command. Putinhin may have been present at the Battle of Slim Buttes in September, in which an army unit bested Crazy Horse and smashed a

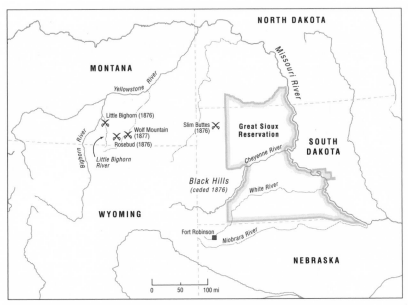

Map 2. The War for the Black Hills, 1876–1877 (Erin Greb Cartography)

Minneconjou village north of the Black Hills. The following January, at the Battle of Wolf Mountain, Crazy Horse again engaged the army, this time under Nelson Miles, in southern Montana. Horn Cloud's boy was already a veteran, having counted coup in the fight with Long Hair though barely old enough to be a warrior.[5]

In May 1877, an exhausted Crazy Horse surrendered and brought in one of the last large groups of free Lakotas. For months the government dickered with tribal leaders and government spies about Crazy Horse's fate, and in early September they went to Camp Sheridan to bring Tasunka Witko back under guard to Camp (later Fort) Robinson, in northwestern Nebraska. Beard was there for the final surrender, which took place at Beaver Valley. The scouts escorted Crazy Horse to the fort, and during the trip a small thundercloud came up as they neared Chadron. Two bolts of lightning flashed from the cloud. Crazy Horse looked up and laughed. "You might as well kill me here," he told his escort, "because the *wakinyan* have said I'm going to die." The *wakinyan* were the "winged gods," the thunderbird spirits that came in flashes of lightning and portended death. Either Beard traveled with Crazy Horse to Camp Robinson when he saw the cloud, or he knew someone who told the story later.

The Horn Cloud family likely came in to the Spotted Tail agency after Crazy Horse surrendered. But they appear to have merely watched the events that played out, not abandoned their freedom. Though close to Crazy Horse, it's doubtful they made the last trip to Camp Robinson. Perhaps they suspected that treachery was imminent, because, on September 5, the great Lakota warrior was killed, bayoneted by a soldier and betrayed by some within his own tribe. Beard believed they killed him out of envy—both the *wasicu* and Lakotas—because of his unparalleled bravery and poise. "A leader is always singled out," he remarked later, "and the leaders will always be killed." They wrapped him and put the body in a tree scaffold in the traditional way, said Beard, painting a red mark on the wrapping to show that he'd been killed.[6]

The world of the Horn Clouds was collapsing. Their leader and relative was murdered; they were menaced by government troops at the agency; winter was drawing near. But surrender meant giving up their guns and ponies to enemies who had been tracking them since the Custer fight. So they headed north, several children in tow, of which the eldest, Putin-hin, was doing a man's work now that he had been tested in battle. The family crossed over the "medicine line," or Canadian border, in late 1877, probably traveling with a larger band. "I rode a sorrel horse," Beard told his friend Jake Herman, "a Calvary horse I captured during the Battle. All the way to Canada they took shots at us." Near Wood Mountain in today's south-central Saskatchewan, about thirty miles from the U.S. border, they met up with the Lakota leader in exile, who was every bit Crazy Horse's equal.[7]

Sitting Bull had directed Native forces in the fight against Custer, and his reputation for bravery in battle was well earned. He was an imposing man with an impassive mien and strapping build. He had acknowledged power as a holy man and as a warrior, fighting various army expeditions into Lakota land for over a decade. In his forties by the time of the Greasy Grass dustup, Sitting Bull was past his prime as a warrior, but as a leader he drew a large following and united the divisions of the Sioux with a firm and defiant hand.[8]

Putinhin lauded Sitting Bull's bravery in the Long Hair fight. Some Beard descendants believe the two men were cousins, though that term can be stretched a long way in Indian country. Ernie LaPointe doesn't think of Beard as a relative, and a blood tie to the Sitting Bulls would have probably been noted during Putinhin's many visits to his house. Whatever the two men may have lacked in kinship, though, they made up for in the shared experience of being refugees. And Beard maintained close relations with the Sitting Bull family for the rest of his life.

For the next few years Sitting Bull and his followers would roam between Wood Mountain and the Cypress Hills, a stretch of rolling country about one hundred miles long. Estimates for the group that trickled north range as high as five thousand, of which about a third would have been warriors. Though most were Lakotas, their ranks were swelled by Yankton Sioux, Santees, and Nez Perces fleeing the violent Indian policy in the south. By late 1877 the Horn Clouds had joined them, among the last Lakotas who held out from going in to the reservation, clinging to a way of life that, when his father was Putinhin's age, would have seemed like it could go on forever.[9]

At first it seemed safe and familiar, a land of generous pastures broken with draws that drained frequent streams, a thinly timbered region bordered with badlands. But it was no paradise, even in summer. "The ruthless mosquitoes, which are a positive plague in that region in the summer months, swarmed by the millions," wrote a Chicago correspondent who visited the Lakotas, "their venomous bites covering our hands, necks, and faces with blotches resembling smallpox pustules." At one meeting he recalled a herd of fifteen thousand ponies and war horses in the backyard of Sitting Bull's camp. Their numbers would soon start to dwindle.[10]

Many in the American press labeled them "murderers" and demanded their extradition. In their defense, none less than abolitionist Wendell Phillips wrote an open letter comparing the Lakotas to another group of oppressed Americans: "Every reason which made England refuse to give up the fugitive slave exists in the Indian case," Phillips argued, before they were "trodden down alike by the greed and neglect of a powerful and grasping people." Everyone had an opinion on the refugees in Grandmother's Land. They were border celebrities in an age when the forty-ninth parallel was a long and simmering strip of contested ground.[11]

What the Lakotas found in Canada must have surprised them: a more flexible government policy and a better-trained brand of men to carry it out. Canada, by and large, hadn't subjected its Native population to lengthy removals and confrontation. Even in the west they rarely resorted to mobilizing forces. Not inclined to see Sitting Bull as a renegade, they met him with cautious acceptance when he crossed into exile. What's more, the Lakotas were no longer confronted by the green recruits so common in the U.S. Army. Now they faced a superbly disciplined group of a few hundred mounted officers sporting kepis and bright scarlet tunics.

These were the North-West Mounted Police, a newly minted paramilitary force led by the capable James Walsh. It was Walsh whose aggressive but even-handed tactics earned the grudging respect of Sitting Bull, a rare feat for a white man. Still famous for their red coats and lone-wolf authority on the Canadian range, the "Mounties" were an efficient and scrupulous unit invested with civil judicial powers. The government gave them the role of making and keeping the peace in an age when Indian wars were still common south of the border.[12]

But Sitting Bull's people were caught in a vise. The Americans wanted revenge for Custer; the Canadians wanted to avoid an international incident with their powerful neighbor. While sympathetic to the Lakotas, the northerners were cognizant of the risks their presence entailed. A single Indian raid on the American side, the government in Ottawa knew, could be a pretext for war. For their part, the Lakotas were trapped between an angry overseer and a nervous host, and the line separating them was only a day's march away.

Ottawa had other reasons to worry. The Sioux were now within reach of several Canadian tribes who were their proven enemies—notably the Blackfeet and Crees—while the government was attempting to settle those tribes on federal reserves. To maintain the peace, it was decided the Lakotas could remain in Canada but only without any direct government help, a passive offer of refuge. Sitting Bull's people were forbidden from crossing over the border, even to hunt buffalo. In late 1877 a visiting American commission, led by General Alfred Terry, failed to change Sitting Bull's preference for asylum. They offered a pardon for past actions, but only on condition the Lakotas give up their horses and guns. Sitting Bull dismissed them rudely.[13]

By the next winter, the Lakotas were starving. They broke up into small parties to hunt the dwindling *pte*, or buffalo, the center of their culture. The occasional illegal foray was made across the border when the herds drifted south. Holy man Black Elk later recalled it was so cold in Canada that a group of whimpering porcupines huddled in his camp to keep warm. Some Lakotas died from eating diseased flesh, not the last time they would be reduced to consuming their horses, the very animal that had given them the freedom of the plains. "Game was scarce in Canada," Beard recalled; "we nearly starved, we had to live on roots and birds."[14]

Before long, Ottawa was trying to push the Lakotas out. With famine likely if they continued in the north, many, but not all, began to filter back across the line. "Finally Sitting Bull decided to come back so we came back to North Dakota up in the Bull Horn Country," in 1880, Beard remembered, after an exile of three years. They went to Fort Buford on the Missouri, and the soldiers brought them downriver in a vessel. "The boat came to Fort Yates. That's where it stopped, and we got off."[15]

It was in Canada that Putinhin came of age. Marie says his mother was wounded at Little Bighorn and limped north with the family across the line. Tradition has it that she died while in Canada, and Marie insists she's buried in Moose Jaw. But Horn Cloud would soon have another wife, or had one already, since the Lakotas practiced plural marriage. It's possible that when Putinhin came to Cherry Creek on the Cheyenne River he had left his birth mother behind in Canada, a stark reminder of a time when the refugee Lakotas belonged to no nation and no place.[16]

By late 1880 the family was settled at Standing Rock agency, a part of Hump's band. Horn Cloud and his new wife, Nest, had five children. The eldest appears on the census as Many Wounded Holes, the teenager who would later change names like a suit of Sunday clothes. The youngest of his brothers, White Enemy, was two years old and had been born over the line in Canada. None of them yet had a Christian name. They were dirt-poor refugees with a horse and four dogs.[17]

Soon they would move further down the Missouri to the Cheyenne River country and a place called Cherry Creek. Today, near Cherry Creek, a stretch of green carpeted badlands lines the river, capped with a tree-lined ridge. An island of cottonwoods and willows and a washed-out bridge mark the last stretch of BIA Route 12 that winds along the river from Highway 63. To the north are undulating badlands, the kind of country that would have supported hunters of deer and buffalo, the rolling hills screening the approach of hunters from a grazing herd.

So the Horn Clouds settled near here, along the river, and built themselves a house of logs. They went through a transformation within sight of their old life, the past in plain view on the bluffs above, and started to till the soil with the memory of starvation fresh in their minds. Theirs was a new project, accompanied by new names, new animals, new neighbors, a school, a church, a government agent, a ration of beef and coffee. They wouldn't have accepted it all at once, but step by step they took what was useful during those first years at Cheyenne River. The American conversion of the Horn Clouds, though much of it was only skin deep, had begun.[18]

5

WOUNDED KNEE

If you glance off to the horizon for just a moment, or reach down to tune the radio, you might miss Wounded Knee. It's just a flat of land on the road that dips from Porcupine to Pine Ridge with no sign of fuss or bluster. A small museum shelters some ragtag exhibits off the road. A two-track path leads up to a church with a large, fenced patch of earth and a marble monument. Inside the chain-link fence, stuffed with tobacco offerings and flowers, about 150 people are buried in one of the most notorious graves in America. "Horn Cloud, the peacemaker, died here innocent," an inscription on the shaft reads. That's the way the Horn Cloud boys wanted their father remembered.

In May 2010, about a century after that stone was put up, a flock of three Black Hawk helicopters manned by the Colorado National Guard descended on the grave. Their mission was to visit the site and learn from an Oglala representative about the day that more than two hundred Lakota people died at the hands of the U.S. Army. As the copters descended, they were met by a throng of Indian protestors who started yelling and waving them off. "We don't want United States military here!" they shouted. "This is our land!" Some women ran underneath the whirling metal blades and tried to keep the choppers from landing. Only one bird had the temerity to set down at all, and it stayed for less than a minute.

The pilots hightailed it back to Rapid City. It wasn't the warm welcome they were expecting in light of the tribe's invitation. It seems that word hadn't gotten out to local people that a few guardsmen would be dropping in for a visit. Sensing a public-relations fiasco in the making, Captain Michael Odgers tried to explain the purpose of the ill-timed sortie: "While the Battle of Wounded Knee is a dark chapter in the history of the Army," he acknowledged, "without learning from the mistakes of our past we are doomed to repeat them." He called it a "battle," something most Oglalas would never do. Soon after, the tribal council passed a resolution forbidding the military from visiting the site where the dead of Wounded Knee are buried.[1]

As they tried to land, a woman was waiting for them on the hill. She wasn't one of the protestors. She was upset by all the commotion, in fact. She was there to greet the soldiers and give them a tour of the site, to tell them what happened that day and to honor her grandfathers. Waiting for the choppers that never landed was Marie Fox Belly, practicing her story of the massacre, a tale she knows better than any other on earth.

The Horn Clouds returned from Canada to Dakota Territory and settled near the Cheyenne River agency in the early 1880s. The hardships in the north forced them to grasp an unavoidable truth: the old way of life was over. They had nearly starved to death in Grandmother's Land, and the return across the border meant the surrender of ideas and habits as well as ponies and guns. As strange as it sounded to people who had hunted and gathered for generations, even centuries, it was time to work the land rather than live off the fat of it. The Horn Clouds were ready to become Indian farmers.

The family made a separate peace with the white world. Beard's grandfather homesteaded on the east side of the Missouri about ten miles above Pierre, but taxes forced him to move west of the river. The rest of the family would take up residence in a log house, not a buffalo-hide tipi. They ran horses and cattle and harvested hay. On Sundays they went to a church and stood along the back wall while Joseph, Beard's younger brother who had been the first in the clan to be schooled in English, would have been the only one who could translate into Lakota the songs and prayers of a Christian god.[2]

Before the decade was out, the Horn Clouds had worked hard to build a small ranch on the Cheyenne. They owned a wagon and harness, four saddles, a tipi, and nine quilts. The Cheyenne River country is biting cold in winter, so their possessions included two heavy beaver shawls and three overcoats. Nomads no more, they accumulated a log house full of dishes and cups, guns and bridles, a lariat, an ax, a coffee pot—and a pile of well-thumbed schoolbooks for Joe's edification.[3]

Beard (still known as Whiskers on the census) married a young woman named Wears Eagle about 1888, the ceremony performed by the Indian agent at Cheyenne River. Putinhin was in his mid- to late twenties; she was six years his junior. Their first son, John, died in infancy, cause unknown. The young couple settled near Horn Cloud and set up house as the father had, surrounded by a crowd of animals, quilts and pipes, kettles and cups and guns. If an inventory from 1896 is accurate, they had ten horses, twenty-five head of cattle, and twenty tons of hay, not a bad spread for the upper Missouri country. In one corner was a cookstove, in the other a buffalo-calf robe trimmed with porcupine quills. The great-grandchildren of Black Buffalo, as Joe would have it, were anchored to a plot of earth about forty-five degrees north latitude on the banks of the "Big Cheyenne."[4]

But the land of the Lakotas was shrinking. The Great Sioux Reservation, created in 1868, comprised all of today's South Dakota west of the Missouri River. Arm-twisting forced the Lakotas to give up the Black Hills in 1876. For the next decade, the government badgered the tribe to surrender even more, but a commission in 1888 was turned away empty-handed. The following year Congress passed appropriations to buy nine million acres on the reservation, pending approval of three-quarters of adult Lakota males, a formality required by treaty. Because Washington had already opened its pocketbook, their "approval" seemed unavoidable.[5]

In the summer of 1889 the government men came to carve up the reservation. They promised horses and cows and plows and schools—in return for a dip of the pen. The parley at Cheyenne River, attended by hundreds of Lakotas, had the atmosphere of a desperate tent revival. Led by General George Crook, Indian fighter extraordinaire, the commissioners held forth and the chiefs wrangled over the wisdom of signing away "excess" acreage.

But the Lakotas were under heavy pressure to cave. Epidemics like measles and whooping cough had broken out. The withholding of government rations was threatened. Lakota stock was trampling untended fields as they listened. And the men from Washington gave them only a week to decide.

The negotiations began slowly. The Lakotas were stoutly opposed at the start. Even the mixed-bloods and white men married to Indian women were dead set against the proposal. The commission had been barnstorming through Lakota country since May, and word was spreading that those at Rosebud and Lower Brule had given in, and their Crow Creek relatives weren't far behind. But the Cheyenne River Lakotas were ready to take a stand.

The Lakotas had long relied on chiefs and headmen to reach consensus for the tribe. But the 1868 treaty stipulated a new kind of democratic rule. A supermajority (three-quarters of adult males) seemed like a cautious way to prevent electoral mischief. But by 1889, a shady side of democratic voting surfaced. The headmen and chiefs had little influence anymore if each man had a vote. And individual votes could be begged, bought, bullied, and cajoled—especially since the ballot was public. In a sense, the body politic of the Lakotas had been broken up in anticipation of breaking down the land base.[6]

The referendum, if such it was, was nearly marred by a riot. On July 17, Hump, a relative of Horn Cloud and chief of the Cheyenne agency police, rose to announce he wouldn't sign the agreement. When a few Lakotas, encouraged by Crook, started to make their mark on the paper by way of assent, several Indians with clubs, at Hump's urging, tried to stop them. Crook blocked their way. Though Hump resisted, the fight soon went out of the police. Chasing Crow got up and signed. Then High Eagle and Ground Hog. Takes His Blanket consented, as did Three Legs. Fights the Bear went up, and Afraid of Nothing, and Black Chicken, and John Blue Cloud—all of them rose and did the long walk to the front of the tent in spite of the warnings from many of their own headmen.[7]

The kith and kin of the Horn Clouds, like Hump, feasted on the government beef for a week. Then, for two weeks after the commissioners left, the votes were re-tallied. When the count finally ended, the pliant

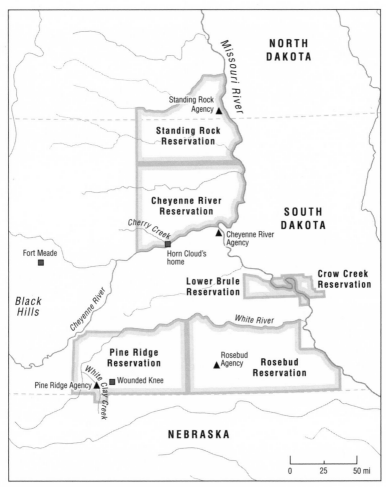

Map 3. The Lakota World, 1890 (Erin Greb Cartography)

ones at Cheyenne River had agreed to sell much of the treaty land and chop up the remainder of the Great Sioux Reservation into a series of smaller reserves. Of 750 adult male Lakotas at Cheyenne River, more than four-fifths—Minneconjous, Sans Arcs, Two Kettles, and the Black-feet subtribes—stepped up to "touch the pen." A week of haranguing had worn them down. Rumors of bribes were common. Even Hump signed on in the end. But the notion of consensus, deeply woven into the pattern of Lakota life, had been pushed aside.[8]

Not everyone did the government's bidding. "Grandpa Beard never signed a treaty," Leonard Little Finger told me proudly. And the Horn Clouds didn't sign this one. Their refusal was probably one reason why they were targeted when the big trouble came in 1890. Still, the family's snub of the commissioners didn't mean they rejected white ways—only that they wouldn't open tribal land to settlement at the paltry rate of $1.25 an acre. They were learning that living on the land was a bitter test, even for white men who abandoned their fields amid clouds of grasshoppers and weeks of drought in a stretch of dry seasons.

Almost ten years after the return from Canada, the Horn Clouds would soon be on the move again.

It all started with a man who went to heaven—and came back to tell about it.

His name was Wovoka, a Northern Paiute shaman from Mason Valley in Nevada. Rumors spread in 1889 that Jack Wilson, as Wovoka was known to whites, claimed to be the son of God. Native leaders traveled hundreds of miles across the West for a glimpse of proof. What they saw and heard when they got there astonished them. The disappearing buffalo would soon return, Wovoka told them. All Indians who had died would come back to life. He showed his new disciples the stigmata on his hands, just the way Christ had been pierced. It was said he could even make animals talk. Best of all, he said, the white man would disappear and the old way of life would return. They danced in his honor, a new kind of dance, and the practice spread like a prairie burn in dry summer. By the spring of 1890, the Ghost Dance reached South Dakota.[9]

The Ghost Dance was a mix of old and new. The Lakotas fasted for twenty-four hours and did a traditional sweat bath—then went out and danced on Sundays. They planted a flowering tree in the middle of a large circle of men and women, as they did with the sun dance, and often tied an American flag to it, traditional religious leaders gathered at the center. The male dancers in the circle were clothed and wore muslin ghost shirts, painted red with eagles, sun circles, and thunderbirds. The women were garbed in "ghost dresses" and wore eagle plumes in their hair. They refused to use any metal or other white-made objects.[10]

The dancers would lock hands in a circle around the tree, shuffling in the dirt, moving right to left. As they danced and sang, they sought a vision of their relatives in the other world. They used no drums. The dancing was ecstatic and lasted four days and nights, many dancers dropping to the ground when the spirit—or sheer exhaustion—overcame them. The falling were dragged along by the others until they couldn't go on, and most would faint away, later to rise and recount their visions. When they finished one dance, they would get up and start again.[11]

The Horn Clouds, who had heard about the dance, had more pressing matters. In late summer they obtained a pass to leave the agency and hunt antelope on Dog Teeth Butte, near the Missouri. By the time they came back to the agency in October, the soldiers told them the "Medicine Dance" had reached Cheyenne River. Wears Eagle was about eight months pregnant, and Beard was preparing to dig in for the long frost when, in the dying weeks of autumn, the last act of the Indian wars overtook them.[12]

To say the Ghost Dance War that followed was about a dance is like saying the Battle of the Little Bighorn was about a river. Most settlers didn't know the difference between a Sioux and a Cherokee, much less a scalp dance and a religious sacrament, and few were inclined to learn the difference. More to the point, the Lakotas were deeply mistrusted. They had never been forgiven for the Custer fight, and many people were bent on avenging the fallen members of the Seventh Cavalry. Newspapers in Rapid City and Omaha competed to exaggerate the likelihood of an Indian outbreak. Published accounts of attacks on settlers were frequent—and false—but that didn't stop the presses. The "Ghost Dance War" was a newspaper war if there ever was one, a partly calculated event that flooded the area with soldiers, stacks of money, and an abiding taste for payback.[13]

By late November the army had planted its troops in a constellation of camps stretching from Fort Meade in the Black Hills up to Fort Yates in the north and down to Rosebud and Pine Ridge agencies, slowly encircling the Lakotas. Commander in chief Nelson Miles had at his immediate disposition some three thousand troops; half the infantry and cavalry of the U.S. Army were posted to the area. Their mission was to stop the Ghost Dancers and make them trade their guns and bows for a life of plows and pitchforks. But many, like the Horn Clouds, had already done that. There was something strange and frantic in the mounting reaction. As Indian physician Charles Eastman commented later, "One might almost as well call upon the army to suppress [evangelist] Billy Sunday and his hysterical followers."[14]

It's no surprise that many Lakotas chose to dance. The buffalo were gone, and the beef ration had been cut in half. If the drought didn't ruin their fields, the grasshoppers ate them. Their great leader Crazy Horse was dead. The other, Sitting Bull, was camped out in a log cabin on the Grand River like a prisoner of war. The old ways were doomed, the new ones unproven. The dance was the only thing left that recalled the world of their elders.

The Horn Cloud family went down to White Clay Creek to have a look. "I and my father and all my brothers danced," Beard recalled. "When we danced, some Indians acted as if they died, and some acted as if they were holy." There were dancers who "saw mysterious things" and even the Savior, who promised to restore their old way of life. But Beard had a nagging doubt.[15]

The family returned to Cheyenne River, where Putinhin made a ghost shirt and painted his magic on it. The medicine men promised him that bullets couldn't pierce the muslin fabric. He danced alongside his family and listened when the dancers cried out again that they'd heard the voice of the Savior. But the magic was missing. The men who couldn't be trusted were the ones who saw the visions and described them the loudest, he said. Beard conferred with Horn Cloud. In the end, said the eldest son, "Nothing mysterious would come to any of my father's family." There was a reason for their skepticism, Marie thinks, since they had entered the white world ten years before: "They knew that there was another way of praying besides just the Ghost Dance."[16]

In the early days of December, Wears Eagle and Beard welcomed to the world their second son, Wet Feet. No doubt they would have preferred to stay put on the banks of the Cheyenne and see the new baby through his first winter, and later they must have wished they had. But the extended Horn Cloud family was soon trapped by a different kind of winter storm that was blowing from the east.

The Horn Clouds were close to Big Foot (Si Tanka), headman of the Minneconjous, and as members of his band they now sought his guidance. Big Foot had camped near Cherry Creek to draw rations in November, and the second week of December he was urged in a letter from Red Cloud to go down to Pine Ridge and meet with the main contingent of Ghost Dancers. The Oglala chief offered him a hundred horses to come and help make peace with the whites.[17]

It was a fateful offer. Big Foot planned to go down the Cheyenne and draw annuities at Fort Bennett before making his way to Pine Ridge. On his way down the river, though, a pair of men rode into camp, one of them badly wounded. They had devastating news for Si Tanka from Grand River in the north: Sitting Bull was dead. Several dozen policemen had stormed his camp at dawn on December 15. When the officers entered his cabin to arrest him, Sitting Bull submitted. But once he was taken outside, the Sioux defenders began to muster. He shouted for help, a rifle fired, and then a fusillade exploded that killed at least eight of his entourage, six policemen, and the leader of Little Bighorn himself. His killers had been "metal breasts," members of the Indian police. As with Crazy Horse, the Lakotas had a hand in the death of another of their heroes.

Si Tanka didn't hesitate. On the next day, the nineteenth, he sent ten men, including Beard, to ride back and get the remnants of Sitting Bull's band, now in shock and mourning. Beard met his cousin Hump at the camp. It was the same Hump who had rallied the Lakotas to deny the agreement the year before, only to finally sign it. But Hump turned Beard and the others away. The infantry marched east up Cheyenne River under Colonel H. C. Merriam, and the cavalry, led by Colonel E. V. Sumner, closed from the west, keeping the Minneconjous within striking distance. The pincers were about to close.

Big Foot's convoy included about four hundred men, women, and children, most of them Minneconjous, with a few Hunkpapa refugees from Standing Rock. They had not raided any homesteads or taken any cattle along the way. They probably had no more than a few dozen guns, many of them antique muzzle-loaders. Some walked, some rode horses, some rode in wagons filled with the few possessions of their crumbling world on the Cheyenne, and some brought cattle. They resembled nothing so much as an emigrant wagon train. The younger ones, like Beard, were anxious to avenge Sitting Bull, but the elders, who had seen the devastation the *wasicu* wrought, no longer had the resolve for a fight. Beard's newborn son was barely two weeks old.

Big Foot was hardly a hostile. He signed the 1868 treaty, he'd traveled to Washington, he missed the Little Bighorn dustup, though perhaps only by accident. He promised Colonel Sumner he would remain encamped at Deep Creek and go back to Fort Bennett the next morning, but he sensed danger. The night of December 23 he broke his promise to Sumner, and his band slipped away for Pine Ridge, descending south into the wasteland known as the Big Badlands. As the old women sang their death songs walking behind the wagons, Beard camped on a hill and watched for soldiers until dawn.[18]

The passage through the lunar, eroded landscape the next day, known by the Lakotas as *makhosica*, "bad lands," was brutal. The spectral peaks and slopes of the main "wall" were a formidable obstacle, and the wind was bitter and raw. Big Foot decided not to turn west to enter the Stronghold, the elevated redoubt of the Ghost Dancers from Rosebud and Pine Ridge who were spoiling for a fight with the soldiers. Instead, the Minneconjou men used axes and spades to hack out a path for the wagons, looking over their shoulders for signs of the army. When they made their breach and reached the bottom of the pass, the gaunt Big Foot had his men slaughter some of the yearling colts to feed his band.

They didn't finish crossing the nearby White River until dark. The Lakotas roped their cattle and dragged them across the ice. It was Christmas Eve. The next day was holy, the churchgoers knew, but that wouldn't deter the soldiers when they found out Big Foot had run. By then, Spotted Elk, as Big Foot was also known, had been taken sick with pneumonia.[19]

On the twenty-sixth they camped at Red Water Creek on Pine Ridge. It was a site Beard marked well, for he would one day build his ranch there in honor of that camp and that night and those people. Big Foot sent scouts fanning out to the south looking for soldiers. Many bands were drawing near the agency in Pine Ridge, they reported back, and the cavalry was waiting for them along the way. The coughing disease left Big Foot weak and in no mood to defy them.

The next day he led the ragged train of Minneconjous toward American Horse Creek, a few miles southwest of Kyle. On a faraway ridge they spotted some army scouts, Sioux men who were doing the bluecoats' bidding. A few of the young men galloped off to catch them and brought one back, leading him by his horse's reins, but he reassured them everything was fine.

The morning of December 28 they saw the soldiers from a distance, forming ranks along a row of pines at the base of Porcupine Butte. The soldiers had deployed two large Hotchkiss cannons and were lined up in a row, as if for battle. Big Foot knew that to break and run would only be taken as a sign of guilt. They had done nothing wrong, they had stolen no goods, they had killed no animals except their own. They proceeded forward toward the village of Pine Ridge.

The young men were more quarrelsome, though. Beard rode ahead with several others and approached the line of soldiers. They trotted slowly. They were cautious, because Sitting Bull had been killed only two weeks before. The bluecoats jammed the cartridges into their guns and waited.

Then Beard did a strange thing.

He got down from his horse and held out his hand. He wanted the soldiers to know how brave he was. Then he made a prayer. "Grandfather, God have pity on me for what is going to happen," he said. "I may die today, or I may not. Whatever it is, grant me the strength to persevere."[20]

He walked up to a Hotchkiss cannon and shoved his hand down the barrel. Ha! It was as though he was counting coup on the *wasicu* gun. He defied them all to respond. He would let them know he was no treaty Indian. It was aggressive, perhaps foolhardy, for a man with an infant son. The soldiers looked on, confused, because to fire on one man was folly. Before anyone could decide what to do next, Big Foot's wagon was heard rolling up along the creek behind them.[21]

The wagon, flying a white flag, stopped in front of the soldiers. An officer approached and asked if Big Foot could talk. They traded words that Beard, standing nearby, could hardly have grasped without an interpreter. Big Foot had been bleeding, and the officer was moved with compassion, knowing he was near death. "I want you to give me twenty-five guns," said the bluecoat, anxious to disarm the Lakotas before they reached Pine Ridge.[22]

Big Foot looked away and said he was afraid. He promised to give up the guns when they reached the agency. The soldiers wrapped him in blankets and called for an ambulance to come up. Then they placed him tenderly, like an injured child, in the wagon bed. Horn Cloud took his scarf off and tied it on Big Foot's head for warmth. But it was hard to understand what the soldiers wanted. Beard heard the officers laughing when they carried Si Tanka away. They drove over the rising and falling swells of the prairie to a small valley where the army had camped, on a creek called Wounded Knee.

The ambulance stopped at a large Sibley tent near the creek, where they stowed the chief for the night. A white flag flew from the tent crown. The Lakota women began setting up camp nearby in the twilight.

That night, December 28, was a long one. The soldiers unloaded sugar, bacon, and hardtack in the Indian camp, and Beard helped distribute it. The bluecoats began dragging cannons and ammunition up the hill overlooking the tipis. Beard could see the fires of the Indian scouts burning nearby, the men who decided to ride against their own people. He didn't sleep at all that night. He had no appetite. He was filled "with fear and foreboding."[23]

He had every right to be. The worst day of his life was about to begin.

A few years back Marie Fox Belly was diagnosed with breast cancer. She put off the chemo and radiation treatments as long as she could. She can remember the days when a sip of water tasted bitter, when a soda was undrinkable, when, the day after a chemo session, she felt like someone had beaten her whole body with a stick. "I'm a survivor," she says proudly, the cancer in full remission, at least for a while. And the survival ethic runs deep in the Dewey Beard clan. For years, in fact, she was secretary and president of the Wounded Knee Survivors Association, founded by the Horn Cloud boys to press the legal claims of survivors and their descendants after 1890. In 1990 she testified before a Senate committee on Wounded Knee reparations, much as her great-grandfather would do during the Great Depression.

Born in 1951, Marie missed the massacre by more than half a century. Her youthful laugh and butch-cut hair (which disappeared after the chemo) make her seem younger than her years, though she has a grandson out of high school. But elder she is at the ripe old age of sixty-three, already pushing the average life span on Pine Ridge. Like many others on the reservation, she can't let go of the day Big Foot's people camped at Wounded Knee.

Marie lives with her husband, daughter, and grandchildren in a trailer park near the old hospital, just above a dreary housing project in the center of Pine Ridge. A wire fence with a dirt yard leads to the front door, while around back is a barbecue grill, some towering cottonwoods, and a yard scattered with bikes and toys, a shady preserve I didn't see for many years. I had to come knocking several times before Marie trusted me. On my fourth or fifth visit, she shyly brought out a faded photograph of her parents, happily embracing in front of what looks like an old Model T.

You don't want to get Marie started on Wounded Knee unless you have an afternoon to spare. She doesn't see the Horn Clouds as enemies of white people, she'll tell you up front. They were only called "hostile" because they refused to sign treaties. They'd been to a Congregational church, sent Joe to school, built log houses. But then the drought came. And the government cut rations. When a people are under stress, she says, "They resort back to an earlier form of worship." And that was the beginning of the dance that almost destroyed her family. "The Ghost Dance was a dance of life," says Marie, even if it didn't end up that way.

The military was called in to put an end to it all, so you'd expect resentment against the army to run deep among the Oglalas. Sure enough, a National Guard helicopter landing at Wounded Knee 120 years later can provoke the outrage of elders and an emergency tribal hearing. But Pine Ridge, where the surviving Horn Cloud children would settle, is a profoundly patriotic place. The Lakotas honor their veterans at powwows. Old Glory flies from many a house and yard. To be a veteran—on this and other reservations—is the highest honor someone can earn. Military service fulfills the credo of a warrior tradition. It also means a job and a paycheck on a reservation where the unemployment rate runs higher than the temperature most of the year.

Putinhin wasn't a patriot in the usual sense. Kaka Beard, as Marie calls her great-grandfather, used to tell her mother, Celane, that if she ever had sons she should never send them off to war. What happened at Wounded Knee he could never forget, a memory he passed on to his family. "It's them that killed your grandparents," he would remind Celane, a granddaughter he raised as his own child. And Celane's sons didn't enlist.

Marie's life took a different turn. She married Luke White Stone, who did two tours in Vietnam and won a bronze star. He lost part of his hearing as a helicopter door gunner, and on his second tour he was in the Americal division, where such luminaries as Colin Powell served. (One of the other units in Americal committed the My Lai Massacre.) Luke and Marie have been together for about forty years, since she was a teenager.

They know every crack and pothole on the road to Wounded Knee, at least before the BIA got around to repaving it. Sunday nights they would pass the place on their way to the tribal radio station. Before she got sick Marie was a disc jockey at KILI, ten or so miles from where Big Foot's people camped their final night. The tribal voice for the Oglalas, KILI mixes health tips and political hearings in Lakota with smart and sassy hip-hop and Buddy Red Bow ballads. And they do it all from Porcupine Butte, about a mile from where Beard shoved his hand into the Hotchkiss cannon on the way down to the creek. Marie could almost see the place from the studio.

Her grandfather always mourned what happened there, "but he wasn't bitter to the point where he taught us to hate or to dislike. All he ever said was this: 'You have to be careful of the *wasicu* because even in the blink of an eye they can defeat you. You watch them carefully, but you learn what they teach you and use what they teach you against them. That's how you defeat them. Not by guns, but by what you know.' That was education."

Marie was a "dormer" student at Pine Ridge Boarding School who graduated and went to Oakland about 1970, part of the voluntary government relocation program. By moving to urban areas, Indians would learn valuable skills to make them self-supporting citizens, or so the theory went. Marie learned how to take apart business machines for repair and put them back together again—what turned out to be a useless trade when computers replaced typewriters, and processors made camshafts obsolete. "They put us in the cities to perish," she mourns. Relocation for Marie's generation and that of her parents was what allotment had been for Putinhin's—a grand piece of social engineering fostered by good intentions but sabotaged by lousy foresight.

Marie is loaded with stories that range from the deeply touching to the mildly implausible, with lots of secondhand tales thrown in for seasoning. A small girl when her great-grandfather died, she insists that her vivid memories of Putinhinla, as she calls him, are true. Each one, bright and sparkling, she brings out to show like a fresh-cut gem. Not everything she says is borne out by the record, I realize over time. But much in the record about Wounded Knee is false or distorted in the first place. It may be the nature of the oral tradition to puff and embroider. That's where written history begins—by choosing one of the spoken versions and repeating it. But writing down a story doesn't disprove the alternatives, it only silences them. I look for places where the two ways of telling overlap.

Grandpa Beard must have seemed like a ghost from another age to a little girl in the 1950s. Marie was taught to show deep respect for him in the Lakota way. "I put my ear to his chest, and I could hear his heartbeat. Then I could feel his breath on top of my head. His hands were big hands, and I thought, 'Gee, this man held his child, a newborn baby, and he held weapons of war. But he also shook hands in friendship.' His eyes were the color of coffee, brownish, really clear. Ninety nine years old and he was still able to hear very well. He had all his teeth, too . . ."

As her voice trails off, she starts to tear up.

"The same blood that runs through his veins runs through mine."

There was another thing about Dewey Beard that was unforgettable, especially for a four-year-old with a vivid imagination:

"I sat on his lap and felt that scar in his leg where he was shot. I could put my hand in where the muscle was torn away."

She says he used to talk about that a lot.

At dawn on December 29, 1890, a bugle sounded reveille, and the cavalry began to mount their horses. It was a cautious welcome to the day: over five hundred troops and scouts had assembled under command of Colonel James Forsyth, including the Seventh Cavalry, George Custer's old unit. Several had been in Custer's rearguard in 1876 and escaped the fate of their unlucky comrades. The soldiers, on foot and horse, had drawn a ring around Big Foot's camp.

Horn Cloud had had a premonition of battle. The night before, he warned his sons to stay put if a few Lakota people started mischief. But he was firm about what they should do if the white men started something instead. "If you die at once, among your relations defending them, I will be satisfied." During the night his father had asked a medicine man what the Ghost Dance Messiah would do to protect them. It was more a taunt than a question, coming from a man who doubted the power of Wovoka's magic.[24]

Much had happened in the fourteen years since the Greasy Grass. It had been summer then, the Moon of Making Fat, and the buffalo were still plentiful. Now it was winter, and they were surrounded by lines of soldiers whose ranks would never bend. Cannons were pointed at them from the hill above. Some of their own men had decided to ride with the soldiers. The Lakotas were poorly armed, made their village at a place of the soldiers' choosing, carried their leader on a stretcher, and hoisted a white flag above their leader's tent— not a row of war lances gathering for a charge into the ranks of their captors.

Early that morning, the army's mixed-blood interpreter, Philip Wells, ordered them to surrender their weapons. A group of soldiers barged through the Indian camp, seizing guns, knives, axes, and awls. Beard returned to his lodge and grabbed his gun. First he dug a hole and laid down the arm, covered it with dirt, and draped quilts and blankets over it. A soldier suddenly stepped in and told him to come to a council in Big Foot's tent. Putinhin buried a handful of cartridges by the door and covered them with manure before he left.

For the time being, they were safe. Since the soldiers had encircled their camp, Beard figured, they couldn't shoot without firing into their own ranks. But the bluecoats were acting strangely. They ordered the Indians to line up in the ravine next to the camp. The soldiers came up with the guns they had taken, now empty, and pointed them at the Indians and pulled the trigger. Some of the Lakotas and white civilians nearby thought they were drunk. It was a crude punishment for not surrendering their pieces sooner, and Beard watched, offended by the spectacle, as the weapons piled up in the center of the council.[25]

There was a bad feeling in the air. Some of the warriors said they would surrender only their cartridges. One of the holy men began to sing a prayer. Some people cried out, "The soldiers are going to shoot!," and the women and children stood to one side, watching nervously. Another Lakota sidled up to Wells and threatened to kill him if he told a lie while translating. Then the medicine man Yellow Bird began scooping handfuls of earth and tossing them skyward like the Ghost Dancers. An officer came out of a tent with another gun (Beard breathed a sigh of relief when he saw it wasn't his own). It was as if all these things, clear and necessary, each one leading to the next, were moving on a crowded train down the steel rails the white men built across the prairie with no one able to stop where it was going.[26]

One man didn't hear the order to surrender. Black Coyote, a deaf Lakota, gripped his rifle defiantly. Before anyone could explain to him what was happening, some bluecoats grabbed him from behind. Horn Cloud called for an interpreter, and the squads of soldiers pointed their guns at the council. The old people, wrapped in their blankets, were sitting and smoking. The sergeants tussled with Black Coyote, who cried out that he didn't want to be killed.[27]

Then, with the muzzle pointed up, the gun went off.

Many Lakotas later on didn't recall hearing the single shot before the booming volley that followed. Rough Feather remembered the sudden noise of the guns like "the sound of tearing canvass." Afraid of the Enemy said it was "like a lightning crash." Dewey Beard only recalled later that "it was like when a wagon wheel breaks in the road." Most agreed that the men and boys sitting in council, Horn Cloud among them, were mowed down in an instant. Even the white flag of truce was shredded.[28]

The battle, if battle it was, was on. Armed only with a knife, the eldest son of Horn Cloud started to run.

Beard picked his way blindly through the black powder smoke as the firing continued. Ahead he saw a row of brass buttons suspended in the fog. A soldier raised his muzzle from the clearing haze and fired over Beard's shoulder, deafening him momentarily and singeing his hair. Beard wrested the gun away and stabbed the bluecoat in the chest and the heart, until the man fell, screaming, tearing at Beard's buckskin. He straddled the bluecoat and plunged the knife into his kidneys up to the hilt—and the soldier expired. Now he had a gun of his own, and he ran toward the ravine where the women and children had fled. He had to find his family.

Beard ran the gauntlet under fire from every direction. From what he could tell, the soldiers were killing each other in the crossfire. He took a bullet in the right arm and crumpled. In front of him, out of the smoke, another soldier rose up. They aimed their guns at each other and snapped, but the pieces didn't go off. As Beard lunged for the ravine, he stumbled into another enemy. He fired at the man, who fell down kicking his legs wildly. The shots, Beard said, "sounded like firecrackers and hail in a storm." By this time the bluecoats stood above the ravine and fired down on the scattering Lakotas, like taking target practice in a heavy blanket of smoke.[29]

Putinhin was badly injured. "I began to breathe very hard and every breath hurt me very much. I got up and tried to run but could not, so I walked. I was strangling with something warm in my throat and mouth. I spit it out and looked at it, and it was blood, so I knew that I was shot." His throat began to tighten, and he was bleeding through the nose. Then he was hit again, this time "in the lap," above the left knee. The wound staggered him, and he sat down to collect himself. He got out the cartridges he pocketed from a dead soldier and began firing above him.[30]

Wounded at least twice, Beard continued shooting until a shell jammed in the gun. He hopped on one leg toward the ravine and fell when he put pressure on the wounded limb. He threw the now useless gun away and hobbled, like an old man twice his years, through the choking pall of smoke.[31]

It was much worse than the Long Hair battle. That was a fight; this was a slaughter. Beard could see clumps of dead children scattered across the ravine, and the sight sickened him. A Lakota gave him a carbine stripped from a dead pony soldier. So he scrambled up the draw chasing soldiers and firing, then climbed back down and ran into an Indian scout. They fired at each other and missed. A Lakota grabbed Beard's buckskin and tried to hide behind him, but the soldiers killed him, too.

Too weak to run any further, Beard collapsed. A man with his jaw shot away offered him a cartridge belt. "While I was lying on my back, I looked down the ravine & saw a lot of women coming up & crying." He hadn't seen his family since the firing started, but what he saw next made him fear the worst. A group of children were running along the cut bank, and soldiers on both sides were shooting into the crowd. Their bodies soon littered the ground like carcasses around a bad water hole.[32]

As the wounded Beard was resting, a young woman nearby was shot through the throat and shoulder. He beckoned her to move closer, and she struggled to fall within reach. Catching her dress and pulling her in to shelter, he stood up a little unsteady and told her to follow him up the bank.

Then, as if in a dream, he heard something . . . It was . . . it was a song. He could hear someone singing up above him.

He followed the voice up the gulley. He was sure he knew it. It was female and sad, and it felt like it had been shattered into pieces in the cold air.

At the top of the ravine, a woman staggered across his path. It was his own mother, Nest, lurching ahead with a hole in her side. Waving an army pistol in one hand, she made a strange apparition among the smoke and whizzing bullets. She saw Putinhin. "My son, pass by me," she said. "I am going to fall down now." Soldiers from the ravine ridge took potshots at her. She fell beside him, clutching her intestines spilling out of her side. Beard watched as his mother slowly bled herself into the earth. He fired back until he emptied the magazine and moved on through the gulley, a man made an orphan in the very small part of an afternoon.[33]

A Lakota man stumbled into him. He was wounded in the knee and gave the grieving Putinhin a Winchester with cartridges. It was hard for Beard to fire, since he couldn't use his right arm. He strung the gun over his left shoulder, stuck his right thumb between his teeth to ease the pain in his arm, and ran toward where he heard his brother White Lance had been shot. Unable to aim the weapon, he urged the young men to protect the women nearby.

He could barely see his own hands. "It was now in the ravine just like a prairie fire when it reaches brush and tall grass and rages with a new power; it was like hail coming down . . . and nothing could be seen for the smoke. In the bottom of the ravine the bullets raised more dust than there was smoke, so that they could not see one another."[34]

Beard jumped into a large depression in the low ground. White Lance rolled down the hillside and joined him. He'd been shot in the leg and was half-dead, but their brother William had it worse, a bullet lodged in his breast, and he was lying there next to them, breathing painfully. Beard remembered his father's words from the night before: "All you, my dear sons, stand together and keep yourselves sober," Horn Cloud had said, "& all of you, if you die at once, among your relations defending them, I will be satisfied." So White Lance and Beard picked up their brother and brought him to his feet, and White Lance struggled to carry him to the edge of the ravine. They shook hands as he set him down there, but William would not survive.[35]

The Hotchkiss guns were pouring two-inch shells in their midst from the opposite bank. Beard rested for a moment as the big guns pounded the sides of the gulley. The smoke had grown so thick it was suffocating the wounded. He saw one Lakota whose stomach had been ripped open by a Hotchkiss shell. A woman laughed loudly and fell down with a wound. A Lakota armed with bow and arrows tumbled, too, and Beard admonished some young men to use his weapons, since the soldiers were afraid of arrows. The ravine was filled with the sound of Lakotas singing their death songs, preparing for the spirit world.

In the smoke and thunder that swallowed them, Beard gathered his nerve. He worked his way back up the ravine in search of his wife, Wears Eagle, and his son Wet Feet, barely a month old. He found a crowd of women and children hiding in a small pit, while some bluecoats were lying prone and taking shots at them. His strength returning, Beard picked one of them out and shot him clean through with the Winchester, his right arm throbbing. He fired and wounded another. As he reloaded, a horse clattered along the top of the ravine above, and he heard a voice shouting at the soldiers.

Putinhin stood up and looked at the horseman, something like a sword swinging from his saddle. Horn Cloud's son took aim, pulled the trigger, and the man collapsed and hung from the horse by the stirrups. Beard took a step forward to confirm his kill when a missed shot threw dirt in his face. He could hear the bullets zing around him, but he couldn't see anything.

His eyes burning, he crawled back down the ravine until his sight returned. The sun was lowering in the sky. The cavalry was still shooting. He traded shots with an Indian scout and worked his way up the opposite cut bank.

Beard didn't believe in the power of the ghost shirts anymore, if he ever had. He was wounded in several places. Yet it was as if the bullets could strike him but not finish him off. "I felt very sick and wanted to die." He hoped he would find his end there in the ravine, though he didn't have the strength to stand up and even make a full target of himself. His father had told him to die with the family.[36]

The end was coming. More shots rang out. Then several Lakotas rode up on horseback. Beard called out to them, but they rode off again. He hobbled after, and they stopped and came back. One of the riders was his brother Joe.

"'All my brothers and parents are dead and I have to go in and be killed too," Joe said. But Putinhin wouldn't have it. He was the eldest, and he was already covered with blood, so he would stay. But they pulled Beard on the horse and held him there while Joe walked at his side. Beard begged to be left because he was already so close to the end. But they couldn't leave him.[37]

When they reached a hill above the valley, Putinhin looked back and saw "the dead men, women and children scattered about the place where the flag of truce was still standing and flying." He knew what he had to do next. "When I got to the ridge I knew I had escaped that, so I turned and I started to sing." And the words came tumbling out. "My friends, a long time ago you lived this good way of life," he chanted, "and now you are here." His voice arched high and strong above the curling smoke of the guns below. He knew in that moment that everything had changed. "Myself," he finished, "I am going on forward." And he turned and walked over the ridge. Part of Putinhin never left Wounded Knee that day, and part of him would never look back.[38]

He went as far as White Clay Creek, where a big Lakota camp was pitched. His youngest brothers, Frank and Ernest, were there to greet him. Ernest, who had run for miles to escape the melee, later came down with consumption, which he credited to the events of that day. "When we arrived there," Beard remembered later, "I first realized that I was alive again."[39]

For all that he had been through, he was lucky. Seven of the Horn Clouds had died, his father first among them. His mother (perhaps stepmother), Nest, fell too. His brothers William and Sherman. His cousin (or sister) Pretty Enemy. His wife, Wears Eagle. And, a few months after the slaughter, his son Wet Feet, one of many who died long after the smoke of guns had drifted away. The infant swallowed blood when suckling his mother's breast in the ravine, the father said, and "was always sick till it died" the following March.[40]

Each survivor took away a piece of the horror. "We tried to run but they shot us like we were buffalo," Louise Weasel Bear said. Rough Feather's wife saw her entire family mowed down. James Pipe on Head fled from the crossfire with his mother; his sister was killed while carrying an infant on her back. Harry Kills White Man saw his mother felled with a bullet to the head as they ran for cover like "it just happened this morning," he said decades later. Peter Stand and a group of women dug out a trench with their bare hands. Of about sixty who took refuge there, a dozen survived.[41]

Beard would say it succinctly enough, sitting in a chair in a hospitality room at the Hotel Alex Johnson sixty-five years later, wearing an eagle feather headdress and talking to a man in a bow tie interrogating him for *National Geographic*:

"They murdered us."[42]

Like many geographical names, the origins of "Wounded Knee" are obscure. One source suggests the name started as "The Place Where the Man Wounded in the Knee Was Buried," a mouthful probably too big for Rand McNally. Eulogized by Stephen Vincent Benét, Dee Brown, even Buffalo Bill, the name is as much a part of American history as Yorktown and Gettysburg, Plymouth or Deadwood—and more tragic than Laramie or Dodge. The day it remembers would be almost as close to the winter solstice as Greasy Grass had been to the longest day of summer.[43]

Some have called the Ghost Dance a "Messiah craze," but Leonard Little Finger will have none of it. The Horn Cloud brothers were out working in the fields the day they went off to join Big Foot, he says with a chuckle. "You're talking about messianic Ghost Dancers, and they're hauling hay?"

The labels historians use don't describe how complex people really are, he adds. And the labels about Wounded Knee are wrong. "It gets written down," Leonard says, "and it becomes true." Big Foot's people were renegades in the narrow sense, since they were running from the army. They were also a bunch of scared Indian farmers.

Leonard describes himself as the great-great-grandson of Si Tanka, Big Foot, on his father's side. His paternal grandfather, John Little Finger, was wounded at Wounded Knee and later allotted land on Pine Ridge. Leonard owns that land today and hopes to put up a campground and school on the plot. His maternal grandfather was Joe Horn Cloud, Dewey's younger brother. So Leonard's line comes down from Wounded Knee like a pair of bloody creeks joining a river that cuts deep across Lakota country.

After Wounded Knee, the victors took many prizes: pipes, moccasins, horses, guns, tools—and a lock of Big Foot's hair. Some of the souvenirs ended up in a museum in Barre, Massachusetts, where Leonard traveled in 2000 to bring them home in an act of formal repatriation. The hair lock was returned to Pine Ridge and burned in a ceremony, the ashes buried on Little Finger family land. Leonard says he's still fighting to get some of the remaining items back.

Little Finger is a combatant in the Lakota "genealogy wars," the skirmishes that erupt over who can legitimately claim descent from great leaders like Crazy Horse, Sitting Bull, and Big Foot. There is controversy over the real and presumed descendants of Big Foot, and some on Pine Ridge have protested that burning that hair lock destroyed all DNA evidence that would have settled the matter forever. The Oglala tribal court deferred an attempt to challenge Leonard's claim, but the bickering won't end there. The accusations get nasty, and the bragging rights are big on a reservation where descent lines are highly prized. Leonard learned the family tree from his grandfather John and is adamant on the issue of his descent.[44]

Little Finger is a skilled cultural translator. He's a native Lakota speaker who has taught rez kids their roots and lectures about his culture locally and abroad. He is schooled in the ways of the white world, too—he can raise seed money, work the press, badger a congressman for favors. On any given day he might be greeting a descendant of Wovoka, guiding a tour for anthropologist Jane Goodall, or giving a college commencement address. A few of his ideas would seem more at home in a Baptist church than a liberal arts university. Like the day he told me, sitting in his kitchen over a spread of family photos, why he doesn't believe in evolution.

"It didn't seem to mesh up with the creation stories I heard as a child," he said. "I began to learn evolution, but at the same time, see what I had in my own culture. . . . I couldn't fathom the fact that there was something that crawled out of the water and developed gills and started walking and then climbed up into the trees, then came off and started walking upright—and here we are. I couldn't see that."

The right kind of education seemed the answer. So Leonard, retired from his government job with Indian Health Service, turned to the task of alternative teaching. He established the Lakota Language Consortium in 2004 and sought funding help to start a school to teach the Lakota language in Oglala. In 2007 a nonprofit group, Mission for Love, volunteered time and materials to come out and put up the one-story building, which they did with all the pluck and good cheer of an Amish barn-raising.

"On this reservation there is no program that is successfully creating fluent speakers," he says. Most kids today don't know enough Lakota to talk about the weather. "The only way it's going to happen is if it's community based, community assisted, and we find a way to be able to give a child as they progress the same kind of recognition they would get in a different school." Leonard looked everywhere for a model of what might work. "I found an answer through home-schooling concepts."

He courted rock stars, scientists, academics, and curriculum wonks. He used Big Foot as a funding inspiration for the school. He also used Dewey Beard, which bothered Marie, who considers Leonard a distant descendant of a collateral line. He refused to ask for federal funding out of principle. But the operational money never came. So, more unfinished than abandoned, the school sits on land owned by John Little Finger, still unused except for organizing special tours and running a Lakota-language day-care center. Sometimes I meet him in the school office, unoccupied except for a conference table and a patent-leather executive chair. He talks about the school going virtual online. But Lakota Circle Village has a permanent feel of being between terms, its doors barely open six years after the raising.

The conversation never veers far from Grandpa Beard, as Leonard calls him. When Big Foot's people met the soldiers near Porcupine Butte, he says, Beard was one of the edgy ones. He had a young wife and a newborn son to protect, but Big Foot was a treaty signer and Beard wasn't. So Si Tanka chose to fly the white flag and go to Wounded Knee under guard. Big Foot didn't want to violate the pipe, which is what the Lakotas smoked to honor the 1868 treaty. If you use the pipe, "it's as sacred and it's upheld as much as you use the Bible or put your hand on there and swear to uphold the Constitution," Leonard says. His long, pensive face is as somber as it ever looks. "Wounded Knee has many, many different connotations, but one of them is that if I say it, I keep my word. That's what Lakota is."

The Lakotas call Wounded Knee "the place of the great killing," he reminds me, and they call the incident a "massacre." Even that word isn't right for Leonard. Joe and Dewey both referred to Wounded Knee as a "battle," he says. "I know it as a massacre. But the more I began to look at it, it was, from their perspective, a battle for their life." Joe, he says, implored his brother to record his experience of the Wounded Knee encounter, and he acted as his interpreter many times. You can label it a massacre, Leonard says, but the Horn Cloud boys chose to focus on the struggle after Wounded Knee, not what they lost there.

Joe, Leonard's blood grandfather, was lucky to survive at all. He was about fifteen at the time and dressed that day in "English clothes," as Leonard puts it. Before the first shot could be fired, an unexpected benefactor appeared in an army uniform. Captain George D. Wallace took the boy aside and warned him there was going to be trouble. The officer advised him to move over by the horses and help the women get away while they could. When Joe started to leave, some soldiers stopped him, but Wallace waved him through to safety. And so Joe Horn Cloud lived.

It turns out Wallace was the only commissioned officer killed at Wounded Knee that day. He would have known something about annihilation, having barely escaped with Reno at the Little Bighorn fourteen years earlier. Leonard recounts that his own father was named Wallace Little Finger—but that was the other side of the family. It's a mystery to him why his grandfather John, who survived the massacre with multiple wounds, picked that name. Maybe he saw what Wallace did for young Joe, but Leonard isn't sure.

"As a result of that, Joe's the only Horn Cloud of the Horn Cloud family, to my knowledge, that was not wounded"—or killed. Leonard chews on that idea like a dry old piece of jerky. "So basically what Captain Wallace did was save my life. If Joe had been killed, you and I would not be talking." The historical leap almost leaves me breathless. "It's a matter of circumstances for how you got here," he says, "and it's a matter of circumstances for how I got here."

When I leave Leonard's that night, the sun is setting behind me in a fiery ball of orange. I drive back to the motel on Highway 18, into the dusk, and I can see Old Glory flying from a tract house in Pine Ridge. The cloth has frayed away badly to a panel of stars and stripes just a few inches wide. It's as though the owner just couldn't bear to burn or bury it. It looks shredded, windswept, weathered but defiant.

Some things, Leonard reminds me, hang by a very slender thread.

The number of casualties at Wounded Knee has been endlessly picked over. The marble stone at the gravesite, erected through the leadership of Joe and Dewey, is marked with only a few dozen names, most of them heads of families who perished. Captain Frank Baldwin's account reported 146 bodies were buried in the grave. White eyewitness estimates hovered at about 200. But these were only immediate tallies. Aside from those who died later of mortal wounds, a number of fleeing Lakotas perished far from the field and were never logged as casualties. Beard told Dave Miller he thought almost 300 had died. His brother Joe, who made a stab at a definitive list, said 185. The army, by contrast, lost 25 men in its initial count. By any reckoning, the numbers were chilling.[45]

Whether they called it a battle or a massacre, most of the survivors carried telling reminders. Louise Weasel Bear took a bullet and hurt every day the rest of her life. Medicine Woman was hit in the elbow with a slug that rendered her right arm forever useless. Beard's brother White Lance was shot in the head, leg, and foot and walked afterward with a pronounced limp and pair of crutches. Beard had his back wound X-rayed years later on a trip to Washington, Marie says, his lung collapsed and the bullet a permanent companion, a disability he complained of. His original census name, Many Wounded Holes, had come to be eerily accurate ten years later.[46]

Once the shooting was over, many of the wounded made their way to the town of Pine Ridge, eighteen miles away. Agency personnel tore out the pews in the Episcopalian chapel and converted it into a makeshift hospital to receive both soldiers and Indians. Most of the wounded Lakotas who reported the first day were women and children, and the soldiers laid hay and quilts on the floor to comfort them. The Christmas tree was still standing in the chapel when the doctors went to work.

Agency physician Charles Eastman, a Santee Sioux, was charged with overseeing the chaos. The volunteer nurses did their best to tender to the Indians, but the Lakotas were frightened by the mere sight of soldiers. Eastman, an assimilated and devout Christian, had nothing but contempt for the way the government handled the episode. "The 'Messiah craze' in itself was scarcely a source of danger," he complained later. One of his patients was a desperate and depressed warrior, bleeding from the mouth, named Beard.[47]

A blizzard struck the day after, covering the tracks of the bloodbath. On New Year's Day, Eastman was entrusted with a contingent of a hundred civilians, most of them Indian, to ride out and look for survivors. A wagon stocked with reporters and a photographer trailed behind. Dredging the snow that had fallen since the fight, they undertook an archaeologist's nightmare. They found bodies scattered across the treeless terrain as far as three miles from the camp center. "The snow partly melted from over their bodies," remembered Joe Horn Cloud, a member of the expedition. "Babies were found crawling about their dead mothers and dying. . . . The bodies looked like chickens on the snow."[48]

They dug a large trench on the hill where the Hotchkiss guns had been deployed. Into it they tossed dozens of corpses. The contractor got two dollars a body, and the soldiers jumped in to tramp down the dead. "They buried our people in the same way we bury our horses," Beard said later, probably meaning they used no coffins. While he was watching the burial, they picked up a boy about sixteen years old. He was still alive, and his eyes were open. But he was frozen so stiff he couldn't call out. Badly wounded, unable to speak English, Beard felt helpless to stop them, and he watched as they threw the boy in the trench still breathing.[49]

When Putinhin told that story to his family later, Celane said, he would cry.

In the weeks to come, a military court of inquiry exonerated the army of any wrongdoing. Colonel Forsyth was found to have judiciously positioned his troops. No soldiers were found to have been killed in a crossfire, as General Miles himself had alleged. And Indian women and children were killed only when their own warriors mingled with them. "'Treachery' was practiced by the Indians," concluded the original Kent-Baldwin investigation, "whether by a preconcerted plan or by the actions of the Indian who fired the first shot." In fact, the evidence is strong that both sides fired on their own people, though the army had the overwhelming advantage of arms.[50]

The court ruled that the Indians fired fifty shots before the army even responded and that the Lakotas were responsible for the melee. The report lauded the discipline of the soldiers as "exceedingly satisfactory" and noted that "their behavior was characterized by skill, coolness, discretion, and forbearance, and reflects the highest possible credit upon the regiment." If anyone could have written a narrative more at odds with the Indian memory of the episode, it would have been hard to invent. Medals of Honor were later awarded to eighteen soldiers.[51]

The opening action, in which Big Foot and most of the men were killed in the main council tent, probably took no more than ten minutes. The pursuit of men, women, and children that followed lasted for hours. Most white civilian eyewitnesses, including medical personnel, testified that the army fired indiscriminately. Scores of Lakotas were killed in full retreat. By some accounts the first action of Wounded Knee may have been a battle, but a battle that dragged a dreadful tail behind it.[52]

James Mooney, a Smithsonian anthropologist who arrived in South Dakota about the time of Wounded Knee, gave an even-handed judgment for its day, even if surpassing fair to the army. He concluded "that the first shot was fired by an Indian, and that the Indians were responsible for the engagement; that the answering volley and attack by the troops was right and justifiable, but that the wholesale slaughter of women and children was unnecessary and inexcusable." Most eyewitness civilian judgments of the encounter are not so generous to the army.[53]

In spite of passions fired by the newspapers, only one noncombatant was killed by the Lakotas in the entire campaign of 1890–91. And the only noncombatants who lost livestock and other property were Indian. Whatever the provocation, the U.S. Army fired on what was a crowd of apprentice Christian farmers, even though they didn't belong to the Grange or sport broad-brimmed hats and carry pitchforks.[54]

The last of the Ghost Dancers surrendered in mid-January. A week later, General Miles arranged for a military review at Pine Ridge before the units dispersed. Miles would criticize Wounded Knee as an incompetent military disaster. But he was also the commander who directed the encirclement of the Lakotas and prepared for an unlikely winter campaign against them, a strategy that triggered the slaughter. The review took place in a snowstorm on a frigid, windswept day. As Miles watched, wrapped warmly in his fur-trimmed greatcoat from a nearby hill, some thirty-five hundred troops made their way across the parade ground with full colors.[55]

Meanwhile, a bedraggled, pathetic figure walked the streets of Pine Ridge village. His parents, wife, and two brothers were dead, his son was soon to follow. And his own healing was unfinished. So he got it in his mind to procure a small revolver and arranged a meeting with the reservation agent. On the given day he strode through the agency door, the gun tucked under a war shirt. The Lakota man walked past the secretary and entered the room where the official was hard at work. He intended to kill him, says Leonard, and maybe himself, too.

The agent knew the man had been at Wounded Knee, and he asked to see his wounds. The man lifted his shirt. And there was the gun.

What are you going to do with that? the agent asked.

Self-defense, the man mumbled.

Surrender the gun or be arrested, he said firmly.

The Lakota man looked at him. He was a warrior. He had killed before. But never in a room. Or under a roof like this instead of the sky. Never a man in a chair armed only with a pen, especially a *wasicu*. For just a moment he hesitated, circled by the memory of his family, surrounded by ghosts.

He let go of the pistol, and it clattered to the floor.

He turned and left without a word.

"Right then I decided to give my wild warrior days up," Beard would say later. And the decision bought him another life. If he'd pulled the trigger he would have been hung for murder—or killed faster than a rabid dog.[56]

The scars would remain, but Beard's healing progressed in both worlds. Doctor Eastman and a Lakota practitioner of "bear medicine" helped make the warrior whole. His bravery would soon be tested again, though. A few years later, a prominent cattle rancher, Gus Craven, was about to evacuate wife and children from his ranch after an Indian threat when Beard and one of his brothers came to their relief. Offering to protect the ranch from marauding Lakotas, they stood guard over the family for almost a week, earning the Cravens' lasting friendship. For Dewey Beard, the memory of Wounded Knee meant many things, but revenge was not among them.[57]

The Horn Clouds said no to history too many times. They apparently ignored the Interior Department's order requiring that bands come into the agencies in the winter of 1876. They fled north when Crazy Horse was killed in 1877. They never accepted the Crook Commission that came to break up the Great Sioux Reservation in 1889. And they said no again when they broke out with Big Foot and ran for the Badlands the next year. They had taken every path possible to avoid the road to the agency. In the end, resigned to a modest life of stock-raising and hauling hay, many ended up in a common grave on a small hill far from almost anywhere.

Beard didn't go back to the Big Cheyenne country. The government confiscated the Horn Cloud property as spoils of war, if war it was. The family would keep an account of what the government seized, but to little avail. Beard settled on Pine Ridge with what was left of his family, ready to mentor Joe, Frank, and Ernest as an older brother would. In official eyes, they were transformed from Minneconjous to Oglalas, registered now, as many Wounded Knee survivors were, at Pine Ridge rather than Cheyenne River.

But there was one thing the surviving Horn Clouds couldn't foresee. The world—and the technology that drove it—was changing more rapidly than anyone could guess.

Before twenty-five years were out, the victors of Wounded Knee, led by one of the most famous men in America, would be back to make the movie.

6

CODY

When asked by the coroner for her late husband's occupation, Alice Beard described him as a "showman." And Dewey Beard learned showmanship at the knee of one of the great impresarios of late-nineteenth-century America, Colonel William F. Cody. U.S. Army scout, dime novel star, and fearless Indian fighter, "Buffalo Bill" adapted his adventures on the plains for an audience hungry to devour tales of Native depredations and thrill at the spectacle of men who could ride a wild horse with more grace and deportment than most mortals could saunter across a city street.[1]

Bill Cody was everything a red-blooded American could have wanted during the audacious age of Manifest Destiny. He was born on an Iowa farm, rode for the Pony Express as a teenager, killed buffalo by the train carload for the Kansas Pacific Railroad, and scouted for the army starting in the Civil War. In 1872 he earned a Congressional Medal of Honor for bravery, and four years later he killed the Cheyenne chief Yellow Hair (by his own account) in revenge for the Custer defeat. He was said to have fought in over a dozen battles (he arrived too late for Wounded Knee), curried a reputation as a matinee idol, and became the founding father of Cody, Wyoming, where his legacy is still revered. In midlife he developed a keen interest in portraying his exploits on stage, and later, for touring in outdoor arenas that could accommodate rough-riding cowboys and daredevil Indians in pursuit. He was a celebrity before most Americans knew what celebrity-hood was.

The big-tent show that made Cody famous shuttled from podunk towns to strapping young cities to the great capitals of Europe, traveling tirelessly between 1883 and 1913. It was not always, strictly speaking, an American pageant. In fact, Cody eventually brought Cossacks from the Dnieper, Irish lancers, French dragoons, Argentine gauchos, Mexican vaqueros, and German hussars—and of course, the "savages" that sprang full blown from American soil, many of them Lakotas. They were known, by 1893, as Buffalo Bill's Wild West and Congress of Rough Riders of the World, and they had dozens of hangers-on, scores of competitors, and hundreds of thousands of fans who braved bad weather and poor transport for a look at the tribes and nations Cody gathered, a choreographed blend of modern "centaurs" that pranced under the electric lights that heralded a new century.

Cody plucked many of his Indian riders from among the Lakotas. They were less likely to be idle in Boston or Pittsburgh than in Pine Ridge, he figured, where memories of Wounded Knee were still raw. Officials like Nelson Miles, who had orchestrated the Wounded Knee campaign, were quick to agree that the Wild West could keep them out of mischief and even put troublemakers to work for a fair piece of money. In fact, the Oglalas from Pine Ridge, where Beard had newly settled, would dominate the Wild West show for years. Cody and his partners soon realized that a homogeneous group of Indians was easier to manage: they avoided rivalries with other tribes, simplified the logistics of translation, and made recruitment trips cost-effective.[2]

He promoted his Indians as a last hurrah before their noble way of life vanished. Many a Wild West show ticket was sold on the claim that the modern world would soon swallow the Indians and their lifestyle whole. And for years the heavies of the Wild West were full-blood Lakotas, many of them Ghost Dancers who would take a fall and come back to life—this time to the roar of an adoring crowd.[3]

Beard performed on the grueling 1895 tour, an odyssey that ran from mid-April to November and played dozens of cities from Bangor, Maine, to Montgomery, Alabama. When righthand man Nate Salsbury fell sick, Cody turned over management of the tour to James Bailey of Barnum and Bailey fame. The pace they set was furious. It was a two-hundred-day season with 321 performances, matinee and evening doubles common. They covered nineteen states, rode nine thousand miles on thirty-four railroads, and missed only three performances to weather or other mishap. Over the course of a season, Cody's entourage estimated they would play to four million people, more than will go to watch a professional baseball team today in an entire year.[4]

And who could have resisted the lure of "1000 animated tableaux" led by "the best known living romantic character" in the world? The incomparable Cody drilled airborne brass balls with a Winchester. The peerless Annie Oakley shot clay pigeons out of the air. Ruthless Indians attacked a wagon train. An Arab Atlas supported a human pyramid of ten comrades on his shoulders. Mexicans lassoed, soldiers drilled, Cossacks cantered and did headstands in the saddle. Cowboys hung from a galloping horse to pick up a handkerchief or cow-punched a bucking bronc that could jump three feet off the ground. And of course there was a buffalo hunt with Cody at the lead, an Indian attack on the Deadwood Mail Coach, and a rousing cameo of the Custer fight. The two-hour show was the most thrilling spectacle many would see in a lifetime.[5]

The logistics were impeccable. Admen placed articles in local papers and flattered the civic pride of the host city weeks in advance. On the appointed day a crew of five hundred performers rolled into town in fifty train cars of special rolling stock, often in the wee hours. Packed with a motley crew of men, horses, and buffalo, the cars were unloaded after daybreak and the riders moved out in parade formation toward midday, riding up the main street of town in a procession people waited hours to see. Cody rode at the front, holding out his hat in a gesture of supreme goodwill. His hair flowing to his shoulders, a diamond pin from Queen Victoria stuck in his shirt, he trotted up the street on a sorrel gifted him by General Miles after the Wounded Knee campaign.[6]

The cowboy band struck up "La Marseillaise," "God Save the Queen," and "Yankee Doodle," a brassy bouillabaisse for starters. Indians rode by on ponies, shields strapped to their backs and bodies smeared with yellow paint, full of "treachery and strategy," said the Atlanta papers. A walking version of the circus was the best advertisement for the real show that followed. In the bigger towns, electric cable cars ran down the street and scattered the Rough Riders, a world of screeching brakes and engines riding pell-mell through a throng of men who had learned to eat and sleep in the saddle. Though one day Beard would ride in fancy convertibles, famed as a last survivor, none of those later parades could match these marches up America's Main Streets, bathed in the huzzahs of a crowd who had never seen such a menagerie of exotic men and animals.[7]

The outdoor show was a bargain at fifty cents, a quarter for kids under nine. It began with the "Star Spangled Banner," followed by a mounted crowd of Lakotas dashing around the arena singing and whooping, a sound "which sent the shivers chasing down your spinal column if for a moment you shut your eyes and imagined yourself at their mercy in the dead of night," noted one journalist. The Oglalas would rein their horses in, fall silent, and wait for the next troupe that followed on their heels. The arena typically measured five hundred by two hundred feet, and the grandstand was covered for inclement weather.[8]

The performance area was lined with seven thousand feet of electric wire and powered by two portable dynamos the size of small fire engines. A beam projector similar to those used in naval operations served as a limelight. At night under the lights the riders' shadows flitted across the crowd and the arena floor like wandering phantoms. Reserve ticket holders were given high-back chairs; the rest made do with bleachers, and people came in droves to fill them. At Hartford they drew forty thousand (two performances) in one day, sixteen miles of people shoulder to shoulder, or so the *Hartford Post* surmised.[9]

Beard and the Lakotas rode without stirrups or saddles, "guiltless of clothing" as one wag put it, except for a breechclout. In New Hampshire they dressed "in a string of sleighbells and a coat of ocher." But in heavy rain one night, their yellow and blue war paint washed away before the eyes of an audience camped beneath a canvas-covered grandstand. In Boston, one reporter gushed, with an opera glass "you can get a better idea of the noble red man by looking up and down that line [of Indians] . . . than you would by reading a library of Cooper's novels." A spear in one hand and bridle rope in the other, they attacked the Deadwood coach, mauled the emigrant train, or did the delicate dance of Custer's last fight. A standby Cody scene, a hundred-yard race between an Indian on foot and another on horseback, was a feat Beard would later perform at Pine Ridge fairs.[10]

When not performing, they lived simply. There were circus tents for the horses (five tons of hay daily and five tons of straw for sleeping), a circular blacksmith tent, and a dining tent that could feed six hundred men at a sitting. The Lakotas stuck to a regimen of meat, potatoes, bread, and coffee, and occasionally roasted a stray dog if they happened upon one, a practice that revolted observers. Reluctant to employ any eating utensils at first, they were reported to be using spoons quite happily before the summer was out.[11]

The Indians often camped apart from the other performers, one hundred of them living in about fifteen painted tipis. They laid out beds of straw and slept under blankets. They tried sitting on chairs, though most of them didn't get the knack of it. Even in camp they wore their finery—beaded leggings and shirts—and wrapped themselves in blankets. The Indian camp was a crowd favorite, and customers were encouraged to browse through the show village between performances. Many of the Lakotas, one report noted, had been visibly scarred by smallpox.[12]

Sunday was their only day of rest, a time dedicated to playing cards, talking with reporters, and posing for "kodac fiends," wielders of early versions of transparent roll film. (The daylight loading camera was only a few years old.) The rest of the week they worked hard. Beard, like most Lakotas, earned room and board and twenty-five dollars a month. Paid weekly, they counted out their money and returned most of it to the bursar for safekeeping, some of them saving more than five hundred dollars in a season. Others telegraphed remittances to families at home. At tour's end each was given a suit of clothes by Cody's minions, an affectionate keepsake from the colonel.[13]

When not working, the Oglalas could go where they pleased. On Cape Cod they held a ceremony in a sacred place they found near Half Moon Beach. They swam in every swimming hole they could find. Some caroused in city bars and saloons. In Washington a group paid a visit to the assistant commissioner of the Office of Indian Affairs to complain about conditions back home. An older Lakota man told the official that if they took the time to recite the whole litany of unfulfilled government promises to the Indian, they'd have to shut down the Wild West show for two days.[14]

They were at the mercy of the elements everywhere. In Salem, Massachusetts, a pelting rain doused the mess tent, and they started bailing with buckets when it came up to their knees. In Oswego, New York, a storm of high winds collapsed the grandstand in mid-performance, and the roof flew away. People were trampled as they tried to escape, and a panic ensued among flying poles, running children, and fainting women. The Lakotas held ranks and watched the scene quietly, then rode their horses up to the restraining rope and kept the people from fleeing into the arena, where they might have been flattened in the confusion. The Indians performed "nobly," one observer advised, and finished their set while half the audience fled in terror.[15]

Watching over a company of five hundred weather-beaten toughs was an impresario's nightmare. In North Adams, Massachusetts, a French dragoon was thrown from his mount and broke a collarbone, but serious accidents were rare, even for daredevils. In New York, a Cossack with a whip lashed and bloodied a kibitzing Jew in the crowd. In Washington, a sixteen-year old black girl eloped with one of the Indian riders who had promised her marriage and riches.[16]

The Oglala Crazy Bull (also called Jealous) was accused of throwing a brick at a taunting twelve-year-old in Baltimore who later died of his wound. At a hearing in Atlanta, Crazy Bull was fingered by a witness because of a mole on his nose. Cody posted bond for two thousand dollars, but before the trial could conclude, the father of the dead boy decided the incident was accidental. "Since W.F. Cody, 'Buffalo Bill,' has manfully come forward and paid him a sum of money for expenses & c., he is unwilling to prosecute the case further." Cody, who would squander much of his fortune eventually, may have been a mediocre businessman, but he understood better than most the karma of bad press.[17]

The *Washington Post* called Cody an entertainer and an educator. It noted that the Congress of Rough Riders, conceived during a European tour, "may be an important factor in the future establishment of an international peace congress." It was a rare occasion for Frenchmen, Germans, Russians, and Englishmen to ride and camp in harmony and good cheer. While most of the War Department closed down shop to watch a matinee show in 1895, the memory of such an alliance, "promoting the amity of nations and cementing the brotherhood of man" as the display ads cheered, would seem preposterous only 20 years later in the trenches of the Great War.[18]

Cody had complex motives for taking Ghost Dancers like Beard on tour. Not only were formerly "hostile" Lakotas kept busy in peaceful pursuits, but the show educated them about Gilded Age America. Resistance to conquest would weaken in the wake of so many parades, so many packed houses, so many rides across the country and, in other years, across the Atlantic. The Lakotas were on show, of course, but so were the parks and hotels and leafy avenues of urban America, the rolling stock and massive marine yards that must have seemed astonishing to a band of daring hunter-gatherers who had spent most of their lives hunting and riding across the swells of the Dakota prairie.[19]

Beard and the Oglalas were meant to be awestruck and awe-inspiring. They traveled like prisoners of war on parade. They learned how to walk on a moving train. They were impressed by the workings of an elevator. They saw primitive automobiles and cameras. They mastered the art of going up and down a set of stairs. They learned how to eat white man's grub and balance themselves on the seat of a chair. On their off days they toured factories and cathedrals, battlefields and public plazas. They would have seen Independence Hall and Faneuil Hall, Cape Cod and New Bedford, the mills of Pittsburgh and the cotton fields of Carolina, the Green Mountains and the Smokies, the horse country of Virginia and the Capitol dome. They were paid scouts who traveled by rail, wheel, and rudder and returned with information useful to the tribe, even if their trip confirmed, in scope and intensity, the end of their former way of life.[20]

Cody gave them a job doing what they did best—riding a horse, performing (sham) battles, dressing and acting the way a Lakota man was taught from boyhood. And barnstorming with Cody wasn't only lucrative—it was legal. Aside from their tough performance schedule, they could move about as they wished, a freedom often denied Indians on the reservation. The Oglalas and other Indians were like Native guest workers admitted to the East, granted a season or two or three in the spotlight, who earned their way among people whose language they could barely understand and whose lives ranged from the grimy sweatshops of Lowell to the sublime environs of Beacon Street.

Still, Cody took a beating in the press from Indian rights organizations and some government officials. Many reformers preferred that Indians learn to read and write rather than lollygag in a traveling show. The critics seemed oblivious that there was little work on the reservation once they finished school—and little land to farm when they took up the plow. Some Interior Department authorities argued that touring with Cody would only be an obstacle on the road to citizenship, and a painful reminder of a world forever lost. Indian Affairs commissioner Thomas Morgan threatened that any Indians who left to tour with the shows would lose their land and annuities.[21]

They had a point. Several Lakota performers died of disease over the years. Rumors of drunkenness, lechery, and wild behavior, some of them true, were splashed in the press. Such reports fed early critiques of the show, but as the years passed, Cody's generosity of spirit seemed ascendant. He posted a substantial bond for each performer, drew up individual contracts, treated the Lakotas as he did non-Indian performers, and put up extra money for funeral expenses or even for homesick Oglalas to visit Pine Ridge. Cody was a show-off, a canny salesman, a vain and boastful promoter, and, by all appearances, a bad businessman in the long term—but he seems to have generally earned the respect of his Indian riders.[22]

Beard signed on with what was the world's best troupe in a period when there would soon be dozens, if not hundreds, of traveling shows. Some were not so scrupulous. By the early 1900s, companies like the Miller Brothers' 101 Ranch Real Wild West were touring Europe and the East Coast, though Indian performers were given slighter contracts and endured more dubious working conditions.[23]

And so the experience of performing Indians, adorned in regalia and stepping to a relentless beat, became a familiar American sight for the century to come. Expositions, world fairs, rodeos, powwows, and festivals would welcome Native riders and dancers. The Cody "alumni" returned to Indian country with bizarre stories of the world beyond the rez. Those who followed in their path for decades to come weren't as celebrated, but they earned a ticket to see parts of the world—Minneapolis, Denver, Laramie, Chicago, New York—that would have otherwise been beyond their reach. "Waste Chicago, Omaha bad," goes an old Lakota expression. In Lakota, *waste*, pronounced "WASH-tay," means "good," and the adage recalls Indian performers (and even students on their way to boarding schools) who liked to stop off at the Windy City, where the opportunities for carousing were plentiful.

The sights and sounds of six months on the road must have staggered Putinhin, by now in his early to mid-thirties. One of a hundred Indians in the show, mostly Lakotas, he may have had little contact with Cody, especially since his English was poor, but he probably remembered one April performance in Philadelphia the night they reenacted the Ghost Dance. Several of the soldiers who had been at Wounded Knee were reputedly part of the troupe that year. Though for some reason the spectacle seems to have been quickly suppressed, it was not the last time Cody would call upon Beard and his people to reenact a memory associated with Wounded Knee.[24]

What the barnstorming Oglalas thought of their adventures is anyone's guess. A Syracuse reporter on the tour may have come close when he wrote "the Indians, who have traveled and who appreciate the magnitude of the white man's power, when they go back to their reservations impart to the other Indians a most wholesome respect for the government." It probably wasn't wholesome, but it made for some powerful propaganda.[25]

How many times Beard toured with Cody is a mystery. The colonel was known to change riders on a regular basis to keep the spectacle fresh, so it may not have been long. Beard told one reporter long after that it was only a year—perhaps true, but newspaper stories about Putinhin got many things wrong. Marie tells of another show he rode in when he was much older, likely recounted by her mother. For Alice to have called him a "showman," though, suggests he performed many times under the lights. He may have gone to Chicago's Columbian Centennial in 1893 and to the St. Louis World's Fair of 1904—many other Indians did. But as is often the case in his story, Beard seems like a blur at the edge of an old photograph, someone who moved his head just a little as the shutter was being snapped.[26]

Now in the prime of his life, he was a strapping, handsome man. Putinhin had a long, angular face. His teeth were white and pearly, his hair long, coarse, and black, some would say auburn-tinged. He had intense eyes that could be brooding at times, bright and gleaming at others. He would have been, like any boy raised on the high plains in the nineteenth century, a sleek, taut, efficient mass of muscle and sinew. He had uncommonly large hands, and stood close to six feet tall, not particularly big for a Lakota. In full regalia, on tour with Cody, he had to be an imposing, even forbidding presence.

But his years as a showman were limited. Dressed in torn dungarees, flannel shirt, and moccasins, as he did later in life, he had the look of an agile and gritty farmhand.

The decade of the 1890s was a time of transition. In 1891 Beard married Chief Woman, the elder sister of his first wife, Wears Eagle, who died at Wounded Knee. Marrying a sister-in-law in Lakota culture wasn't unusual. Plural marriage was common, and sisters were often married to the same man to maintain bloodlines and minimize jealousy between wives. Though Beard didn't have any other spouses, Chief Woman would have been a natural choice. In her mid-forties at the time, ten years older than Beard, she may have been a widow seeking another husband. More important, she was the closest connection to Wears Eagle. Unlike her younger sister, whose ceremony had been conducted by a government agent, theirs was an Indian custom marriage not recognized by the white world. They simply moved in together.[27]

As the years went by, Beard's horizons widened. His travels with Cody initiated him into a world he would return to many times, though as a plaintiff rather than a performer. Closer to home, other influences were penetrating the reservation. Pine Ridge was being evangelized by Presbyterian, Episcopalian, and Catholic missionaries, and converts were common. The Oglalas were encouraged to add a Christian name as quickly as possible, a fact that formalized church membership and made government bookkeeping, especially the mechanics of inheritance, easier.[28]

Toward the end of 1898, Beard formally added the Christian name that made his identity in the white world final. Family lore has it that he borrowed the last name of Admiral George Dewey, newly feted as the hero of Manila Bay at the outbreak of the Spanish-American War. The story rings true, though not all the evidence supports it. Dewey was a national hero at the time, and it seems fitting that Beard would have honored himself with a great warrior's name, a respected practice among the Lakotas. The new name, wherever he got it, suggested that Beard was officially a Christian. But the conversion may have been more nominal than heartfelt, and he would change denominations later in life.[29]

Chief Woman, who became Mary Beard in 1899, seems to have converted along with her husband. After appearing in the 1900 census, she died of unknown causes. She bore him no children, the only one of three wives not to do so. Mary was in her late forties when she died and may have physically resembled her sister Wears Eagle, what would have been a bittersweet memory for Putinhin. It was a marriage that lasted a decade and saw Beard through the painful struggle of surviving in a world where half of his family had disappeared in a single day.[30]

Beard didn't wait long to find a new mate. On August 15, 1901, he married the woman who would live with him the rest of his life, Alice Lone Bear (One Bear), a local girl from Kyle. Alice was the daughter of One Bear and Four Woman, or Gives Things (aka Lizzie Walks at Night), from the nearby Rosebud Reservation; she was the granddaughter, on her mother's side, of Charlie Kills Enemy and Rose Half Rope. Alice learned some English in school, and she could write well enough, recalls Marie, but slowly. Once she broke some bones in both her arms and wore two casts for a time, but she had them removed early because she couldn't stand them. The arms healed so crooked that writing became a chore, borne out by a shaky signature later in life. Details about Alice are scant. One story has it she met Beard while on a show tour. She liked to roll her own Bull Durham cigarettes and enjoyed a good smoke, even years later with her grandkids.[31]

Though Beard stopped touring with Pahaska, as the Lakotas called Cody, the old scout wasn't out of his life. As the years rolled on, the colonel couldn't forget the Oglalas who had been such a major part of his show. In 1913, news trickled out as far as Pine Ridge that Cody was planning a new kind of performance. This one would be captured and preserved in moving pictures, not recede into darkness the moment the arena spotlight was extinguished. Cody, in fact, was going to make a movie. Not just any movie, but a Western. And not just any Western, but one that would depict the very day that Dewey Beard lost so many of his people.

It was, as it often is, a question of money. Cody's touring days were done, and he had lost his fortune on the Wild West show. But in 1913 he settled on the idea of telling his life story on film. He hocked the property of the Wild West as collateral for a twenty-thousand-dollar loan from the owners of the *Denver Post*. Cody had already leapt from the battlefield to the theatrical stage to the big-top touring business, and another jump seemed only in keeping with his ability to perform in every known theatrical medium in the early modern era, even if he couldn't remain solvent.[32]

Cody and several of his Indian riders had visited Thomas Edison's New Jersey studio in 1894, where the "Master of Menlo Park" had filmed them on kinetoscope. A few flickering images of that meeting remain, one of them a twenty-second scrap of men and boys performing the Ghost Dance. That may have been Cody's original inspiration, but it was nothing compared to what he now had in mind. He was going to film the arc of a long and momentous life—his life—from the Battle of Summit Springs in 1869 through the Warbonnet Creek encounter in which Bill had taken the ceremonial first scalp in revenge for Custer, all the way to the Wounded Knee conflict. It would be an entertainment, an autobiography, and a fledgling documentary rolled into one.[33]

Wearing a snow-white beard, his body gone soft and paunchy, the old colonel could still make the hard sell. He collared Secretary of War Lindley Garrison and pitched him on how chronicling the army's successes would be a public-relations triumph. Garrison concurred and allowed him to use the Twelfth Cavalry, posted at Fort Robinson, as actors. Then Cody cadged permission from the Interior Department for the use of Lakotas on Pine Ridge to play the Indian roles. Secretary of the Interior Franklin Lane asked only that Cody show at film's end that the Oglalas had been modernized at school and home. *The Indian Wars*, as the project came to be known, would need to end on a peaceful note.

Not only did the government sign on to the project, so, too, did many of the original players. General Miles agreed to appear, though he was opposed to filming the Wounded Knee encounter at all, a debacle he bitterly criticized in his autobiography. High-ranking officers like Frank Baldwin, Charles King, and Marion Maus also agreed. But the army had won the campaign of 1890, so their participation wasn't a surprise. The Indians were a different matter. Perhaps the only one who could get the Lakotas to take part was Cody himself, a man with long experience working alongside the Oglalas, many of whom trusted and respected him. But this time Cody had chosen for his venue a piece of contested ground—the place of Wounded Knee itself.

That Wounded Knee was a bitter memory Cody well knew. But his powers of persuasion were extraordinary. The Lakota warriors in the Wild West had done at least one cameo performance of the Ghost Dance, a movement laden with bad memories for many of them. If Cody could get them to do it in Philadelphia, he may have reasoned, why not in their own backyard? "It will be a regular reunion on the ground where we fought and bled together," Miles optimistically told the press. But not everyone shared the sentiment that Wounded Knee would be a grand old gathering of the clans.[34]

Filming in South Dakota for *The Indian Wars* started in the fall of 1913. Buffalo Bill later claimed the filmmakers hired over a thousand Indians for the entire film and dropped forty thousand dollars on Pine Ridge alone, a princely sum for the time. The tipis of hundreds of families spread for acres across the Pine Ridge prairie near Wounded Knee Creek. It was a time in the movie industry when Indians were still used to play Indians.[35]

After weeks of rehearsal the serious work began. A couple hundred troops of the Twelfth Cavalry rode up from Fort Robinson, the place where Crazy Horse had been killed decades before. General Miles, principal military adviser, insisted the two sides be represented in accurate numbers, so director Theodore Wharton was forced to improvise. He marched the soldiers back and forth in front of the cameras to make them seem like a force more than twice their actual size.[36]

1. Leonard Little Finger, a great-nephew of Dewey Beard, works to preserve Lakota language and culture on the Pine Ridge Reservation. He knew Beard as one of his many "grandfathers." (Photo by the author.)

2. Francis Apple Sr., another of Beard's great-nephews, received advice from his uncle Dewey about how to stay alive before going off to fight in the Korean War. (Photo by the author.)

3. The "Peace through Unity" Indian Memorial, dedicated at the Little Bighorn Battlefield in 2003, recognizes the warriors who fought in the battle and the Native cultures that survive their struggle. (Photo by the author.)

4. As a teenager during the Great Depression, David Humphreys Miller made it his mission to interview and draw the Indian survivors of the Battle of the Little Bighorn. Here he paints Joseph White Cow Bull in 1939. (Courtesy of the Center for Western Studies, Augustana College.)

5. Ernie LaPointe, great-grandson of Sitting Bull, worked hard to confirm his status as a lineal descendant of the famous warrior. He remembers Beard as one of the last of a great Lakota generation. (Photo by the author.)

6. Charles Eastman, agency physician in Pine Ridge in 1890, doctored Dewey Beard after Wounded Knee. He later devised a method for Westernizing Sioux names and became a noted writer and advocate of Native causes. (Courtesy of the Library of Congress LC-USZ62-102275.)

7. The consummate showman of the Gilded Age, William F. "Buffalo Bill" Cody hired Dewey Beard to ride with his Wild West and Congress of Rough Riders of the World a few years after Wounded Knee. (Courtesy of the Library of Congress LC-USZ62-2050.)

8. Alice Lone Bear married Dewey Beard in 1901, a marriage that would last for over half a century. (Courtesy of the South Dakota State Historical Society.)

9. The Horn Cloud brothers (*left to right*, Daniel, Joseph, and Dewey Beard) posed in 1907 for a photo in traditional clothing. Note that Joe, schooled from an early age and fluent in English, preferred to dress in non-Indian clothing. (Courtesy of the Nebraska State Historical Society, RG 1227-25-05.)

10. The Horn Cloud brothers also posed in Western clothing in a parallel photo. Depicting Indians in "before" and "after" poses was a common convention for encouraging cultural assimilation, especially at government boarding schools. (Courtesy of the Nebraska State Historical Society, R G 1227-25-04.)

11. Neither General Nelson Miles (on horseback) nor William Cody was present at Wounded Knee in 1890, but both men played an integral part in re-filming the "battle" in 1913—and in shaping Beard's life. (Courtesy of the Buffalo Bill Museum and Grave, Lookout Mountain, Golden, Colorado.)

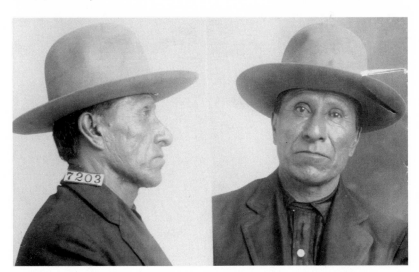

12. Fox Belly was a former U.S. Army scout and agency policeman from Pine Ridge. In 1910 he killed Beard's brother Frank Horn Cloud. Fox Belly died while serving his sentence at the federal penitentiary in Leavenworth. (Courtesy of the National Archives and Records Administration RG 129, Kansas City.)

Derey Beard aug 1927

13. In 1927 Beard was photographed near his Red Water Creek home. Like other Indian males of the time, he was expected to wear his hair short. (Courtesy of the University of Wisconsin–Eau Claire, Adin T. Newman Collection.)

14. The male Lakota survivors of Wounded Knee gathered for a reunion at the mass gravesite in 1932. Beard, the sixth standing from the right, is wearing a white coat and holding a hat. (Courtesy of the National Museum of the American Indian, Smithsonian Institution [P22423], photo by NMAI Photo Services.)

15. The mass grave at Wounded Knee lies beneath a long wedge of grass flanked by a cyclone fence and abuts a small chapel. (Photo by the author.)

16. Francis Case, South Dakota congressman and senator, tried unsuccessfully to get compensation for the Wounded Knee survivors. He was instrumental, however, in getting Pine Ridge land condemned for use as an aerial gunnery range, an act that cost the Beard family their allotments in 1942. (Courtesy of the Library of Congress LC-H 25-234126-DA.)

17. Rex Herman, who earned two Purple Hearts in the Korean War, grew up on a ranch close to the Beard allotment. His father, Jake, was a close friend of Dewey's and frequently acted as his translator. (Photo by the author.)

18. Evelyn Beard Yankton, Dewey Beard's granddaughter (standing in center with white shirt), poses with her children, grandchildren, and in-laws. Her father, Thomas, was the last of Beard's children to survive. (Photo by the author.)

19. The most famous portrait of Beard was done by Bill Groethe at a reunion of Little Big-horn survivors organized by David Miller in 1948. (Photo courtesy of Bill Groethe.)

20. Dewey and Alice Beard enjoy a visit with the Eddie Herman family, relatives of Rex Herman, in the early 1950s. Candid photos of Beard with family and friends are rare. (Photo file: Beard, Dewey, courtesy of the American Heritage Center, University of Wyoming.)

21. In later years, Beard became a familiar figure in Rapid City. He usually dressed in simple street clothes and lived in an Indian encampment near Rapid Creek. (Courtesy of the South Dakota State Historical Society.)

22. Beard's reputation as a Little Bighorn survivor made him a minor celebrity at festivals and parades across the West in his waning years. (Courtesy of the Little Bighorn National Battlefield, National Park Service.)

23. Marie Fox Belly (*right*) and Corliss "Corky" Besselievre hadn't seen each other for fifty years before they met one day on the high ground overlooking Wounded Knee. What brought them together was the fond memory of Dewey Beard, Marie's great-grandfather. (Photo by the author.)

24. Many people came to Dewey Beard's funeral at St. Stephens Church in November 1955. Alice Beard and Corky Besselievre (*second from right*) stand near the cemetery where Beard was buried. (Photo courtesy of Corliss Besselievre.)

25. St. Stephens, near Kyle, is the resting place of many in Beard's extended family, in addition to scores of neighbors and friends. (Photo by the author.)

The Essanay Film Company, producers of "Broncho Billy" Westerns and later, Charlie Chaplin, rose to the challenge of location shooting. They built a platform on wagon wheels to film from an elevated perspective, shooting down into the same ravine Beard had escaped from with a hole in his thigh and a collapsed lung. Some of the cast had to work on acting etiquette, though. *Moving Picture World* reported that "the Indians refused to remain 'dead' after being 'killed,' unless they were absolutely without ammunition and then they would roll over that they might get a better view of the antics of their brothers." The company encountered a blizzard in the Badlands, tiptoed through delicate negotiations between Indians and soldiers, and by trip's end had shot over four miles, or some twenty-five thousand feet, of nitrate film. One Cody biographer says they put up a carousel with wooden horses at Wounded Knee to entertain Oglala kids, though the irony seems too grim to be true.[37]

There was a tragic slant to the production. Gawkers from Nebraska drove up in a hundred autos and buggies to watch the reenactment. "Many Indians were gathered there also," reported the *Chadron Journal*, "and their wailing for dead friends was most pitiful." "There came again yesterday," echoed the *Denver Post*, "the ghost song as those who had lost the ones they loved sought again the death place and mourned. Again as the wailing cry mounted higher and higher, again as the sobs came one by one the warriors stalked forward to lay their heads on the shoulder of some weeping Indian woman and then stalk on again." And the *Post* correspondent wasn't done yet: "Again there were the tears and the clasping of hands, for memory and grief can live long in the heart of an Indian."[38]

Among those who contracted to play in the movie was Dewey Beard. Most Lakotas were paid $1.50 a day, full board, and feed for horses, what would have been good money on Pine Ridge, especially for several weeks running. (The colonel boasted to a reporter he paid the Oglalas $2.00 to $5.00 a day.) But why would Beard have acted in a movie that replayed the slaughter of his family? To reenact the day his wife and parents were killed would have required a man immensely brave or extremely thick-skinned—or both.[39]

Perhaps the reenactment was a kind of redemption. Like many Lakotas, Beard trusted Pahaska, had ridden with him on tour, had seen how he sympathized with his people's transition to the white world. Leonard Little Finger thinks his grandfather's main motive was to truthfully document the event for future generations, and he's probably right. Beard may well have been driven to correct the historical record, to have a role in seeing that people would finally know, in Cody's hands, the truth about Wounded Knee. If that was his intention, it was a naive one.

Through it all, General Miles was ambivalent. He didn't think the Wounded Knee episode should be filmed at all, and he remained at the agency in protest during the shooting. The wife of Pine Ridge agent (later, superintendent) John Brennan later said that "Gen. Miles would not allow them to show the women and children in the fight and that was left out." Keeping women and children out of Wounded Knee footage may have been good publicity for the army, but it struck many of the Oglalas, Beard among them, as a lie.[40]

Miles had a long and glorious reputation to protect, having distinguished himself in every major war during the second half of the nineteenth century. His résumé read like a dime novel plot. He was wounded at Chancellorsville (1863) and later awarded the Medal of Honor. He was instrumental in the capture of Chief Joseph (1877) and Geronimo (1886), and harried Sitting Bull along the Canadian border. After directing the Wounded Knee campaign, though not appearing at the battle, he led the troops that crushed the Pullman strike (1894) and commanded the invasion of Puerto Rico (1898). President Wilson practically had to put a bit in his mouth to keep him out of World War I.

Beard's first personal encounter with Miles was shortly after Wounded Knee. They had in common a profound warrior ethic, though their fates couldn't have been more divergent: one a triumphant commander, the other a badly wounded and despondent fighter. One can only imagine what they found to talk about. Given his dissatisfaction with the way Wounded Knee unfolded, Miles must have sympathized with a gritty Lakota warrior who claimed to have fought Custer. And if Putinhin was at Wolf Mountain in 1877, they would have been able to talk about a battle they actually shared.

With his credentials as a survivor and Cody veteran, Putinhin approached Miles at Pine Ridge during the filming. The general was glad to comply with his request for a testimonial, and it was the second time he did so. "This is to certify that twenty-two years ago I gave Dewey Beard a certificate of good character," Miles wrote on October 21, 1913, "and am much gratified to learn that he has maintained that character ever since. He is one of the survivors of the Wounded Knee Massacre, in which he was twice seriously wounded and lost his father, mother, two brothers, sister, wife and child killed. I recommend him to the sympathy and kindness of all." Notably, Miles called it a "massacre," not a common sentiment among military officers, then or now.[41]

Beard was proud of that letter and kept it for years. But it left out a good part of the truth. More than any other officer, Miles had orchestrated the 1890 campaign that cornered the Lakotas, whipped up the frontier press, and made the debacle at Wounded Knee possible. His testament to Beard was double-edged. Miles may have rendered moving homage to Putinhin, but the general had helped drive his family, his band, and in a deeper sense, his people to near ruin. His note, a substitute for the original lost in the intervening years, was tinged with guilt and condescension.

It was also a professional courtesy. There is honor among warriors, and Beard, by some accounts, now bore the name of Admiral Dewey.

Cody's bio-documentary was released as *The Indian Wars* in early 1914, a nostalgic look back at a frontier war while a gruesome modern one was about to explode across the ocean. In Washington, a special screening drew a thousand dignitaries and commissioners. War Secretary Garrison and Interior Secretary Lane "expressed the deepest satisfaction with the pictures." Out west, the Denver press recommended *Indian Wars* to "every father and mother in Denver" and even their children, too. When the lights came up after one performance, *Moving Picture World* reported, "a thousand people [were] awaking to the realization of having witnessed the most wonderful spectacle ever produced since motion pictures were invented." Advertisements called it a "five-reel thriller that will live forever."[42]

Not everyone was so moved. M. R. Gilmore, curator of the Nebraska State Historical Society, witnessed the location filming and alleged that much was false in Cody's version and that the government planned to file it as "historical data." Some Wounded Knee survivors, who may or may not have seen the finished film, were angry. Edward Owl King, a young boy in 1890, lost his sister and mother at Wounded Knee and took a bullet himself. "The picture was all wrong," he said years later. "The Indians without thinking went ahead and performed in the ways that were directed by some white people, not truthfully but just the way they wanted it presented in pictures." Afraid of the Enemy was in his thirties when the firing on Wounded Knee Creek began. He was shot "all through the body" and forty years later had the bloody cloak he wore that day, ripped by nine bullet holes. The government still owed them the truth about the slaughter, he told an interviewer, "not like the picture show that came here and had the Indians to act just like they wanted but not the truth."[43]

Chauncey Yellow Robe, a Sioux educated at Carlisle Indian School, heaped scorn on the project in a speech before the Society of American Indians, a new Native rights organization, not long after filming ended. He chided Cody and Miles, neither of whom was at Wounded Knee the day of the massacre, for their pretended heroism in the movie. "You will be able to see their bravery and their hair-breadth escapes soon in your theaters," he sneered to a crowd of two hundred, though the finished film didn't suggest they participated in the battle.[44]

Beard and his family had serious doubts of their own. As the filming wore on, it began to dawn on the Horn Cloud boys, who had lost so much at Wounded Knee, that Pahaska, for all his promises, was putting on a show no more real than the cavorting that Putinhin had done on horseback before crowded grandstands in Boston or Atlanta. Dewey and Joe joined fellow Oglalas in petitioning Washington to suppress the film after it opened in Omaha. They criticized the producers for not showing the death of Indian women and children, who fell in large numbers. They frowned on the movie for failing to show that the Lakotas were taken by surprise (they were wearing war paint in the film) and for depicting the two sides as equal in numbers. It was worse than pretending to rob the Deadwood stage or the tired shtick of killing Custer by following a spotlight before a grandstand full of admirers. They were filming on the very ground where their parents had been killed and then dumped in a grave with all the ceremony of fallen horses.[45]

Above that grave, overlooking the killing field and the Essanay camera-men, was the monument to the Wounded Knee dead. But for Joe Horn Cloud, it might not have been there at all. Savvy in the ways of the white world, Joe had a major role raising the money for the marble stone that listed many of the victims. They dedicated it ten years before Cody and his company even got there. On a late-spring day in 1903 a large crowd huddled around the monument as an old woman walked up the hill to the grave. She held out her arms to the sky and began to chant for the dead. Her keening lament was taken up by all the women present until the valley around the hill was filled with an unearthly sound. When their mourning stopped, they set bright pieces of prayer cloth over the top of the grave. Joe gave a short speech while the men looked on, the old ones passing around a pipe, the young ones puffing on cigarettes.[46]

It was in the shadow of that memorial that Cody replayed the last "battle" of the Indian Wars. Horn Cloud's sons would prove helpful allies. Joe was one of four translators on the project, and Dewey was named in many news-paper stories for his heroic acting. The *Denver Post* described Beard during the filming as a man who "saw his brothers fall one by one, but kept fighting on." The *Duluth News Tribune* reported that he "saw his eight brothers fall one by one in the real battle, again fighting against the onslaught of the Seventh cavalry." And "Dewey Beard, still considered a hero among his tribe, appears in his ghost shirt, which still bears the mark of five bullet holes," another source remarked. The only way his name would have been known is by the credits, or more likely, the intertitles the audience would have read during the performance. The film seemed to be picking up momentum by late 1914, playing New Orleans, Salt Lake City, Omaha, and Washington, even the Electric Theater in Emporia, Kansas, where the evening show was twenty cents, and Boy Scouts (in uniform) got in for a nickel.[47]

But the newspapers could never get Dewey Beard right, even in reporting a quasi-documentary. One review said he held off the soldiers for fourteen hours at Wounded Knee, when in fact he rode off long before that, even by his own account. And Beard didn't lose eight brothers but two, even if his actual loss was just as horrible. If the facts weren't exactly right, however, the gist of his role was. Cody believed that Beard had fought bravely, a notion that must have been corroborated by other survivors, of whom there were many. His was one of the few Indian names featured in news stories, and perhaps in publicity. "Pictures that never will be reproduced," bragged the *Emporia Gazette* of the coming attraction, a boast that had more truth in it than anyone at the time could have guessed.[48]

The finger pointing wasn't over, especially as the film began to lose popularity at the box office. Some Indians argued that the Lakotas hadn't understood what Cody was filming, and they gathered to reenact a battle that had nothing to do with Wounded Knee. Pine Ridge superintendent Brennan countered that "the object of the reproduction was fully explained to them" and "the Indians entered no protest nor did they enter protest at any time during progress of the work." Philip Wells, a mixed-blood Lakota and army scout present at both the original Wounded Knee and the filming, was more pointed. All the participants, including Joe Horn Cloud, he wrote, knew for months in advance that Wounded Knee was the subject of the film. "To deceive them all so completely," Wells wrote to a local paper, "would lead one to believe that we are living in the age of miracles."[49]

It's dubious that Cody would have lied about the subject of his film to the very tribe that had been so crucial to his Wild West show. He was known and trusted by many Lakotas who had been at Wounded Knee. But the aging showman probably wasn't above putting out rumors that would heighten the drama of the filming. Some sources later claimed that the Indians were planning to load their guns with real bullets instead of blanks and, when time came to roll film, turn their guns on the soldiers and gain their long dormant revenge—until dissuaded by Cody. The story was a patent falsehood. Still, padding publicity for city slickers in Denver was a far cry from hoodwinking the Lakotas who rode with him across much of America and Europe.[50]

The critical reaction, as time went on, was mixed. While some reviews raved, the film never picked up enough momentum to stay in circulation for long. In fact, it soon disappeared from everywhere. Today, there is no record of copyright for *The Indian Wars*, no copy registered in the Library of Congress, no known extant copy anywhere. Though some have claimed the army decided to ban the film for its depiction of Wounded Knee, a more likely reason for its disappearance is the disintegration of the nitrate stock it was filmed on. An array of stills and a few feet of footage are all we have. *The Indian Wars,* and Dewey Beard's struggle to avenge his fallen brothers—even if there were not eight of them—probably just disintegrated on the shelves of a Washington vault.[51]

The Indian Wars were over, the wounds still tender to the touch.

But for Putinhin, Bill Cody's *Indian Wars* turned out to be just another piece of make-believe.

7

FOX BELLY

When Marie changed her name to Fox Belly several years ago, it was a choice loaded with Horn Cloud family history. I had little idea the Fox Belly name would unlock a family secret when she first told me, but as the story unfolded I began to piece together a bizarre tale of cowardice, betrayal, murder—and reconciliation. When Leonard found out she'd become a Fox Belly—and what that meant—he was speechless. It was a name his grandfather Joe Horn Cloud hated until his dying day, and Dewey Beard couldn't have felt much differently.

Fox Belly, an Oglala, was born about 1856, the son of Running Horse and Her Holy Blanket. Probably older than Beard, he was already an adult when the Black Hills were sold in 1876 and the Lakotas were called in to settle on the reservation. He would set up house later in the Potato Creek area of Pine Ridge, a not-too-distant neighbor of several Horn Clouds. The two families farmed and ranched in the same country, traveled the same roads by team and wagon, sent their children to the same isolated day school.[1]

A tough and quarrelsome man by reputation, Fox Belly directed his aggression through approved channels. In the fall of 1876, while the Horn Clouds were on the run after Little Bighorn, he enlisted as a U.S. Army scout at Camp Robinson. There were powerful incentives for Indians to ride with the army. Scouts earned a steady income and had permission to carry a firearm, otherwise forbidden to members of hostile tribes. Even

Crazy Horse enlisted shortly before he died, proof that scouting was a respectable trade for men from a warrior tradition. As an army scout, Fox Belly would have upheld the warrior ethic of his ancestors, even if he had to sign a paper and carry a white man's gun.[2]

Some scouts rode against traditional tribal enemies, an enviable prospect. But others were used as translators and guides to subdue their own people and allies, sometimes even fight them. Fox Belly, one of the latter, acted as a translator in the campaign that pursued the Lakotas and Cheyennes after the Little Bighorn. Resentment toward the government "wolves"—as scouts were known in Plains Indian sign—ran deep. Although Joe said their father scouted for General William Harney in the 1850s, there's no record of Beard and his brothers ever riding for the government. Fox Belly's enlistment couldn't have endeared him to a family that had been driven into Canada after Custer fell and was later mowed down at Wounded Knee.

A farmer and rancher by trade, Fox Belly found other gainful employment in his spare time. He worked as a herder (cowboy) for the government and served time as a tribal policeman. The Indian police force, established in 1878, was another respected profession for reservation males. They served in large numbers at Pine Ridge on short-term enlistments and performed something like the duties of the traditional *akicita*, or Lakota police, who aggressively enforced law and order in the old days. The son of Running Horse had a history of working as an enforcer.[3]

He would marry Julia, born in 1862, the daughter of Big Star and Red Woman. Together the Fox Bellys had four children and lived on Pine Ridge in relative peace—until the winter of 1910. It was Jennie Blue Legs, Fox Belly's daughter, who complained to authorities one winter day that her father was beating her mother. Marie says it was about whether the children should have to go to school, but the official report is more pedestrian— and ugly. The argument started over fixing a doorknob, it seems. Fox Belly kicked his wife hard between the legs, twice, knocking her senseless, and Julia told her daughter to find help. She testified later it hurt so much because he was wearing a new pair of shoes.[4]

Frank Horn Cloud, Beard's younger brother, was a tribal policeman, and it was Frank who was assigned to ride out to the Fox Belly place to investigate the complaint. No stranger to trouble, Frank was born in Canada about 1880 while his family wandered in exile after the Little Bighorn. As a boy of ten he was present at Wounded Knee, escaping to safety in a hail of gunfire. He learned to read and write in local schools, was allotted land, and settled in the Potato Creek area, a neighbor of the Fox Bellys. Of his four children, one had already died in infancy, while another, a month old, would pass away before the year was out, infant death being a common event among the Lakotas.[5]

Frank went out to the Fox Belly place and arrested his man, apparently without incident. They rode over together to Pine Ridge, and the authorities held the prisoner for several days. It was March 1910, and far from the end of winter on the plains, where the season might drag on for weeks. When his wife wouldn't come in to testify, the authorities let Fox Belly go. But they scheduled another hearing in Medicine Root District, closer to the family abode. Fox Belly was said to have had a grudge against Frank ever since the government assigned land allotments a few years before.

Marie contends that Fox Belly had whipped Julia on occasion, and his wife's testimony bears that out. When Frank arrested him, Marie says, he called Fox Belly *winyan*, a "woman," for hitting his wife. "In those days that was a bad thing to call somebody," Marie explains, a massive understatement about a culture that glorified every aspect of male combat. "When he did that, Kaka Fox Belly got mad."

Horn Cloud rode back to the Fox Belly homestead on March 8 before the scheduled hearing. As he approached the ranch house, a woman came out and mysteriously waved a towel and went back inside. Frank was dismounting when he looked back and saw Fox Belly standing with a rifle on a cut bank thirty yards away. Before the policeman could react, the old scout fired at him and missed, and Frank got back on his horse and started to ride. Fox Belly's second shot went through the saddle, penetrated Frank's back, and exited through the intestines. The assailant fired several more times, and Horn Cloud rode off across the prairie badly wounded.

Frank made his way to the house of a nearby farmer who got him in a buggy and drove back to his home before going to find a doctor. Brothers Dewey Beard and Joe Horn Cloud were summoned when it became clear he wouldn't make it. Frank swore out a final statement testifying to the assault, while, as Joe put it, he "was lying in a bed full of blood."[6]

Fox Belly would later claim that Horn Cloud fired first. But Frank denied that, and Joe, who saw his brother off that morning, said he left with six cartridges and came back with the same number. Joe would never forgive Fox Belly. He told Frank on his deathbed: "'He ought to have killed you right there, for it would have been better. Wherever he go, he is going to die.'" Frank, who had evaded dozens of army bullets at Wounded Knee twenty years before, couldn't dodge the one fired by a close neighbor twice his age who had been a "metal breast" himself, as policemen were called. On March 10, Dewey Beard watched as his brother slowly bled to death.[7]

"He died in the line of duty, Indian police," Marie murmurs proudly. But she seems as awed by the man who fired the bullet as she is by her great-grand-uncle Frank, who took it. Like many Lakotas, Frank had little to his name but land. His wife said he left three horses and nine head of cattle, but the cattle soon disappeared, and she had to sell one of the horses to feed her family. It was a hard fate for calling a man a woman.[8]

Fox Belly held the local community of Potato Creek "under siege" for ten days, Marie says. Everyone was scared. Women would tell their children, "Get back inside, Fox Belly is coming.'" He went up to Fox Belly Ridge, the other side of Bear Creek, onto family land, and the law sent people up with food and tobacco to talk him in. He stayed about ten days. I notice Marie seems to like the number ten, an easy number for a storyteller, but some of the records bear out her math.

Fox Belly couldn't stay out forever. He came down one day and went to the Randall place, Marie says, where he knocked on the door—which seems a polite thing for a desperate murder fugitive to do. Mrs. Randall shooed the children off and opened the door.

"Who are you?"

"Fox Belly," he grunted.

Her husband fainted away.

She splashed some water on him, and the three of them sat down to talk.

Marie turns all solemn. She's telling a story her mother, Celane, must have told her a dozen times. "They gave him a bowl of soup and a cup of coffee. But every time he took that soup to drink it and looked in the soup, in the reflection he could see Horn Cloud's face. Then he would go to drink his coffee, and he could see his reflection there, too. So he knew Frank died. No one told him, but he knew. They sat there and talked all through the night."

Fox Belly understood it was time to give it up. "He told them to burn everything, because he had killed someone. So they burned the chair he sat on. They burned the utensils he used. They put it all outside and burned it. He killed a man." Then they got on a horse and rode all the way to the agency police office in Allen. The police cuffed Fox Belly, moved him to Pine Ridge, and put him in solitary confinement. A few months later they took him under guard by team and wagon to pay a visit to a judge in Deadwood.

The trial was short. Fox Belly pleaded not guilty at first, then changed the plea for reasons that aren't clear. On September 12, 1910, he was found guilty of murder in the second degree and sentenced to a life of hard labor.[9]

When he entered the federal penitentiary in Leavenworth, Kansas, one week later, Fox Belly (Coyote Belly in prison correspondence) gave his occupation as "policeman." He was reputed to be fifty-nine years old, though the official number is dubious. He had a wife, four children, and property valued at about $10,000, almost all of it land—he would have three children and no wife when he finally died. Prisoner 7203 had never been behind bars before.[10]

Fox Belly was a specimen of the hardscrabble prairie farmer. He was five foot five, about 137 pounds, had light copper-colored skin and was missing two upper teeth. He smoked and chewed tobacco and drank. He was scarred all over his body—on his left middle finger, his right elbow, the edge of his scalp, and he bore a row of pitted scars from his left shoulder to his wrist. The toes of both feet had been frostbitten, and he'd lost a joint and a half of two toes on the right one. He had the look of someone who'd been tortured by life. A warrior for rent (scout), a policeman, and farmer, he'd spent many an hour practicing how to keep his body in one piece.[11]

He lived in cell block C, unit 121, and wasn't eligible for parole for fifteen years. He started in the crusher gang, breaking rocks in grunt labor, and in

1912 he was transferred to kitchen duty, where he remained for the duration of his term, suffering occupational injuries like a burned leg. As the years wore on, Fox Belly rarely took a day off, and in 1915 he was promoted to trusty. He was prescribed eyeglasses two years later, and a photograph he sent his brother in 1921 shows the toll of a decade in the pen. In all that time, Fox Belly would never be written up for even a minor violation.[12]

After years of thinking it over, he changed his mind about the Horn Cloud affair again. "It is alleged that during 1910 I committed murder," he wrote one correspondent, but "I plead not guilty." He argued that Frank Horn Cloud had fired first. Fox Belly sought a transfer to a South Dakota facility to be closer to his family, and then he hired lawyers to gain a pardon for reasons of ill health. But the warden denied him on both counts, maintaining he had only the early stages of arteriosclerosis. In 1918, Julia divorced him.[13]

Eventually, friends and neighbors petitioned for Fox Belly's release. But Joe Horn Cloud bitterly opposed them and begged the Pine Ridge superintendent not to relent. In some ways, life for Fox Belly went on as normal. He received per capita tribal payments from the reservation, signed grazing leases, and collected rent from his allotment. Fox Belly stowed away credit to the amount of over two hundred dollars, and in 1921 he began receiving twenty dollars a month for his service as a U.S. scout. He dictated letters to the Indian Office commissioner, numerous lawyers, the U.S. Senate, and the Pine Ridge superintendent, but his release never came.[14]

Marie tells me with a hush, "The day before he was to come home, he died." But the story is too good to be true. Fox Belly was never granted a transfer, and he was years away from parole. He did his time quietly until the end, and in January 1922 he died of a urinary tract and abdominal infection. He was said to be sixty-four years old. Like Beard, he sent his children to Day School 23 near Potato Creek and was an outstanding horseman. But they parted ways there. Fox Belly had scouted for the military and served as a policeman. He didn't expect to find himself on the wrong side of the white man's law.[15]

The Horn Cloud clan must have been relieved—and satisfied—when the old inmate died. But a funny thing happened in the generation that followed the Horn Cloud/Fox Belly feud. When Marie's mother was about seventeen, she made the acquaintance of Fox Belly's illegitimate grandson, Jonas, who went by his adopted name of Not Help Him. And, almost as in a Hollywood script, Jonas and Celane fell in love. When Jonas started courting Putinhin's granddaughter, Beard pulled the young woman aside: "His grandfather killed your grandfather," he reprimanded her. But it didn't make any difference. They kept seeing each other, whether Beard knew it or not.

One cold day in December, Celane was acting nervous, "sweeping, washing dishes, cocking her ear with one ear to the door," as Marie tells it. "Just about that time someone whistled outside. Unci [Grandmother] Alice said Mom dropped everything, and she dashed out the door. So Unci ran out behind her, and there was Jonas on a white horse in the snow." He spurred his horse when he saw Alice, and Celane ran beside him until he reached down, grabbed her by the arm, and pulled her up on the mount. Jonas took his jacket off and covered her with it, and they galloped off into . . . well, the sunset. "That's what we call eloping," Marie laughs.

They were married by a nearby justice of the peace. Since the magistrate doubled as a butcher, the ceremony took place in a meat locker filled with pigs, chickens, and turkeys hanging from hooks. Dewey and Alice didn't like the match, but they accepted it. Celane, for her part, admitted she was scared. Four days later, the Beards delivered her clothes and luggage to the couple's new home. "They kind of made it official that that was where she was going to be," Marie says. "It was like a Romeo and Juliet movie."[16]

Unlike Shakespeare's lovers, these two survived to raise a family. "There would have been thirteen of us," Marie says of her siblings, counting quietly through the names. She's the eldest daughter of eight who survive. Junior died of meningitis at age two. Herbert Harrison died at four days old. A sister was stillborn, another died of neglect after delivery. Even today, infant mortality on Pine Ridge is almost three times the national average. That was something her great-grandparents would have understood.[17]

I think about what the Fox Belly story means. Marie's great-grandfather killed the brother of one of her other great-grandfathers. It's as though the family tree had been split by a bolt of lightning. Life on Pine Ridge was

complicated for a conquered people given little respect, a primitive education, and a marginal cut of land. Jealousy, bitterness, and feuding arose.
And the legacy continues. Of all the Beard family members I interviewed,
most have little to do with each other, often owing to a perceived slight
from years, even decades, before.

When I told Leonard that the original Fox Belly was the one who killed
his great-uncle Frank, he was shocked. I'm not used to seeing Leonard
astonished, but he was that day. "It don't make sense," he said softly, that
someone who lost a family member to Fox Belly would take his name.
But for Marie, there was no question. Her father, Jonas, asked her to do
it before he died. "That's who I am," he told her, and "you should change
your name to who you are."

Her great-grandfather Dewey Beard was never able to escape the long
reach of the Indian wolves. At Little Bighorn he no doubt saw some of
Custer's Crow and Arikara scouts, or at least their remains; he confronted
Lakota scouts as Big Foot's band moved down from Cheyenne River in
1890; another scout killed his brother Frank twenty years later. And he
was, in a way, still negotiating with them in 1955, when Johnny Bruguier,
former Wounded Knee scout, rendered Beard's Lakota into rough and
woolly English, the Native hired hand still the assigned shadow, still the
messy go-between, still the thankless middleman of the Indian Wars after
all those years.

8

PINE RIDGE

Every summer, I go west to Pine Ridge to visit the place where Dewey Beard lived and died. I love the slow crawl of the land as I cross the country, where the brilliant emerald cornfields of Iowa, lush and prehistoric, give way to the short-grass prairie on the far side of the Missouri, a place where the land changes its face from the open bounty of the earth to the dry gulches and breaks and rugged draws of the plains.

I breeze across the Midwest, basking in the pattern of silo, pasture, and field. The grain elevators fix the traveler's view miles ahead, the way a medieval spire marks a faraway town in Europe. As you move west, the horizon empties itself. Across the Missouri are long, sweeping hills dotted with livestock, a cattle and range landscape both parched and peaceful to the traveler from afar.

The rise in elevation is so gradual you barely notice. By the time you get to Mission, South Dakota, you're twenty-five hundred feet above sea level, and by Wounded Knee, three thousand. You have the sense of being pushed toward the Rockies, lifted up an escarpment by an irresistible force. Across this land, considered trackless by non-Indians in the old days, lies the grid of telephone poles and power lines of today, a map cross-hatched by county roads that cinch the earth like an asphalt-and-gravel corset.

You get to badland country long before the mountains. You can see miles to a distant ridge, but a ravine fifty yards away is invisible. The cut banks and draws make you feel cornered in spite of the big vistas. "Broken land" is what they call it. A rusted Ford is parked in the shadow of a scrubbed-out gully. A row of mailboxes are planted at the end of a long road, as if shouting "Don't forget us!" Three white crosses on a ridge sprout against a blue sky. Behind an abandoned house you can look through an empty doorframe and see a cloud floating by.

The badlands have a gutted look, scraped and slashed around the edges. Or stolen by small chunks and pieces over the course of a million nights, what scientists call erosion. The Lakotas say the bones of monsters can be found there. Or maybe, I think, the creator one day got tired of kneading and shaping the soft rock and moved west to attend to the more exacting labor of the Bitterroots and the Bear Tooth and Bighorn Mountains, leaving the balding terrain of Pine Ridge forever undone.

The drive that began as forbidding and sullen in the morning can be bright and glorious by sunset, the sun working its way down in the west, horses grazing by the road, combines standing in the fields, a lone tree holding up the horizon. I tune the radio to KILI, and there's that ungainly mix of urban shuffle rap, heavy metal, George Straight ballads, and those tribal council meetings with the interminable roll-call votes.

I'm back on Pine Ridge, home of the Oglala Lakotas, where Putinhin spent the last, and by far the longest, of his nine lives.[1]

Beard and his brothers enrolled as Oglalas at Pine Ridge in 1891. The Horn Clouds had nothing left at Cheyenne River. The family homesteads had been abandoned at Cherry Creek, their possessions lost at Wounded Knee. They were among the last refugees of the Indian Wars, and their decision to settle in the south would keep them forever close to the place where their parents had fallen.

Pine Ridge was a big place to settle—about sixty miles wide by a hundred miles long, some three million acres in total. It was the girth of four good-sized western counties and almost as big as the state of Connecticut. (The loss of Bennett County, later opened to homesteading by non-Indians, has decreased, by some accounts, the official size of the reservation.) It was an unfamiliar place for hunter-gatherers used to roaming a land with no obstacles but bad weather and broken terrain, soon to be faced with rows of fence line that ran across the land with no apparent logic or visible end.[2]

Making a go of it on the Pine Ridge was a slog. Much of it wasn't worthy of a plow—and still isn't. One superintendent estimated that only a third of the land was cultivable, and most of that was declared submarginal by the government in the Depression. Temperatures vary from minus-40 in winter to 105 in summer, and rainfall is scattered and unpredictable. Insurance brokers red-lined the area for being in the "hail belt," and plagues ranging from locusts to early frost to hot winds, drought, grasshoppers, and blister beetles on the treeless prairie sound like a roll call from Pharaoh's day, with the crumpled barns and abandoned houses to prove it.[3]

Dewey Beard was a warrior, not a farmer, and the thought of turning over a plot of earth to feed and clothe a family was something he never warmed to. He had made a start of sorts on Cheyenne River, but many of his birth family, his wife, and son were now dead. Though hobbled by wounds he was still a man in his prime, eligible by law to be initiated once again into the mysteries of owning a piece of American earth.

The land available to Indians like Beard was developed through a policy called "allotment." Practiced on many reservations, the plan was formalized by the Dawes Act of 1887, widely believed at the time to be as progressive a piece of Indian law as Congress ever passed. In effect, the statute carved up the land base of a reservation and awarded a patch of earth to each family or adult who could work it. Allotment, its supporters argued, would make industrious, hardworking citizens of the American Indian. Nomads no longer, they would be rooted to a plot of land that provided them with food and cash and a small estate to pass on to their children. Starting in 1904, Pine Ridge was carved, like an enormous prairie pie, into more than eleven thousand allotments.[4]

To protect allottees, the land was placed in trust with the federal government. There was a strong rationale for letting Washington make decisions on behalf of its Indian "wards." Stories of Native people getting bilked by traders were legend. Few full-blood Indians could speak English, much less read or write it, which made them easy prey for fast-talking conmen. So when an Indian allotment was placed in trust, no one could buy it without

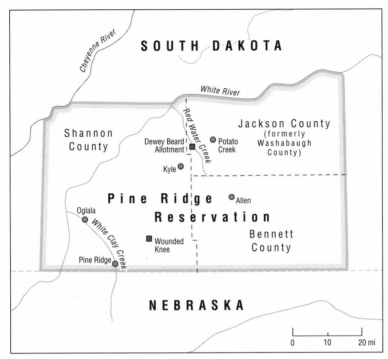

Map 4. The Pine Ridge Reservation (Erin Greb Cartography)

Washington's consent. The only problem was that Uncle Sam's protection was a labyrinth of arcane rules and lethargic foot dragging, a paternalism that viewed Indians as permanent adolescents, or, in legal lingo, "wards."

A family allotment in Lakota country, according to the Great Sioux Agreement of 1889, was 320 acres, double that if it was grazing land. The allottee received two mares, two milk cows, tools including a plow and wagon, and a fifty-dollar cash bonus. Most of them, like Dewey Beard, put up a log house with a dirt floor and roof, erected a small barn, and wound a spool of fence around them. But since most Oglalas didn't have enough cattle to keep their lands grazed and make them productive, they ended up leasing their property. By the time of World War I, the vast majority of the reservation was under lease to experienced non-Indian ranchers. Leased land stayed in Indian hands and earned its owners rent money, though usually a paltry sum. And some landowners were even paid a working wage by operators who ran big herds on their sprawling chunks of the Oglala estate.[5]

But leasing had serious drawbacks, too. Joe Horn Cloud appeared before a House committee in 1920 to protest the fiascos of renting Indian land. White cowboys drove herds that overgrazed the land, he told the Committee on Indian Affairs in Washington. Indian cattle got lost in the herds. The lessees didn't put up fences as promised. Some Indians were forced to lease by the Indian Office. And Oglala ranchers couldn't always get payment when they were sick and needy. A family might have to sell a horse for the price of a coffin, grumbled Joe, so "Why not give it to him when he was alive?" Dewey's brother harangued the committee in a sharp, edgy English that wasn't yet common from the mouth of a full-blood Lakota.[6]

For someone like Joe, who had survived a starving time in Canada and gunfire at Wounded Knee, a group of cigar-chomping pols from Chicago or Akron couldn't have been too intimidating. He bragged how he nearly came to blows once with the Pine Ridge superintendent. He then turned and dressed down the Indian Office's assistant commissioner, E. B. Meritt, seated in the room, who "just goes by what is reported to him, but aside from that he does not know what's going on." The committee hemmed and hawed over the fate of the Indian after 130 years of tutelage, and Horn Cloud hammered back that the reservation agents were layabouts interested in little more than padding their pockets with graft. "They all do just what you are doing," he snapped, "smoking a cigar." The first of the Horn Cloud boys to read and write, Joe, a proud Catholic catechist, preached fire and brimstone in his thirty minutes of fame in Washington.[7]

His words hardly mattered in the end. Pine Ridge was supervised for decades by agents with close ties to the cattle business. John Brennan was a wealthy businessman and rancher who pushed leasing wherever he could. His successor, Henry Tidwell, condoned trespass by outside cattlemen and what amounted to virtually free grazing rights for many non-Indians. In 1919, Oglala leases earned less than $200,000 for two million acres, a measly sum when divvied up among those whose land was being mismanaged and eaten down to the roots. The wide-scale allocation of Oglala land for leasing during the war proved devastating to Oglala ranchers in the long run.[8]

White cattlemen also didn't have to endure the prickly rules of the Indian Office. Before an Indian could slaughter an animal, he needed approval by the Interior Department. Cutting timber required a permit. Herd size was managed by federal fiat. Even personal grooming was regulated. Indian men had to cut their long hair, and for years Putinhin wore a head of shorn locks. Though Native people, if cooperative, were technically free to leave the reservation by the Standing Bear decision (1879), their movements were monitored. And they were quietly tallied by bureaucrats at every turn. Dewey Beard had an allotment number, a ration number, and a tribal census number, and the last two changed every year. Indians across America were counted and recounted, reckoned and enumerated, polled, projected, toted up, added up, surveyed, tested, and sampled. Through allotments, censuses, and annuities, the American Indian was pinned to the proverbial wall like a frog on a stick.[9]

But there wasn't enough decent land on Pine Ridge to allot everyone. In fact, it had the smallest per capita acreage of the various Lakota reservations. The population rose from seven thousand in 1912 to nearly eight thousand by 1930. In another decade, the birth rate was higher on Pine Ridge than any district in the country, and some five thousand Oglalas were unallotted. Dewey Beard was one of the lucky ones. But as the tribal rolls expanded, so did the number of landless Lakotas. The people of Crazy Horse weren't vanishing, they were increasing—and getting poorer in the bargain.[10]

In a prairie hollow a few miles southwest of Kyle, a mile or two from where Beard lived for some years on American Horse Creek, are the headquarters of Oglala Lakota College. Anyone curious enough to look can find the original allotment books in the college library, a squat, prefab metal building that shakes and rattles when a hard wind blows. In the basement, I drag the tomes off the shelf to a nearby table. The big Doomsday books, thick ledgers bound in rough black hide, look more like they belong in the catacombs of a monastery than a college archive.

The Office of Indian Affairs Tract Book says Beard took out allotment number 1775 in 1907. He was allotted a virtual full section of 631.8 acres, the grant signed by President Theodore Roosevelt. For a man who didn't like the idea of fencing his land, the layout must have felt cramped: Section 18, Township 41 North, Range 40 West of the 6th Principal Meridian.

"Dewey Beard" is written in a flowery hand on the ledger; "Putinhin" is listed for his Indian name. Nothing has been scratched out, and annotations are made in different-colored ink in the margins.[11]

Many Wounded Knee survivors took their allotments in the Kyle area, a good sixty miles by wagon from agency headquarters in Pine Ridge. That's probably the way they wanted it. They were a long way from the reach of the Indian Office in a time when automobiles and telephones were rare. Dewey Beard had selected his homestead with special care. Not only did it have a well-watered stretch of creek and good stands of timber, but it was close to where he had camped with Big Foot in 1890 on the road to Wounded Knee. The night they camped on Red Water Creek would have been one of the last he spent with his parents and his first wife, Wears Eagle.

Around the turn of the century, Beard built a one-room log cabin on Red Water, years before the land was allotted. Over time his claim was formalized, and the land became his—at least under the trusteeship of the Interior Department. By the time of World War I, Dewey and Alice Beard were making a go of it. They grew potatoes on three acres of plowed ground. They owned ten horses, two cows, and a wagon. The creek and a nearby spring supplied all the water they needed, and a couple miles of the ranch were fenced. It was "rough land" according to one appraiser, but there the Beards had put down their roots. Son Webster, born about 1906, and daughter Eva, born in 1910, were both allotted 160 acres, while Alice Beard was accorded 320 more, making a family spread of nearly 1,300 acres by 1913.[12]

But the years had been hard on Putinhin. His battle wounds, not least those of Wounded Knee, hampered him. He dragged his feet when he walked. In his early fifties he was diagnosed with chronic articular rheumatism by an agency doctor and found incapable of manual labor. "I do all I can for make my living," he wrote in 1915—or rather someone with a legible, practiced hand wrote for him, in a survey of the period. "I do this all my life." He had been earning a living since 1901, he said, and was only in debt periodically at the general store in Interior. He appraised his annual income as "fair to good," and valued his livestock at close to two thousand dollars, but he had no money in the bank.[13]

Money was hard to come by if you were Indian. Putinhin, as was typical, had an Individual Indian Money account through the Interior Department. The superintendent held all funds on account for Indian wards—land sales, per capita disbursements, leasing income, war bonds—and he loosened the purse strings with consummate caution. In 1920, Putinhin had to run a bureaucratic gantlet to cover transportation costs, $43.81, for an official trip to Washington made three years earlier—and an extra one hundred dollars for farming costs. He had to beg by proxy to get even a fistful of dollars, and the money was typically given out in purchase orders instead of cash, redeemable at the local trading post. It was as hard as going to a banker for a loan—only the money was already his.[14]

Like many Oglalas, Beard received government rations. The Black Hills agreement in 1877 provided, in recompense for the land the tribe ceded, beef, coffee, flour, and other staples until the Oglalas became self-sufficient. Those without jobs or unable to work were put on the ration rolls, where Beard appears with regularity through the end of one century and into the next. Given his age, his war wounds, and recurring rheumatism, he may never have left the list for long. In 1939 he was still on the rolls, a common fate for people on Pine Ridge, and elsewhere, at the time.[15]

Like thousands of other Indians, Dewey Beard was only a "provisional American." The point of allotment was to introduce Indians to farming or ranching, give them a grubstake in the economy, and reward them with citizenship. When the trust period of twenty-five years expired, the land was theirs free and clear, though the right to vote came with the actual allotment. But citizenship, for American Indians, was a mixed blessing: when the trust period of the Dawes Act expired they had to begin paying taxes, and the land was no longer safe from mortgage or repossession.

In 1906 the Burke Act made it possible to patent an allotment before the twenty-five-year waiting period elapsed. Anxious to see its wards "progress," the Indian Office began forcing many mixed-blood Indians to patent lands prematurely. Beard was recommended for "competency" in 1920, though since he was a full-blood and didn't speak English, the superintendent was probably reluctant to push him into the world of tax sales and foreclosures. The Burke Act, passed only a year before Beard was allotted, withheld citizenship and voting rights until allottees had outright title to the land. Putinhin wouldn't officially become an American until the Indian Citizenship Act of 1924, which made citizens of all Indians. By that time he was an elder.[16]

Horn Cloud's eldest outlived allotment, which was discontinued in 1934. But in the three decades the policy was practiced on Pine Ridge, the Indian land base withered. After the twenty-five-year waiting period, the land was scheduled to be patented in fee and assessed with taxes like normal property. Almost 90 percent of patent owners on Pine Ridge ended up selling their allotments for cash. And the results were tragic. "On the whole, they act just about like white people do when they come into possession of a piece of easy money," one superintendent complained.[17]

The perennial problem, between occasional per capita and lease payments, was where to get a bundle of money all at once and put it to work on the land. Like others, Beard sold part of his allotment in order to make improvements on the balance of his property. In 1919 he patented and sold 155 acres to two Nebraska ranchers for $1,100, a windfall for the time. He was leasing the section for $56 a year, but the trickle of money wasn't enough. By 1922, 25 percent of Pine Ridge had been patented and sold to outsiders, and the ranch on Red Water Creek wasn't immune.[18]

Dewey and Alice improved their spread with the proceeds from the sale. By 1925 they lived with their three children—Webster, Thomas, and Carrie—in a shingled one-room log house. They built a sod barn that held a wagon, harness, and plow. They had a roost of a dozen chickens. A herd of three hundred horses—Indian ponies—rounded out the ranch. But ponies were frowned on by the Indian Office, which regarded them as incorrigible grass eaters that dominated water holes and were unable to pull a plow. "An Indian is prouder of fifty ponies than he would be of a thousand head of good cattle," groused one superintendent, who estimated there were twenty-five thousand ponies running wild on Pine Ridge in the early 1920s.[19]

Those ponies were Dewey Beard's joy. He had been a superb rider, of course, good enough to tour with Buffalo Bill. And the rugged physical training he learned as a boy allowed him, even as late as the 1930s, to jump on a pony from a standing start while clad in a pair of moccasins. The

Beard herd was unorthodox, to be sure. He had an inborn stud that used to sire crooked-legged colts, one neighbor recalls. And as his great-nephew Francis Apple saw many times, the old man could talk a stray back to the corral with a tongue of silver.[20]

The Beard family was absent that day in 1925 when federal agents came to survey their property. But if they heard the government was going to be snooping around, they might have wanted to be gone anyway. The Beards were reported by the surveyor to be in good health, though he apparently didn't meet them. His final pronouncement on the ranch was disapproving: "He does not farm and very little effort is shown." But Dewey Beard was no farmer. He may have planted potatoes, but just enough to get through the winter. Dewey and Alice were living on the land, not taming it. And maybe that was a good thing, considering what the appraisers would do the next time they came to Red Water.[21]

The old Beard allotment was at the end of a series of two tracks that disappear into the prairie grass northeast of Kyle. I'd heard about the place from Marie. Francis had promised to show me the way out there years before, though I knew, like everything on the reservation, it was a matter of finding him in the right frame of mind. I saw him one day sitting on a bench in front of the senior citizens center in Kyle. It's the best seat in town for gabbing, since it's next to the post office, which, in a place with no home delivery, everybody visits once a day. Francis, wearing an Obama hat, flashed a toothless grin when he saw me. "Do you think I'll ever amount to anything?" he teased. He was in a good mood.

We got in my old Honda and headed north by northeast. We started on pavement, moved to gravel, then descended to a run of two tracks that zigzagged like a lazy stretch of zipper. We plied one fork after another until the dirt two-tracks gave way to high grass. After a while, we seemed to be driving through open fields. Francis chose the route, knowing exactly which fork to take, which fence to leave open and which to close, how to maneuver each dip and rise.

Whenever I asked Francis how he was doing in those days, the answer was "not too good." He was going out to Hot Springs for treatment at the

Veterans Administration once a week. He was diabetic. He had hepatitis A. And he was being treated for cancer after they found a couple of spots on his bladder. Ever since the Walter Reed fiasco in 2007, he said, they'd been getting good treatment at the VA. His life, I soon discovered, dips and bobs like the road between Sharps and Kyle: down one ridge, up another, cruising from crest to gully. There are thirty-two medicine men on the reservation, he says, "So we shouldn't be this sick."

Francis doesn't like his surname—Apple is slang for an Indian who's red on the outside and white on the inside. Back in the Fort Laramie days of the nineteenth century, he had a white grandfather named La Forge. La Forge decided he needed an Indian name for family gatherings, so his people called him Bad Apple, or Rotten Apple, to tease him. But at the next census, Francis says, "When he came through the roll line the interpreter knew his Indian name already." He shortened it to "Apple," and when LaForge tried to explain it was just a joke, the interpreter said "Keep moving."

"That's how we got stuck," says Francis, a little glumly. The stories behind many Indian names are just as strange.

The trip to Red Water took longer than I expected, and I was getting a little restless. "Tell me a story about Grandpa Beard," I said. Father Apple didn't need much prodding.

"Beard was on his way to visit some friends in Minneconjou country," he started. "They spent the night on the west side of the Black Hills, found a high spot to camp in, then hobbled the horses and went to bed. Grandpa got up early to go out and hunt something for breakfast when he saw a plume of smoke coming from down in the valley. He came back and woke up his friends. They went down to check it out and see if they had any food."

Francis had my close attention. "What they found were three prospectors. They were frying bacon, and Beard had been downwind. The Indians went with good intentions." Francis made that last point like something bad was coming. "But the miners went for their rifles, and Grandpa and his friends had to shoot them.

"The prospectors killed one Indian. That's why they shot back. Otherwise they wouldn't have. They were just begging for food. One of the prospectors had a gold watch, and they put it on their friend's chest before they buried him. They ate their flapjacks in a hurry and took the bacon." He paused, but I could tell he wasn't done yet.

"Then one of Grandpa's friends picked up some rolls of money. They were big and brown on one side—hundred-dollar bills. He said they should take them to a storekeeper, but they let most of them fly away in the wind. All they wanted was the rubber band holding them together, good for braiding hair. Grandpa got hold of one of the bills and kept it.

"They also dumped the leather pouches the donkeys were carrying. There was dust in them, gold-colored powder and nuggets. They dumped it right there on the ground, lifted the little pouches, and took off."

We were skimming the slalom trail north of Kyle, the car running through high grass on the fading two-tracks. We passed a big stand of pines. Red Water Creek was dry. You could see the Badlands off in the distance.

"So they went to a storekeeper and gave him the piece of paper. He said, 'You can charge stuff from my store all winter, and tomorrow you can come by and pick out any horse of your choice.' They said, 'He's a good man, he gave us a horse for that piece of whatever it is.' After the snow melted they planned to go down and find that gold, at least after they figured out what it was. Meanwhile, they kept charging against the bill."

I had the feeling that Francis had told this story many times. And it had as many turns as our sinuous route to Red Water. "Anyway, to make a long story long, they came back with shovels, picks, and a lot of food. But they couldn't find that place later on. They looked and looked. 'It's right here. No, it's over there . . .' There was a dugout before, and they couldn't even find that.

"I used to tease Grandpa about that," Francis said with a laugh. "'Grandfather, they make some things now called Geiger counters. We can rent one and go find that gold.' But he was smart. He says, 'No, if *tunkashila* wanted us to have that, we would have found it. He hid it because there's trouble attached to it.'

"Didn't fool him," Francis mused. "I was just testing him out."

The story struck me as intriguing. Actually, I'd heard it before. I tell Francis the same story about Beard killing white people I heard from his cousin Birgil Kills Straight. When Birgil told it, though, the main characters were stagecoach passengers, not miners. "It could be," Francis said. "The stories get changed around. Every time they tell it it's different. Maybe they were horses, maybe they were donkeys. Who knows?"

The story was starting to make me feel a little funny. "Grandpa told me that story many times. He would have been real young. He may have even heard someone say that. Maybe then he applied it to himself."

Now I was confused. I asked, "You mean it may have never happened to *him*?" I could hardly contain my disappointment.

Francis just shrugged. "A cowboy told me once, 'If you're going to tell a story, you got to add something to it.' We're that way, too."

It was the story that mattered, not who was in it. Somewhere in the Hills three white guys got killed and some crazy Indian threw away a saddlebag of gold dust. I was beginning to feel like David Humphreys Miller, Beard's adopted son, the errant historian.

Father Apple was giving me just what I asked for.

Francis guided us the last few miles over a road he hadn't been on in years. I tried to imagine Beard riding this distance to town, or his children going to school on horseback, traipsing over a sea of prairie where the only thing that followed you was a fence line or a stray cloud. It wasn't barren or uninviting, but rolling rangeland where badlands come into view when you come up over a draw. We passed fields of wheat and alfalfa and stands of cottonwood and pine until we reached the meadow where the Beards made their home.

The old log buildings were gone. We drove across the flat where the barn stood. Then we moved up the ridge and parked near a modest frame house. The yard was filled with half a dozen auto carcasses and a stack of tires, and Francis went over to talk with a tenant at the back door. The land had gone out of family hands in the 1940s, and they didn't know the name Beard at all. The corral was over there, Francis pointed, and he recalled a herd of at least a hundred head. It was an anticlimactic trip for me, the original buildings long absent, but Francis seemed moved by the visit. "When you come back next year, I won't be here," he said as we got back in the car. He meant the cancer was going to get him.

On the drive back to Kyle I didn't recognize a thing. The land was twisted all around and backward. The clouds had changed shape. Like someone blindfolded, I could have drifted for days without finding my way back to the main road. But Francis never hesitated, the forking paths as clear to him as a teacher turning the pages of a school reader. The road meandered as much as the conversation, a fact that suited him just fine.

I asked him about Wounded Knee, a family preoccupation. It made him angry, he said, that the family never got anything in the way of reparations. "The government called it a war so they didn't have to pay us anything." Sometimes Grandpa Beard talked about that day, Francis said, but you couldn't get him to do it on your own. If people pestered him, he would say, "I left all that, and I don't want to mention it." Francis was impressed that Beard went to church every Sunday, considering all he'd been through.

As often happens on Pine Ridge, the lure of military service trumps the tragedy of family history. The future Father Apple did a stint with Uncle Sam himself when he enlisted in the 101st Airborne in the early 1950s. "When I went to the Korean War," he recalled, "Grandpa Beard gave me some advice."

I asked him what it was.

Francis got real quiet. A long silence passed as we rolled down a two-track. He didn't want to answer me, or he just wasn't ready yet.

Instead he told me how he transferred to a demolitions unit and worked with blasting caps. They blew up bridges and detonated mines, and the mines were dangerous work. Most guys couldn't carry the metal detector, they were so scared. "Saw two guys blow up in a minesweeper. They were careless. No one wants to do that job, but they gave it to me." Francis explained why he liked it: "I was young, and I didn't care. 'So what if I die, I'll die over here on the battlefield,' I said. That was the warrior instinct."

When you found a mine you'd put in a little pin for a marker so it could be disabled. Francis and a Crow Indian did all the sweeping in the outfit. When the unit had a tough assignment, the officers would say, "'Where's the chief at? Get those chiefs out here. Go get Apple,' they'd say. They looked for me on dangerous patrols. They thought I could smell the enemy and I knew the terrain, which I did."

His Crow companion was chicken, Francis said, a prejudice Dewey Beard might have shared about the Crow scouts who brought Custer to the Little Bighorn. They were traditional enemies of the Lakotas. "The Crows are great warriors," Francis scoffed—"after you get back."

One day the unit was ambushed by North Koreans. "I suggested they go around one place, but the leader didn't listen. We got hit. Rifle fire all over. There were a hundred Koreans chasing us and hollering. You could hear the tracers bouncing off close to our shoulders. They killed everybody but me and that Crow Indian. I still have bad dreams about it."

Francis grew quiet. I asked him again about the advice Grandpa Beard gave. This time he softened.

"He said, 'Be brave, don't be scared. Don't even be scared a little. Those that are scared and run are the first ones to get shot. Always try to be up front. And pray a lot. Pray when you get up, and pray all during the day.' That's all he told me."

Francis made corporal in three months. But he started drinking with his Crow friend and got into trouble. He left the army after two years, in 1954. He was never even wounded, he says proudly. "'Cause I prayed, I did like my grandfather. Not just prayed, prayed hard."

It was only years later that he realized a strange coincidence. Francis is called Kuwapi (Pursued) in Lakota, after a grandfather, a brother of Beard's who died at Wounded Knee. One day Francis was talking about the Korean War on KILI, the reservation radio station, when it came to him. He saw again the image of the Koreans chasing back his unit. "That's where I lived up to my name Pursued," he said on the air, the first time it had ever occurred to him. Francis cackled. "I lived up to my name and didn't even know it."

On the way back we stop at St. Stephens cemetery, north of Kyle. Francis shows me the family plot where his parents, wife, brothers, and son are buried. Father Apple, now in his eighties, is a reformed alcoholic and an Episcopalian priest, facts that may get to the heart of the man, except there are so many hearts. He's a sun dancer—the traditional Lakota religious rite. He's a demolitions expert, a language instructor, a war veteran, a guy who studied to be a CPA. His wife, Freda, was a "cradle Christian" who had a master's in social work, and his son still sponsors a sun dance. He comes to St. Stephens often to spend time with those who have moved on. People put candy on the graves for the dead to eat; in the old days his own kids used to hang out there to swipe it. A couple times when I visit, horses are grazing inside the fence. Francis says they find the grass sweeter near the graves.

Leonard and Francis are literate and fluent in two languages. But their great-uncle Dewey probably never had a day of schooling in his life. Beard's education happened under the sky, hunting buffalo, breaking horses, learning to read scat and break trail. In Canada he was an adolescent in exile, hardly welcome to an education in Grandmother's Land. And by the time he got to Cheyenne River, he was already well into his teens. His poor English and ever-present thumbprint on official documents are evidence that he never opened a McGuffey's reader in earnest.

Dewey and Alice would have had no choice but to send their own children to school. The government was bent on assimilating Indian youth and even threatened the parents of truant children with the prospect of decreased rations. Putinhin probably approved of his kids learning how to read, but it would have helped that a daily hot meal was a reward for attending the Indian day schools. Still, progress was slow. In 1927 the average eighth grader on Pine Ridge was eighteen years old.[22]

The Beard children went to Day School 29, near Kyle, just as Francis's mother, Susie White Lance, did. When the teacher died of typhoid one day after drinking water from the school well, the building was moved into town for a post office. (Today it serves as a rickety café on the road to Potato Creek.) Thomas and Carrie Beard changed to Day School 23, more happily known as Medicine Bow Day School, in 1931. Set on thirty acres of tribal land, the buildings stood in a small valley on a bend of Potato Creek, the gullies of the big Badlands barely a mile away. Canyons filled with pines ringed the perimeter, and at night in summer you could hear the sound of playing children, yowling coyotes, and barking dogs under the stars.[23]

The little schoolhouse on the prairie, built in 1895, was inaccessible in heavy rain or snow. They used oil lamps to light the main building, used a coal-burning stove for heat, and had no water or sewage hookups. They had a barn, but it didn't have lights. A canning kitchen with running water was added in 1938, as well as a root cellar, a goat shed, and a chicken house. Six acres were irrigated. They gardened, milked, did handicrafts, and put out a school paper. Attendance averaged around twenty through the Depression, but sometimes they had only twelve chairs. English was the sole language of instruction, and Lakota was forbidden. The lessons they learned would have meant little to Dewey and Alice.[24]

Since the school was only a few miles from the Beard ranch, the kids would make the trip on horseback. Francis remembers the family would camp near the school in bad weather, sometimes for a week. But it was a long way to anywhere else. They were sixty-five miles from the agency in Pine Ridge. Kyle, the nearest town, was about fifteen miles. They had to take a wagon and team to Pine Ridge twice a month to get rations, at least until the 1930s, when they could finally get them in Kyle, still a tough trip in bad weather. Students were issued a pair of shoes and suit of clothes every fall, government homespun they wore until threadbare.

Frank Horn Cloud, Dewey's younger brother, and Joe Horn Cloud Jr. enrolled at the school in the early years. So did the Fox Belly kids. The children of Dewey and Alice followed suit: Tom was taught manual trades and gardening, while Carrie learned the mysteries of sewing and sweeping, both given a strict regimen of the three R's. In 1939 Dewey went to Kadoka as part of a school delegation to request relief funds for a Potato Creek commissary. It was, in the larger sense, a very long journey. The man who watched as his mother sank to her death in a bloody ravine at Wounded Knee had gone on to become a loyal member of the Medicine Bow PTA.[25]

By the early 1930s, much of American life had taken root on Pine Ridge: 4-H, the YMCA and YWCA, even the Boy Scouts. But for all the appearance of normality, the Lakotas were poor in ways rural people usually aren't. Few had a single milk cow (lactose intolerance was common). Root cellars were rare. Farming tools were primitive. You have to wonder what Dewey Beard would have made of one superintendent's remark that "every possible effort is being put forth to make the Oglala Sioux realize that his only salvation is within himself." The new ideology of individualism didn't go far in a culture built on consensus and extended family.[26]

Putinhin wasn't a political man, but politics engulfed Pine Ridge in the 1930s. In 1934 the Wheeler-Howard Act (Indian Reorganization Act, or IRA) was voted on in Indian Country, the pearl of FDR's New Deal Indian policy. In a series of referenda, individual tribes decided whether to adopt or refuse reforms introduced by the new law, including creation of new tribal governments and written constitutions. Many Lakotas accepted the reforms as necessary adjustments to a new world. Others argued that IRA, which required that many ordinances be approved by the secretary of the interior, made tribes more dependent on Washington than before.

After a bitter fight, the Oglalas voted to accept reorganization in 1935; Beard's Medicine Root neighbors, who cast their ballots at the day school, had voted overwhelmingly for the bill in a referendum the year before. But there was a great deal of distrust among Lakotas about voting, especially given the long string of treaties in which they had come to regret having surrendered rights and territory. In the end, almost half the eligible voters on Pine Ridge declined to come to the polls, perhaps a de facto rejection of the law. But since an overall majority didn't vote against it, as the legislation mandated, the IRA reorganized Oglala political life.[27]

Most claims groups, like the Black Hills Treaty Council and the Wounded Knee Survivors Association (WKSA), opposed the legislation on grounds it would erode the sovereignty of their claims against the government. We can't be sure how Beard voted—or if he voted at all. The Horn Cloud family refused to sign the 1889 agreement, so the impulse to resist Washington had precedent. For someone who remembered the old days, Horn Cloud's eldest may have decided that not participating in the vote was a way to reject it. After all, the 1889 agreement had been modeled on a program of assent—the only ones who "voted" were those who agreed. Since Putinhin lobbied for the WKSA through the Depression, it seems unlikely he would have found the new law acceptable, much less its spirit, even if some full-bloods supported the referendum.[28]

Politics on Pine Ridge changed noticeably over the years. The *tiyospaye* Putinhin knew as a boy was replaced by a new form of organization that elevated geography above kinship. By the early 1890s, the political unit on Pine Ridge was shifting from the extended family band to a series of seven reservation districts based on watersheds. From early in the twentieth century, these districts became the electoral units of the tribal council, a format solidified under the IRA. Beard was a member of Medicine Root District (named for the creek), and his political life came to be defined by a small tributary of the White River—and a distant council of representatives— rather than an extended group of friends and kin.[29]

Politics was transformative only on the surface. Life went on no matter who was elected in Pine Ridge or Washington, DC. The Oglalas lived in the difficult round of rural life, ruled by seasonal variation, pockmarked by sudden loss. The paper for Medicine Bow Day School tells us that in February 1939 Mark Spotted Horse ate six apples at a school dance and that they played bingo at the Episcopalian Church at five cents a card. Charles Swimmer had a baby girl named Louisa Shot with Arrows. Dr. Walla Tate held a weeklong dental clinic at School 23, and the children chopped ice on Potato Creek morning and night so their animals could drink. The paper didn't shy away from noting that the Earl Blue Bird baby died of unnamed complications, and Charles O'Rourke was found frozen to death in a snowbank.[30]

Contagion and want of care were common. The flu epidemic of 1918 took more than three hundred lives. The biggest threat to health was tuberculosis, estimated to afflict almost half the population at the turn of the century. Between 1896 and 1906, one-fifth of the population died from TB, and by the 1920s the malady caused 40 percent of reservation deaths. Officials bemoaned the lack of proper nutrition, the poor ventilation in log housing, and the obstacle of rural distances. For many years, only four doctors covered a reservation the size of four counties, and before 1930 there was no hospital. Many Oglalas grew fatalistic and wouldn't bother to consult a doctor.[31]

It's doubtful that Beard was cynical about *wasicu* medicine, since he'd been treated by Charles Eastman with some success after Wounded Knee. The Beards were stricken many times nonetheless. At least two of their children died officially of TB, including Webster, the eldest by the time of the Depression. Before that was a string of infant deaths: Jessie (1904), Eva (1914), the first Tom (1914), and Paul (1921). The Beards lost children at every stage of life: infants a few days old, toddlers, a growing teen, mature heads of family. Since Dewey and Alice didn't write letters, and the interviews he gave were usually about massacres and battles, we know next to nothing about how they bore this loss. We know in dollars exactly how much Putinhin drew in annuities in 1903, but nothing about toddler Jessie, the firstborn, before she passed on the next year. A child who reached its majority in the Beard family was uncommon. Except for Jessie, I've never found pictures of the young ones.[32]

Webster, the secondborn and eldest son, died in 1931, having attained his mid-twenties. He was the father of Marie's mother, Celane, and something of a legend in the family. Leonard's mother used to say that Webster was like Tarzan because of his easy way with animals—even birds would fly up and perch on his shoulder. Marie says he was found dead in his barn, and her parents suspected foul play, a story repeated by other family members. She says doctors used TB as a generic diagnosis to avoid stirring up trouble, and on this point she may be right—the death certificate says he'd suffered for years with pulmonary TB and finally succumbed to it. But a contemporary letter, penned by a white merchant who knew the Beards, says Webster's body was found two days after he died of a heart attack.[33]

The loss of an eldest son was among the worst calamities that could befall a Lakota. Some three hundred people attended Webster's funeral, his father said, a sign that his son was well known in the community. The death certificate identifies him as a "farmer," and the tall, shy-looking young man seems to hide under the shadow of his own cap in a Depression-era photo. Putinhin no doubt made his grief public and vocal, in the traditional Lakota way of grieving. He gave away belongings, wept publicly, probably cut himself with a knife.[34]

Dewey Beard, like most Lakotas, found refuge in the church. By 1920, Pine Ridge had more than fifty Christian places of worship. The reservation was heavily missionized by Episcopals, Catholics, and Presbyterians, and even small communities had an array of sacred houses. The churches replaced the traditional *tiyospaye* in terms of social organization, and they provided men with an opportunity for leadership and administration. By the Depression, half the reservation was Catholic. Before his untimely death in 1920, brother Joe was the catechist for Medicine Root District and traveled nationwide for the church.[35]

Though Dewey and Alice married in an Episcopalian ceremony, the Beards also ended up Catholic. They would stay with the Apples outside Kyle and walk the mile or two to the one-story white clapboard St. Stephens on Sunday mornings. But Putinhin wasn't a convert in the strict sense. Many Lakotas married the sacred teachings of scripture with the religious tradition of parents and grandparents, much as Francis has done. Beard no doubt mumbled Christian prayers in Lakota, but he never gave up the pipe ceremony and sweat bath.

What he did beyond that he did in darkness and under cover. Healing ceremonies went underground and were held at night. Sweat baths were forbidden. The sun dance, the central Lakota religious ceremony, was banned, but not eradicated, by Washington for much of his adult life. Sun dancers pierce their flesh with a skewer and engage in several days of rigorous and painful dancing to fulfill a spiritual vow, usually made in thanks for a blessing. As an elder, Beard attended sun dances in the 1950s, and it's possible he danced in them when younger, given his Ghost Dance experience. In fact, he recalled being present at the last great sun dance, in 1881, before the ban went into effect. Even in matters of the spirit, Putinhin was a man of two worlds.[36]

As a traditionalist, he didn't have much liking for one of the worst scourges on Pine Ridge, then and now. Many relatives and acquaintances say they never saw Dewey Beard take a drop of alcohol. But the truth isn't that simple. Francis, who says he joined the VFW in Rapid City when young because the beer was cheap, saw Beard take a drink on occasion. A BIA report says he imbibed alcohol "moderately."

If so, he was an exception to an alarming trend in Lakota country in which, by the end of his life, public binge drinking was becoming commonplace. First introduced for profit during the fur trade, alcohol consumption was noted in Lakota winter counts by the 1830s. The *mni wakan* ("powerful water") was a popular, if regulated, substance that was particularly favored by Lakota males. Selling spirits to Indians had been banned since the nine-teenth century, even after Prohibition was repealed in 1933. In fact, alcohol use remained a relatively moderate health issue on Pine Ridge before the Depression and didn't become a chronic problem until after the war.[37]

In 1953 the prohibition on liquor sales to Indians was lifted. The results were devastating, even on reservations like Pine Ridge that remained dry. Beard's nephews would get drunk and start fighting, Marie says, and Alice would chide her husband for having supported President Eisenhower, who signed the new policy into law. "I did bad," he admitted to his wife on one occasion, before he got out his pipe and went up on the hill to pray. He could not have imagined the full brunt of the plague that would befall his people, and his own family, in the decades to come, a world where fetal alcohol syndrome was widespread, where stumbling drunks on payday were a common sight, where a malt liquor named for Crazy Horse could be sold over the counter to an inebriated elder.

No matter how much the Beards prayed, the illnesses never went away. Carrie Beard, who barely lived to adulthood, had "coughing sickness," Fran-cis remembers. When the Beards would spend the night with the Apples on their way to get rations, he says, "I used to hear her cough all night. We used to wonder, what's wrong with Carrie?" Anybody who had TB back then was done for, he adds. In the summer of 1940, Carrie, born on New Year's Day, passed away at seventeen, a student at Day School 23. By the time America entered World War II, the Beards had only one child left.[38]

One Sunday I met Francis at his church in Kyle, a small, one-room chapel near the water tower. No one else came for the "service" except a college student from Minnesota who was learning Lakota. The door was flapping on the hinges in the wind, and we sat in a pew and jawed about the busi-ness of preaching. Even in his church he wears a cap, ever since he lost his hair in cancer treatments. The hymnals are in Lakota, and Father Apple knows the Communion prayer by heart, having done it for thirty years. The mainline Episcopal church is up by the college turnoff, he tells us. Still, I wonder how a respected man of the cloth could have a flock so small. Francis says the cost of gas keeps a lot of people home.

It's only over the course of many years that Father Apple tells me the story of how he was "defrocked." A wealthy Episcopalian parish in Paoli, Pennsylvania, it turns out, sent his parish over $300,000 in the 1980s in a gesture to help a poor Indian community. It was supposed to buy a building for wayward kids, an alcoholism-prevention program, and seed money for a cattle herd. No one was made accountable for the money, though. But Francis was the point man, and someone finally noticed that his family had been driving a new pickup and getting school scholarships for relatives. None of the money was ever accounted for, and the Paoli church recoiled. Then they went public. Francis said the reports of fraud in the press were lies.

The church decided another Apple had turned bad. Francis was accused of conduct unbecoming a priest, he says, but his superiors couldn't pin the charge of misallocating money on him. So they settled on a "phony" complaint that had to do with his pushing traditional Lakota culture and the sun dance. Francis remembers well the day of the defrocking, a ceremony in itself, like breaking an officer's sword. Each time the bishop told a lie, as Francis tells it, he and his wife looked at each other. The defrocking didn't break him, though. Like his great-uncle told him before he went to war, he didn't run. For years he held monthly meetings at his chapel (as St. Stephen's does), and sometimes he was called upon to give a religious reading elsewhere. Francis didn't go off to hide in a corner. For all its size, it's hard to hide on Pine Ridge anyway.[39]

We have breakfast later at my motel. Francis talks about the old Lakota, the way people used to talk, the "jargon" of Beard's time, much of it now forgotten. "I have paper and pencil, words come to me at night, I jump up and write it. Sometimes I turn the phrases these modern teachers don't even know," he says. Francis is shrewd, and a little suspicious. He published a dictionary of Lakota phrases and proverbs a few years back and left out some of the translations so other people couldn't plagiarize him. Some of the book's retailers weren't too happy when they found out about that.

It's white people who sometimes don't get the truth about Lakota culture, he says. He asks for another cup of coffee and shoots me a funny look.

"White people are so smart they're dumb." The "kid priest," as they used to call him, sizes me up.

"I hope you're not like that."

The Progressive Era, the Jazz Age, and the Great Depression came and went. During all that time, Dewey Beard never stopped trying to get the government to come clean about Wounded Knee. Even into old age he traveled to Washington as an official representative, pestering politicians, testifying before Congress, and regaling reporters with his grisly tale. He never gave up hope that compensation might be granted those who witnessed and survived the events of that long-ago December day. "I feel that every time that I recall this history," he testified in Washington in 1917, "the matter is so vivid in my mind that it seems to me as though it had happened just yesterday." He dragged the weight of that memory with him for two-thirds of a century.[40]

Not many years after the massacre, the Wounded Knee Survivors Association was born. They put up the monument at Wounded Knee in 1903 and sought reparations for survivors and heirs. But Washington moved slowly to investigate. In 1920 a group led by the Horn Cloud brothers formally petitioned the Indian Office for compensation. James McLaughlin, erstwhile rival of Sitting Bull while superintendent at Standing Rock agency, was sent to Pine Ridge with the mission of assessing the veracity of the survivors' claims.

Other than eight horses they rounded up later, the Horn Clouds had lost all of their possessions on the field at Wounded Knee, aside from a few belongings they left behind on Cheyenne River. Joe provided McLaughlin, the Interior Department inspector, with a list of claims, including a wagon, harness, saddles, quilts, pillows, beaver shawls, overcoats, a kettle, coffeepot, and twenty-four dishes and cups. That wasn't to mention two guns, a shotgun, four bridles, lariat ropes, an ax, a wagon cover, and a tipi. To judge from their inventory, the Horn Clouds straddled the fence between the world of hunting buffalo they had been born into and the one with leather harnesses and teacups they adopted on their return from Canada.[41]

But McLaughlin was hardly moved. Among those he interviewed was Beard, who showed him the character testimonial Nelson Miles had written years before. Dewey Beard "bears a good reputation and impressed me very favorably," McLaughlin reported, an unusual remark for a skeptic who considered the Lakota claims dubious at best. He went on to recommend that the claims be dropped, since "the crazed condition and heedlessness of the Indians involved in the Wounded Knee affair was largely responsible for the unfortunate occurrence." The non-hostiles had already been compensated through the Sioux Depredations Act of 1891. But since the survivors of Big Foot's band didn't talk about the matter any longer, he advised, it was better to drop the whole affair. McLaughlin then hedged his bet when he recommended a judgment of $20,000, if the government ever saw fit to pay.[42]

Rather than die out, the Wounded Knee claim picked up momentum during the Depression. The WKSA drafted an early list of demands in 1934, and bills were proposed in Congress the next several years to "liquidate the liability of the United States for the massacre of Sioux men, women, and children." The language of "liquidation" made it sound like a business transaction, which, in the larger scheme of things, it was. But calling it a "massacre" was controversial, a characterization the military never accepted. In fact, the acting secretary of war argued that the Sioux themselves were responsible for the disaster. It was bold legislation for Francis Case, the new representative from Custer, South Dakota, to sponsor.[43]

H.R. 2535—and subsequent bills—called for $1,000 to be awarded the heirs of anyone killed, and $1,000 for any wounded survivor or heir. It may have seemed like a lot on the floor of Congress, but the WKSA had wanted more: $5,000 for each person wounded, and $10,000 or more on behalf of each deceased, depending on the circumstances of death ($15,000 for anyone killed after the encounter ended, and $20,000 for the loss of each child). Their demands were whittled down in meeting and committee until Case settled on a round number that would apply to everyone.[44]

Beard left for Washington in the winter of 1938, sent by the tribe to plead for the bill on behalf of forty-four Wounded Knee survivors. He departed with James Pipe on Head, the WKSA chairman, and an interpreter. Near

Warsaw, Indiana, they wrecked their car in an accident and made the balance of the trip by train. Once arrived in the capital, they paid a visit to Congressman Case and Indian Affairs commissioner John Collier, who was also supportive of the legislation, and made a *Washington Post* photo op in full regalia.[45]

The survivors came to say their peace before Congress in early March. "The United States has done what we call one of the biggest murders," began Beard, speaking through interpreter Charles White Wolf to the House Committee on Indian Affairs. "The United States must be ashamed of it, or something, because they have never even offered to reimburse us or settle in any way." Now in his seventies, Beard recounted the loss of his wife and young baby and reflected on his own wounds: "I never found out why they did that to me—shot me like that; and some time I would like to find out what was the reason why the American troops . . . should ever injure anybody unless anyone was bothering the law." Beard told the congressmen he got his second gunshot wound while lying on the ground.[46]

By the time the committee adjourned on March 7, Beard hadn't finished yet. In a signed statement he reminded Congress that the Lakotas sent many men to Europe to fight in the Great War, some of them descendants of Wounded Knee victims. The old warrior rubbed the irony in: "They helped to defend our country, gave up their lives and fought for this Government which some 47 years ago shot down their helpless unarmed grandfathers and grandmothers at Wounded Knee Creek." He signed the testimony with his habitual thumbprint and headed back to Pine Ridge.[47]

But as Case pointed out to his Oglala constituents, the timing for reparations was all wrong. The Wounded Knee bills first surfaced when much of America was out of work, which didn't boost the chances for settlement. As the war effort consolidated in the 1940s, a bill proposing pensions for Indian victims fifty years earlier seemed belated at best. Even more, to finger the U.S. Army as the culprit, in the eyes of many congressmen, was bad wartime politics. By the time rationing was under way and casualty lists were in the papers, Congress wasn't in the mood to appropriate money for a warrior people who had ridden with Crazy Horse and annihilated several companies at Little Bighorn.[48]

Two months after Beard's testimony, the committee haggled with an army representative over the meaning of Wounded Knee. Case defended the Lakotas, contending that Wounded Knee, not Little Bighorn, was the real "massacre." The point seemed to hit home, but the fear surfaced among committee members that Wounded Knee might not be unique. "I am not sure whether the door should be opened or not," said John Murdock of Arizona, "but I am wondering whether this is only one instance, or whether there are a number of others like it." The supposed end of the Indian Wars, Wounded Knee might end up being a costly precedent instead, as the government meditated over a string of controversial encounters with Native peoples.[49]

"We are waiting for you, my friend," Beard implored his congressman in 1940, having again engaged the talents of a scribe. "I would like to hear from you soon how you get along with my case now." Two weeks after Pearl Harbor he dictated another note: "The soldier begin to shoot into man and women and children many were killed wounded and I was wounded my self in that time too," he reminded Case. And he kept writing. "This I am still lifer now," he echoed awkwardly in 1944. "We are waiting for many years so answ me soon." Even his ghostwriter was hard put to get the words right.[50]

The New Deal didn't offer anything new on Wounded Knee. Nor, for that matter, did any Congress that followed. In 1990, close to the one hundredth anniversary, Marie testified in a Senate hearing to plead the survivors' case for an apology and compensation, but Congress wouldn't budge. The Survivors' Association chapter on Pine Ridge, she tells me, isn't very active anymore. She's the vice president and a member of the board of directors, but it's been a long time since they sat down to talk seriously.[51]

9

GUNNERY RANGE

Dewey Beard stood up in the big hall and looked at the row of men seated before him.

"I would like to say something," he said carefully. He acted as if he was going to begin a speech he knew by heart. The visitors shifted in their seats to look at the tired old Indian addressing them. He spoke in Lakota with a frail voice, but his bearing was tall and firm. "For 50 years I have been kicked around," he said hoarsely, pointing an accusing finger at the men. "Today there is a hard winter coming. I do not know whether I am going to keep warm, or whether to live, and the chance is that I might starve to death." Somebody coughed. The congressmen looked around nervously. They were in his territory, not theirs.[1]

Beard gazed out at the members of a subcommittee of the House Committee on Interior and Insular Affairs, gathered in the American Legion Hall on Pine Ridge on September 12, 1955. It wasn't the first time Putinhin had pleaded with politicians over something taken years before without recompense. The last time, when the subject was Wounded Knee, had been a waste of effort. He nodded at Jake Herman, his interpreter, and continued in Lakota.

"I am hoping you gentlemen," Herman translated politely, when the time came, "if you do not give me back my 980 acres, you will reimburse the people for the loss so they can feel better in time to come." Putinhin

143

wasn't dressed in war bonnet and buckskins, the way he sometimes did for tourists. He was wearing the hand-me-down clothes that made him look like a scarecrow in a field of Washington suits. Even U.S. senator (and former congressman) Francis Case was in the crowd.[2]

Herman tried to make Beard's point clearer. "Remember this disaster to our Indians was not brought on by ourselves. It was brought on through needs of war. Just as today, through needs of war our people need rehabilitation in [other] countries, so we are asking the same thing." The analogy would have made sense to the audience: It was a plain-speech request to bring the spirit of the Marshall Plan to Pine Ridge. "If you don't give me the money," Beard added, "I hope you will pay my people so my grandchildren will have a better education."[3]

Even at the end Dewey Beard was looking to the future. But Uncle Sam seemed to keep dogging him no matter where he went—an adolescent at Little Bighorn, a father at Wounded Knee, and now, out at the wind-swept range on Red Water Creek, a grandfather who had ridden away from his land in 1942 thinking he would one day get it back.

The War Department, now the Department of Defense, had never let go of him.

In 1942, Pine Ridge wasn't a likely target for military maneuvers. Red Cloud's people, the Oglalas, had once resisted the army for decades. The disaster at Wounded Knee, barely fifty years old, was still bitter in the memory of several dozen survivors and their families. But Pearl Harbor changed all that. The American entry into World War II saw a surge in American Indian patriotism, just as had happened in the Great War. Some forty-four thousand Indians served in the military during the conflict, and a fifth of the Native population participated in the armed forces or the war effort. On Pine Ridge alone there were fifteen hundred Oglalas serving out of a population of ten thousand in 1943, most of them enlistments.[4]

But the war effort needed more than recruits. Air bases, landing strips, prisoner-of-war camps, training grounds, and gunnery ranges had to be carved out of the American map in preparation to defeat the Axis powers. The country's least-productive landscape would become the setting for a military revitalization that forever changed the demographics of the American West. The government scoured the arid and semi-arid regions of America for likely terrain, and much of it, like the northwestern tier of the Pine Ridge Reservation, turned out to be Indian.

By a conservative estimate, a million acres of Indian land, greater than the size of Rhode Island, were seized by Uncle Sam for the wartime effort. The appropriated land was condemned, leased, borrowed, or bought outright. Indian land wasn't the sole target of the War Department, to be sure. People of many cultures and races were called on to surrender property, willingly or not, in the interests of protecting the republic. But the Indian estate was particularly vulnerable.[5]

Native people, proportionally, bore more of the burden than any other group. To begin with, much of Indian country was already in federal hands, making land transfers to the War Department fairly simple. Given that reservations were established in regions with minimal economic value, the terrain tended to be some of the least-productive land in the West. And as World War I had proven, Indian people were highly patriotic. Their sense of sacrifice for country was widely recognized and likely anticipated.

They were vulnerable for less attractive reasons, too. Many did not speak English. Most were uneducated. The vast majority were poor. And almost all were accustomed to having their lives ruled by federal regulation. In many ways, they were an ideal population to exploit. They had been made passive by economic dependence and possessed minimal resources to ensure due process.

It happened to the Walker River Paiutes, and the Cheyenne River Sioux, and the Shoshone-Bannocks. It befell the Tohono O'odhams of Arizona, the Sitka Tribe of Alaska, and the Cherokees of Oklahoma. But it was the Oglalas of Pine Ridge who would witness the largest Indian land seizure of the World War II era. It was to become the home of the Pine Ridge Aerial Gunnery Range, a vast spread of badlands, farming plateaus, and ranging ranchland that covered roughly 340,000 acres across the northwestern top of the reservation. That came to roughly forty miles long by fifteen miles wide, the size of a big county east of the Mississippi.[6]

Dewey Beard would be deeply touched by World War II, if in unexpected ways. And all his training as a warrior and showman could not have prepared him for what would happen. Putinhin would have needed a bundle of cash, a car, an English translator, a little book learning, and a profound cultural change of heart before walking into a lawyer's office to contest what the government did to him in the summer of 1942. Like 125 other families on Pine Ridge, he would barely have enough time to round up his horses before the storm hit.

When I cross the Washington Channel on the way back and forth to Virginia twice a week, where I teach, I use the Francis Case Memorial Bridge. The view from the bridge is enchanting, especially when the light is dying late in the day and a pale glow crawls across the marina and the crowded fish market across from the Jefferson Memorial. Thousands of drivers cross the bridge on a busy weekday, but I doubt more than a handful of them know whom it's named for: a South Dakota Republican who made his way to Washington and served as a member of Congress under every administration from FDR to Kennedy.

The Honorable Francis Higbee Case served in the House and Senate from 1937 to 1962, an advocate of sober appropriations and efficient government. A newspaper editor and publisher by trade, he was highly regarded in Washington for his work on weather research, highway development, and the dispersal of farm commodities overseas. Case knew Dewey Beard, and no doubt remembered him, from the Wounded Knee hearings. As it turned out, Iron Hail would rue the day the congressman ever set eyes on the Washabaugh County rangeland he called home.

An Iowa native, Case had a convert's passion for his adopted state. He once argued that the United Nations capital should be established in South Dakota's Black Hills, a place, it so happened, considered sacred by the Lakotas. It was at the geographical center of North America, Case argued, and afforded a temperate climate free of mosquitoes and flies. The Hills lacked the blight of industry, offered wonderful recreation, were awash in healthy spring water, and had the advantage of nearby Mount Rushmore. Even "racial discriminations are unknown" in the Hills, he bragged to the Truman White House in 1945.[7]

But race had played a part in how Case lobbied for a different barrel of pork in the months before the war. In 1941 the War Department had been mulling over where it would establish a large bombing range to train pilots before they went overseas. In July, Case was arguing to Secretary of War Henry Stimson that South Dakota was a choice spot for the range. The military needed flat land without mountains. They required sparsely inhabited terrain. They sought a broad strip long enough for a plane to fly at least five minutes on a bombing run. Large parts of western South Dakota were eligible on all counts.[8]

The choice was driven by simple economics. South Dakota was clamoring for government help, given the experience of a decade-long depression. The state had lost 7 percent of its residents during the 1930s, Case noted, and "Labor is idle and crying for work." People were leaving the state in droves to work at defense installations elsewhere, and an even greater exodus appeared imminent. Case saw many advantages to bringing in the military. "The range will be used by groups from other bases and will automatically bring thousands of additional fliers or personnel into Rapid City during the course of a year."[9]

The bombing range was only the first step in reviving the economy. In fact, there was talk of creating a permanent air base near the Black Hills if the range was approved. "Rapid City is the biggest little city in the country," Case boasted three weeks after the Pearl Harbor attack, "and we feel its selection for an Air Base site is more than justified by reason of special opportunities for a large aerial gunnery range nearby." The range, he reassured one Rapid City businessman, would guarantee the existence of a larger base "many years after you and I are gone."[10]

Other things being equal, there should have been no problem finding the army a comfortable home on the range in Dakota. But other things weren't equal. A strip of land between Scenic and Kadoka had very few families— but was crossed by a scenic highway that had been a favorite project of the late senator Peter Norbeck. Other areas were dismissed out of hand, since "probably they are plastered with oil leases," lamented Case. What the congressman needed was a stretch of country that lacked deep pockets, powerful friends, and political muscle. That was Pine Ridge all over.[11]

The reservation was notably poor and remote. Case was sure there were so few residents that the proposed land could be vacated within ten days. "With a population not exceeding 500 in the 750 square miles, and most of it Indian," he wrote General H. H. Arnold, "there are very few farm buildings of substantial character. The agriculture is largely stock raising and there are only a few cultivated fields." Six weeks before Pearl Harbor—before, in fact, the tribe had any idea of what was going to happen—Case was angling for an army contract that would bring the Black Hills out of the Depression at the expense of a hundred or so Oglala families.[12]

The congressman from Custer County, a marine private in World War I, was a cagey player. He wrote the Rapid City manager that "there was no use in stirring up someone (who might not get the full story) to raise some objections and start a song and dance about the inability or difficulty in getting any particular piece of land. Such a thing coming right now might be very hard to overcome." He advised the Indian Office in November not to let the Oglala Tribal Council know too much early on. The fact that it was largely Indian land figured in Case's calculus. In the end, however, the army officially chose Pine Ridge for its remoteness from Rapid City, its open terrain, and the lack of significant highways and railroads in the area.[13]

By the next summer, rumors of the impending land seizure had spread. Many on Pine Ridge thought it was unfair, especially in a place where patriotism ran high and military service was common. "Mr. Case, this is sure hard on us," wrote Louis Mousseau, one of Beard's neighbors north of Kyle. "Some of us have lived here for 30 + 40 years, building up our homes on our allotments." Case duly answered him the next month: "I am sure that you and the other Indians realize that it is up to the War Department to decide whether they need the land for a [sic] aerial gunnery range," he rejoined, and "it is not fair to the boys to send them into battle without practice." He concluded by emphasizing it was the War Department's business, staying mum on his own role in the affair.[14]

On July 7, 1942, it became official. The War Department would take possession of the land by August 1, and the bombing flights would start immediately. Details about how the land would be acquired were left murky. "It is a real crisis in the lives of these people," noted Pine Ridge agency superintendent W. O. Roberts. "The patriotic urge of these folk makes them acquiesce in their dispossession, but their attitude is quite similar to that of parents watching their sons take off for military duty. There are tears, expression of genuine sorrow at losing their homes."[15]

Many, including Putinhin, wouldn't have much more than a week to clear out of them.

Just about everybody on Pine Ridge knew Jake Herman. Born the year of Wounded Knee, Jake went on to play football at Carlisle Indian School in Pennsylvania and claimed to have attended more government schools than any other Sioux Indian. He jested once that he decided to drop out of school because he didn't want to show up Abraham Lincoln, a president with a "common education."[16]

Jake eventually became a bronc rider and fancy rope spinner in Jack King's Wild West Show and the Rodeo Royal Circus. The shows were descendants of Cody's bold spectacle, the godfather of American rodeo. But getting thrown from a temperamental bronc was a hard way to make a buck. Jake got tired of being a serious cowboy and turned to rodeo clowning instead—lots of folks were laughing at him anyway, he figured, for all the time he spent in the dust. So he dressed in tails and baggy pants, sported a fake nose, whiskers, and black derby, and ended up in the arena resembling a poor cousin of Charlie Chaplin's Little Tramp. Beard and Herman, both experienced showmen, became fast friends.

Jake had a way with animals, too. His assistant was Creeping Jenny, a Shetland mule that took verbal orders, opened gates, and was notoriously hard to rope. Jake taught her how to tell her age, lie down, and sit up; he even trained a dog, Tag, that would jump on the mule and ride it around a rodeo ground. Then there were the skunks. The Herman family would catch them and hold them up so they wouldn't shoot their scent. Jake would take a razor blade and cut them and then pull the stink bag out until they healed. He'd clown with them in the arena, pretending they were shooting him with white powder. One time he picked up a skunk that he thought they'd fixed, and it squirted him in the face—his wife made him bury those clothes. "When the skunk hit me in the eyes," he used to say, "I think it made me see better."[17]

Herman, who toured through the 1920s and 1930s, could make seventy-five dollars a month, a pretty sum for the day. He dogged Brahma bulls for a while, and in 1924 rammed a bull head-on in a fake fight—and carried the scars for a lifetime. Rodeo clowns "remind one of the old Roman days," he said, "when Christians were thrown in the arena for the lions to tear to pieces and everybody got a big kick out of it." He retired from clowning because he couldn't stay on the bulls anymore and thought it wise to quit while he was still in one piece. Jake went on to become an artist, a writer, a long-standing member of the Oglala Tribal Council, and a translator for his friend Dewey Beard.[18]

The Hermans and Beards lived about four miles from each other, west of Potato Creek. Jake spoke Lakota and listened to Beard tell stories about the old days. He said the old man told "father to son" stories, and an abiding affection took root. Dewey told him about how Bear Butte got its name and how the sun dance came to the Lakotas. Jake knew the old language, the "jargon" of the elders, the kind Francis has tried to rescue in his books. Putinhin wouldn't have used him as a translator unless he did.

Herman had a few good tales himself. He would tell about the time his brother Edward was attacked by his own prized black stallion. The horse reared and kicked him one day while he sat on another mount and trampled him after he fell. A few hours later, curled in his mother's arms, he died. To lose an eldest son was a disaster, so the mount was given a trial by seven elders. They considered killing the offending horse, but settled on a different fate. The stallion should be ridden and worked to death by its owners, they decided, and Edward Herman's black beauty was given to a neighbor and toiled like a mule until it died.[19]

Beard told Herman his own tales about the *sunka wakan*, "holy dog," of the Lakotas. There was the year they were wintering in deep snow in the Black Hills, and food was scarce. A group of scouts located a small herd of buffalo near a frozen lake. The Lakotas surrounded the herd on horseback, he told Jake, and by waving their robes and yelling, stampeded them onto the ice. The buffalo slipped and fell and sprawled on the lake, easy prey for the hunters, and the Lakotas moved in for the kill. They rode across the frozen surface, but the horses slipped and their riders crashed to the ice. Some broke arms and legs, Beard said, and a few even died. But as they scampered after their prey, they killed many of the bulls, and the meat allowed the band to survive.[20]

The days of reminiscing and storytelling near Potato Creek soon came to an end. In July 1942 the Beards and Hermans got the bad news that their allotments were going to be part of the new gunnery range. The allotted and fee land was condemned in short order, and about 125 families were given marching orders in the name of a national emergency, at the quiet behest of Francis Case. Even if Beard had sworn none of his grandchildren would serve in the military, there was no resisting the appraisers who descended on the small ranchers of Potato Creek.

The families didn't have a lot of time to pack. The Hermans were given ten days to vacate their mother's allotment, a 160-acre farm with a large stand of corn. Jake's son Rex, about ten at the time, remembers moving day: "My dad, mother, and my sister rode on the hayrack, and us three boys rode what few horses and cows we had. I rode my dad's trick mule out of there." They rode to Kyle and camped under the stars at Red Water, then moved to No Flesh Creek. They made several trips back to the old place to tear down the house and move it log by log south of Kyle.

The training flights started soon after. A plane would pull a target of nylon tied by a cable, and other planes would dive at it. Some of the bullets would overshoot. Cattle outside the range were killed, and sometimes houses were hit. When the gunners were done, they would dump the shells they didn't use. As kids they used to pick up whole belts of live shells, Rex's brother Paul Herman remembers, a burly rancher dressed in plaid shirt and coveralls when I meet him. You can still find them out there, he says.

People had to sell livestock at firesale prices. Looters made away with implements, logs, and tools. Jake and his wife never got over the taking. "They really felt deep injustice," says Paul, now a great-grandfather with seventy-eight grandchildren and great-grandchildren on my last count. "They took the prime land, the cattle land. People used to say 'Why didn't they cross the river and get those badlands out there, nobody lived out there but prairie dogs.' That's the kind of land they took. They took the best. Maybe it was easier to deal with Indian people than white people cause probably the white people had lawyers and backing in Congress."

Paul's younger brother Rex, who lives by Allen on a small ranch, shows me family photos and keepsakes every time I visit. Born in 1932, Rex remembers Dewey well. He had pearly white teeth to the end, he says, "They just got worn like an old buffalo bull." His hair was coal black and didn't turn grey. Dewey was reserved, never spoke unless spoken to. But Rex doesn't speak Lakota, and the old man liked to talk and laugh in his own language. He told Jake a strange story about Wounded Knee once. There was a team of horses tied to a wagon wheel in camp, and when the shooting started, one Lakota man got excited. He jumped up on the horse and was whipping it, bouncing up and down, trying to ride away because he thought it was loose. The man went crazy trying to escape, and the soldiers shot him. Dewey and Jake used to laugh about that one. "The way he told it, I guess in Lakota it was funny."

Wounded Knee didn't shake the Herman clan as it did the Horn Clouds. But sooner or later the military touches everyone on Pine Ridge. In a cardboard box Rex keeps a postcard from a brother who served in World War II. "Don't chase the gals too hard," Sonny Herman wrote from Europe in 1944. He was killed in Holland shortly after. It was a hard blow for a family that had already given up its land to the war effort, but it didn't deter Rex. He enlisted in the First Marine Division in Korea a few years later. He spent thirteen months in-country and made corporal. In 1952 he took shrapnel in his leg and stomach along the thirty-eighth parallel and won two Purple Hearts.

Rex showed me the scars on his stomach, which looks like the surface of a sewed-up pigskin. He shuffles around in a bathrobe or his marine corps sweats, chewing gum and telling me about his granddaughter, a scholarship student at Duke who's now in graduate school. He's got stomach and colon problems and spent six months a few years back with a feeding tube stuck in him. The next year it was eye surgery and sunglasses.

The Hermans, Depression-era Indian boys who worked the land, went to boarding school, and learned to ride a horse long and hard, are a dying breed. They knew the Beards from month to month, season to season, but only in the way that a child knows a distant elder. Today an elder himself, Rex is dry and deadpan. When I ask after his health he says, "I'm still above ground." Paul, who has prostate cancer, hasn't lost his sense of humor either. His big shoulders hunched over, a feed cap tilted back on his head, he says to me one day, "I'll tell you a joke. What did Custer say when he stopped off at the BIA agency at Pine Ridge on his way up to the Little Bighorn?"

No idea, I say.

"'Whatever you do . . . don't do anything till I get back.'"

The Beards, who settled at Red Water before the land was even allotted, lived there close to forty years. The gunnery range taking came at a bad time. In 1940, daughter Carrie died of tuberculosis, leaving only Tommy, of all Dewey's children, still alive. Born in 1916, Tommy contracted TB himself and was doctored from an early age. He married Martha Owns the Bear in 1940, and they lost two infants of their own before the war was out. When the army came to serve notice on local landowners in 1942, Putinhin was about eighty, receiving old-age assistance from the State of South Dakota.

Dewey Beard "was a poor man," says Rex. Only on a place like Pine Ridge could the son of Horn Cloud tell an investigator with a straight face that he earned a "fair" income. In 1940, 90 percent of Oglalas were on public assistance. The same year, Dewey and Alice earned $665, half of it in relief funds and Social Security, the balance from ranching (probably horse sales), cutting timber, and leasing land. Dewey had a good-sized ranch and a (dwindling) herd of horses, but cash would have been hard to come by. As times got tougher he sold family crafts to the myriad souvenir hunters who descended on Pine Ridge.[21]

At least the land was theirs, even if Uncle Sam held the paper. The hard, sandy soil at Red Water was good for grazing. There were a few acres of bottomland, and a good trail across the property. The creek was a steady source of water, and the railhead at Interior was only some twenty miles away. They even ran some fence around the main yard, but apparently not enough. Marie says the BIA wrote Dewey one day and told him to fence the whole allotment, though he preferred to see his horses run wild. He played possum then to see if someone might do it for him. Sure enough, when the neighboring ranchers got leases or deeds in the meantime, "they started fencing off their land," she says, "so by the time they finished stringing all the land around his, he had a fence."

On Pine Ridge you had to savor the small victories, because the defeats could suck you dry. And the arrival of the army in 1942 did just that. Though the order to move within ten days was amended to two months, many evacuees, given the lack of phones and good roads, didn't learn of the change until they had abandoned their homes before the original August 1 deadline. The Beards, who learned their fate in mid-July, got out quickly.[22]

It had to be a sorrowful piece of work. For Putinhin, it was another break with the old days. It was at Red Water, after all, that Big Foot's band had spent the night on the way down from Cheyenne River. And the Beards had only a handful of days to gather up their possessions. (I sometimes wonder if the letter from General Miles made it—a bear-claw necklace from Beard's grandfather and a beaded deerskin shirt did.) But they moved like elders, not people in their prime. Putinhin was too old and tired to even round up most of his herd. A report from July 23 put the Beards' situation in a hard light: "10 horses, not much to move. Has tent. Did not know where they were going." It reads like a telegraph from a war zone, which in one sense it was.[23]

Landowners were paid "fair market value" for allotments, but the reckoning was harsh. The appraisals were done by outsiders with limited local experience. The assessments reflected the low price of land during the Depression but seemingly ignored how the war would affect rising agricultural prices. Timber reserves, potential irrigation, and the replacement value of food sources went unconsidered. Improvements were lowballed, moving expenses denied. The assessed value of the Beards' log house, fourteen by eighteen by seven feet, with a dirt floor and no foundation, was twenty dollars—considerably less than the average weekly wage in the manufacturing sector. The land was what they called "improved," though not in any splendid way. The Beards did have a well; a windmill and motor were valued at forty dollars. Once the taking was done, they were offered a buyback of the log house at a "salvage value" of two dollars (relocation required), which they apparently refused.[24]

As if the sudden displacement, the loss of neighbors and community, and the meager appraisals weren't enough, the money for the condemned land wasn't available until the following year. Many evacuees were forced to borrow (with limited collateral) to tide themselves over. In the end, Alice and Dewey Beard received $3,370 for their family allotments near Red Water, about four dollars an acre. That included the land allotted Eva, who died in 1914 when she was four. The one tangible reminder of their dead children, in a place where belongings were few and hardships many, was the land they had been allotted.[25]

A few thousand dollars may have sounded like a windfall, but the proceeds of the forced sale were handed out in installments. More difficult to fathom was that the money was used to compensate the state for old-age assistance payments, which Beard had been receiving since 1938. Of seventy-five pensioners forced off the range, he was one of a minority to settle his account with South Dakota. Beard paid down his "debt" of $963 in August 1943, barely a year after evacuation. Not until a half century later, long after he and Alice were gone, would the state be required to reimburse families for public benefits long misappropriated as loans.[26]

Dewey and Alice were frugal. Aside from the state money, they had less than one hundred dollars of debt when they lost their land. And they spent their sale proceeds with the same prudence. They paid down the small debt and the larger sum they owed the state. They bought a wagon, harness, team of mares, and some building materials. By then they were left with a monthly allowance of sixty dollars. But it was no time to start over again, not for a pair of elders who had raised and lost a large family over the course of forty years.[27]

The Beards settled briefly with son Tom on his allotment, and they had reason to hope the land would return to them when the war was over. In fact, Indian and non-Indian landowners alike testified that they had been told the government was leasing allotted land, not buying it. Nowhere, it turned out, was such a promise written down in any legally binding document. How well the appraisal process was explained to people not fluent in English is unclear. Even the government wasn't sure, as late as the summer of 1942, whether it would lease or buy allotted land. Beard went to his deathbed hoping his ranch would be returned.[28]

The Oglala Lakota Tribe paid a heavy price, too. Much of the gunnery-range land was owned by the tribe, not by allotted individuals. The tribal land, it turned out, was leased by Washington, not condemned and purchased. In fact, the government leased it at three cents per acre per year, a far cry from what the Indian Office considered fair. The tribe seems to have had no effective advocate in the process, other than occasional angry missives to other agencies from the Indian Office commissioner. As Paul Herman says, "We didn't even know what a lawyer was in those days."[29]

The range deprived Pine Ridge of a huge bloc of grazing land important to its prosperity. Perhaps more troubling was that much of the acreage was never used for target practice. As soon as the government leased the land, it invited ranchers—many from off-reservation—to run cattle on it. Washington started charging grazing fees, which even Lakota ranchers had to pay. During the three decades the military controlled the range, the government made a small profit on its balance sheet after subtracting the price of leasing and buying land from what was recouped in grazing livestock.[30]

World War II, like the Great War, had cost the Oglalas dearly. For all their patriotism, Oglala land was once again reduced by hardnosed business methods under cover of national emergency.

The Hermans did better than Dewey and Alice in the end. Jake's family took the money and bought another 160-acre parcel. The land they bought near No Flesh Creek is where Paul and his family live today. But they were lucky. With allotments condemned and tribal lands leased by the government, land prices skyrocketed on the reservation. It was hard for former landowners to buy moderately priced lots where they could settle in and start over again.

Decades later, the army left Pine Ridge and original owners were permitted to repurchase the gunnery-range land at the original cost plus interest. By then, though, "there was nothing left but the land," says Rex. The prairie had been overgrazed because "ranchers had come in and leased it for practically nothing." Few residents re-bought land and got back into the cattle business. Many who regained their property simply sold it back to the tribe. Only in 1956, by which time Beard was gone, did Congress authorize additional funds for evacuees.[31]

"They never did recover," Rex says of the former gunnery-range owners. A 1951 study showed that 80 percent of those who lost their land in 1942 had become downwardly mobile, with little or no land and less income than they had ten years before. Dewey Beard was one of them. He was homeless on Oglala land, having returned to the roaming ways of his ancestors in the days before Pine Ridge knew fences and roads. From tipi to tent, from one-room shack to shantytown, Dewey and Alice would stay on the move for the rest of their lives.[32]

10

LAST MAN STANDING

During the Depression, the Beards had taken to summering in the Badlands. It wasn't "getting away from it all" that moved them up to Cedar Pass to mingle with tourists toting Polaroids, garbed in sundresses and Bermuda shorts. It was a deeply ingrained poverty. By 1939, 90 percent of the family's income came from public relief, and a few years later their allotments were gone. Nothing was going their way: the government wouldn't pay for Wounded Knee, and a long tribal struggle to get compensation for the Black Hills was failing. For years, Dewey and Alice would live on their gunnery-range legacy of sixty dollars a month.[1]

It was hardly enough. But Putinhin's time with Buffalo Bill had given him a taste for the showman's life. Thirty miles from the Red Water ranch, Dewey and Alice settled in to become the "authentic" Lakota residents of the Badlands. For their last twenty years they would pitch their hand-sewn tipi at Cedar Pass, near park service headquarters, and Dewey would pose with tourists near the front flap, dressed in an eagle-feather war bonnet and his grandfather's bear-claw necklace. He was known as a Wounded Knee survivor who, with the passage of time, became one of the last witnesses of Little Bighorn. The cost of a picture, by most accounts, was a quarter.[2]

The "old Dewey Beard" of South Dakota legend was born. He spoke to Boy Scout groups. He posed with boys and girls. The couple stood for color postcards, perennially available today on e-bay. Marie says the park paid Dewey "day money" to be there, and tourists tossed nickels and dimes into a small pot. Mario Gonzalez, a prominent Lakota lawyer on the Black Hills case in later years, said his father told him that when Dewey worked at Cedar Pass, the kids would come up and touch him like a live exhibit of the Little Bighorn. Dewey wouldn't say anything, but they had to pay for the privilege.

Leonard doesn't like remembering his great-uncle that way. It isn't seemly, says a man who traces his lineage to both Big Foot and Horn Cloud. Dewey became something of a small-time spectacle, a walking cigar-store Indian who seemed to have watched as the whole history of his tribe, from the old days to the modern era, passed before his very eyes. "What did he end up with?" asks Leonard, miffed by what became of Putinhin. "He had tremendous gifts. And all he could do was be a showman and have his picture taken for fifty cents. And he had a little shack up there in Rapid City. What a waste of that knowledge that could have been shared."

He was a warrior without a pension. He was a Lakota without land. Unlike Fox Belly, he had fought on the "wrong" side of the Indian Wars. Unlike Crazy Horse, he lived to be an old man. He survived epidemic and upheaval. He was unschooled, unskilled but for his horses and weapons, a family man who had seen most of his family die. He was known on Pine Ridge as one of the last of the old-timers, a reassuring relic of The Days Before the White Man. The local publicity wizards would even bring him out at a powwow to dazzle visiting Russian farm experts at the height of the Cold War.[3]

He was honored in traditional ways, too. Francis recalls the Grey Horse Society dance in the Kyle community center in the 1930s. Each of the dancers carried an elaborately carved stick that commemorated a favorite horse. Three of his grandfathers, including White Lance and Beard, were there. Beard's stick may have symbolized the mount he said he rode at Little Bighorn—or the one he captured there and rode to Canada. "I saw them. They brought sticks and sang the Grey Horse Society song. They rode their little stick horses, and they danced around, and all the ladies did the tremolo," says Francis. "I was small, but I can say that I saw it." He couldn't have been any older at the dance than Marie was when Dewey died. (White Lance passed in 1935; Francis was born in 1931.) Francis is proud that no one else in the family has that memory.[4]

Like many on Pine Ridge, the Beards would never come out of the Depression. The war buildup that fueled American affluence in the 1950s bypassed the reservation. Much of the land had been sold away or leased—or taken by the government. Changing technology made farming and ranching more expensive. Most Oglalas didn't have money to travel to off-reservation jobs during the war, and when veterans came home, unemployment soared. The living standards on Pine Ridge went into free fall during the 1930s and didn't pull out for decades. By 1956, most Pine Ridge residents had no land, and their net worth averaged $121. Even elders scrambled to make ends meet.[5]

That Putinhin would come back to the movies near the end of his life was a surprise. He wasn't a skilled actor, even if Cody's *The Indian Wars* had introduced him to the notion of working in front of a camera. That documentary was Beard's biggest moment on film, at least in terms of billing. He was, for a few weeks, a local silent-screen hero—but one who had to relive a terrible memory in the telling.

It was Dave Miller who snuck Beard back into the movies. Beard adopted Miller in the 1950s in what may have been an act to replace his last remaining son—Tommy—who died in 1954. Since Miller knew Lakota culture, the adoption probably took the form of a *hunka* ceremony. An elder adopted a younger friend in the *hunka*, the two pledging mutual loyalty and sacrifice for a lifetime. Symbolically, the elder agrees to adopt the younger "captive" rather than see him killed, as the rite was originally conceived. *Hunka* was a solemn commitment, even in the mid-twentieth century, and Beard would not have taken the gesture lightly, especially with a man who had proven his friendship many times over.[6]

Miller's job as Indian adviser to Hollywood gave him an inside track with central casting. And thanks to his adopted son, Beard landed a series of bit parts in the 1950s. The films had a pro-Indian stance and at least one homicidal *wasicu*—not uncommon for the new revisionist Westerns of the day. Putinhin's performances were tiny, uncredited cameos that helped an old warrior stay afloat when most of the country was thriving in the Eisenhower years.

Tomahawk (1951) depicts the Powder River War of the 1860s, a struggle that Beard, according to Francis, witnessed as a young boy. The prolific George Sherman directed, and Dave Miller took a bit role as a cavalry officer. There's a lot of Lakota spoken in the film (though no subtitles), a kind of early *Dances with Wolves* in Technicolor. Beard does a cameo turn in a crowd of war-bonneted chiefs who sound like the members of a Greek chorus warning the white man of impending doom just before a squad of cavalry rides out to be slaughtered.

The basic facts of *Tomahawk* are so accurate it's almost eerie, at least by Hollywood standards—a tribute, no doubt, to Dave Miller. The Fetterman Battle (1866) unfolds in the movie much as participating Indians said it did. The Wagon Box Fight (1867) is also portrayed, in which soldiers armed with new breech-loading rifles reported killing and wounding almost two hundred Indians, probably a much inflated body count. It was the classic circle-the-wagons fight that Hollywood loved to film—but rarely happened on the plains. In 1867 it did, and Dave Miller helped them get it basically right.[7]

Filming the battle was good for the Indian economy. Beard's neighbor from Potato Creek, Rex Herman, got a dual role: he played a cavalry soldier in a scene with Rock Hudson and later rode as an Indian in the Wagon Box dustup. The Indians were paid fifty dollars for a practice fall and fifty dollars for the real thing, Rex says of the fight scenes. "You just had to suck it up and keep from falling on your head." Rex was one of the few people who could ride in the buffalo-hunt scene—another precursor of *Dances with Wolves*—because hardly anyone could ride bareback. He was paid $3.50 a day for a hundred saddle horses he ran up to Rapid City for the filming. The original battle may have bloodied the Lakotas, but the reenactment spread some welcome cash around Pine Ridge.

Battles of Chief Pontiac (1952) was in a class all by itself. Directed by Felix Feist, who later did episodes of *Lost in Paradise* and *Voyage to the Bottom of the Sea*, *Pontiac* is B film with a twist from the early 1950s pro-Indian lobby. The casting is imaginative, with Lon Chaney Jr. taking the juicy role of Pontiac. Alice Beard puts in a brief appearance in camp, and Dewey has a few seconds in a headdress and regalia. Though the story is set around the Great Lakes, many scenes were filmed in the canyon and butte country of the West—and the actors speak Lakota! At one point a squad of Hessian soldiers marches across the short-grass prairie as if they'd taken a wrong turn at Detroit and couldn't stop themselves at the Mississippi. No one will ever mistake *Pontiac* for a documentary.[8]

In 1955 *Chief Crazy Horse* appeared, with the buff Victor Mature as Beard's famous uncle. Dewey didn't act in the film, but he did go to see it. He dismissed as preposterous scenes where Mature pitched woo to Suzan Ball, out of character for Crazy Horse, he said. Universal Pictures did go to a lot of trouble, like keeping Mature's headdress in a deep freezer full of dry ice to keep it erect while they filmed during a hot July in Technicolor. Beard told a local reporter he liked the film anyway.[9]

The movie Marie Fox Belly remembers is *The Last Hunt* (1956), another gritty pageant of frontier greed. Shot in the Badlands in the dog days of summer, it tells of two buffalo hunters—good guy Stewart Granger and bad guy Robert Taylor. "Killin's the only real proof you're alive," Taylor grunts, who stops at nothing to prove the point. Screen-idol Taylor captures Debra Paget in a raid he makes on an Indian camp, but she falls for Granger instead, who's determined to return her to her people.[10]

Beard appears in a short scene when Granger goes to deliver Paget to her tribe in the Badlands. The tipi encampment is flying Old Glory (like the Lakotas who were flying a white flag at Wounded Knee), patiently awaiting a herd of government beef. In a pan shot of the village, kids are running and frolicking, one of them probably Marie. Then Dewey and Alice come on screen, showing their disappointment when told the beeves haven't arrived. It's a dour and silent and fleeting image, perhaps nothing strange for a man who'd been posing for pictures in the Badlands for years. If that was what South Dakota Historical Society director Will Robinson meant by "capitalizing" on his fame as a Little Bighorn survivor, it was a pretty thin reward.

They were all extras, Marie remembers. "We got to earn money and eat sugar cubes." One hot day she recalls in particular. They were filming between Interior and Conata, and the techie crew poured plastic or wax over the ground to make it look like ice. Then they turned on a huge propeller and blew Styrofoam around like snow to imitate the dead of winter. Marie got heat stroke, and her nose started bleeding. "I almost died. It wasn't even cold. It was July."

Putinhin was there, standing in midsummer heat dressed for a winter script, watching as the Hollywood corps read through their lines about life and death and love on the plains. But he knew the place from long before. Only a few miles from where the cameras rolled, Beard had come down through Big Foot Pass sixty-five years earlier with his people. They cut gullies and holes in the pass using picks and shovels, working hard to beat nightfall and stay ahead of the soldiers in their rear.

Now he had come back an old man. The Badlands, once on the road to Wounded Knee, had become a make-believe movie set with Stewart Granger getting the Indian girl and riding into the sunset. The soldiers were actors, the snow was Styrofoam, and the bad guy froze to death in the middle of July. Hollywood, by the standards of Beard's life anyway, was a very forgiving boss.

Dewey and Alice lived like modern nomads. In summer they pitched their tipi at Cedar Pass. Part of the year they lived in the Oshkosh Indian camp in Rapid City, a hodgepodge tent village that looked like it never climbed out of the Depression. They had a place east of Kyle for a time. And later they lived in a small two-room house on American Horse Creek, a few miles southwest of Kyle, a place Marie remembers warmly. The day we visited, all we could see were the house foundations. She showed me where the outhouse stood and how they hung the lanterns for a little girl afraid of the dark. She would ride to Kyle in a wagon with her great-grandfather, who would stand up in front as he drove the team of horses.

Her grandfather Webster died before her mother, Celane, was three, and the Beards raised her like a daughter. She must have seemed a blessing for a couple who lost so many of their own children. Alice and Dewey impressed on her the importance of home: "Wherever you live, and whatever you live in," they would tell Celane, "even if it one-room shack, or tent, or tipi, take care of it and try to make it look pretty and nice. Reason why is because you live there and you can do anything you want; sleep long time, or sew, or raise your kids in there, and it represents your mother."[11]

Alice was known as Alice Tasunka Opi Win, or Wounded Horse. As a little girl she lived in a tipi and learned to bead and work with porcupine quills. She'd throw a blanket on an unsuspecting porcupine and pull out the quills by hand until the animal got tired and just gave up. She showed her granddaughter how to tan deer and antelope hides, too. Celane would eagerly listen to their stories, and they would quiz her later, to make sure she remembered.[12]

Dewey and Alice taught her a series of modest and tender lessons about life. Drinking milk would make her lazy, Grandpa Beard warned. Meat was better than vegetables, he advised. Their teachings were part of a tradition that regarded children with love and indulgence. Don't take small children out at night or even hang their clothes for fear of the darkness spirit, he cautioned. And a newborn child should be washed with sage tea: "You wash them with the sage because the sage come from the Grandmother Earth," he told her. "She wants to be the first one to take care of the baby. If you do that, this Grandmother Earth is watching him; make sure that he has a good, clean, quiet life and knowledge."[13]

Putinhin talked to her about the world beyond Kyle. He told Celane to obey the Sisters at Holy Rosary Mission, where she attended Catholic school for years, and warned her not speak Lakota in their presence. But Grandpa Beard always prayed with the pipe, she recalled, and more than half a century of Christian services couldn't change that. Celane, for her part, never learned how to pray the Catholic way after all her years in church. A Sister at the mission asked her once, in a theological test, who made her. She replied, "My father." Asked who her father was, she said "Webster Beard." They punished her for that.[14]

Evelyn Beard Yankton spent a lot of time with her grandparents too, though she wasn't raised by them. Her parents, Tommy and Martha (Owns the Bear) Beard, lost two children before she was born in 1946. Evelyn, who became a child dancer, wore a jingle skirt in 106-degree weather and danced with Dewey and Alice at powwows and parades. It was hot in that costume, she jokes, almost like "child abuse."

She visited her grandparents often in a place they had southeast of Kyle. Grandpa Beard had two bullet holes in his back, and Evelyn used to draw on them like a sketch pad. Alice would warn, "Don't turn over, she's playing on your back," but he didn't always hear. (Once he rolled over in his sleep and smothered her pet Chihuahua.) Animals, in fact, were a common sight at the Beard place. His favorite rodeo horse, Brownie, was docile and difficult by turns. Evelyn could play under his flanks when he was in the mood, but nobody could sit astride him for long. When Brownie died, Alice made dried meat out of him. "We ate him and prayed over him," she chuckles.

Her grandfather planted a round garden with a fence where he grew melons, radishes, and cucumbers. He prayed on it and decided his animal friends could eat on the outside but not the inside. One day a brown bear wandered by for a snack, and Beard chased everyone into the house. Then he ran back out and called to his four-legged neighbor as he lumbered off, "Come back again!" He was sincere—it was bear medicine that helped heal him after Wounded Knee.

When Evelyn reached school age, the authorities told her parents they had to send her to boarding school. Her grandfather didn't trust them. So Beard moved her parents, Tom and Martha, to Rapid City, and Evelyn enrolled in a public school at age seven, speaking no English. She's still thankful she didn't have to be separated from her parents. "He saved me" from boarding school, she says, and she's been pretty much an urban Indian, from Rapid City to Laredo, ever since.

The boarding school, central to the reservation experience, just missed Dewey Beard. But his family and neighbors attended school in a different era. Leonard went to Holy Rosary—and ran away. Rex Herman ran off from the school too, though he says the Catholic nuns were some of the best people he ever knew. Celane said she was slapped and hit with a ruler, and she never learned how to pray during her three years' confinement. For many, it was a harrowing rite of passage in which children were coercively removed from their parents, forbidden to speak their native tongue, and sometimes beaten. Others recall a tough but loving environment where they learned discipline without whippings and received a useful education. Dewey as a boy would have found Holy Rosary unbearable. But it's hard to imagine that he would have sent Celane there if he didn't believe she would be fairly treated. He seems to have had doubts about it the longer he lived, however. By the 1950s, he did his best to keep Evelyn away from the church and school authorities.[15]

Today, Evelyn works the night shift at the Rapid City Wal-Mart. Though enrolled at Pine Ridge, she doesn't have much to do with the old ways. When somebody dies, she tells her kids, "Don't try to worship a grave." In Lakota practice a family gives away copious gifts after a funeral, but that's not her way. "Don't do the giveaway," she advises them. "Do it when I'm alive. Take a blanket right now and give it to an elder," she says, "or take a homeless person to dinner and invite me." She sees value in the way things used to be, but she has raised three children off-reservation and has a granddaughter in college.

In this much, at least, the Beards resemble each other: Nobody has much to do with the rest of the family. Evelyn went away to school years ago and gave show photos of her grandfather and family to Celane for safekeeping. When she came back to reclaim them, "Celane said her family was hungry, so she had to sell the pictures for food." Evelyn was philosophical at the time. "Maybe this is how my grandfather is feeding you," she thought. She had cordial relations with Celane afterward, but she's always thought her daughter Marie held a grudge. For her part, Marie thinks Evelyn's mother, Martha, took a lot of family items that didn't belong to her after Dewey died.

The branches of the family tree have grown apart. The *tiyospaye* Putinhin was born into, and nurtured after Wounded Knee, was a fragile thing. Evelyn is proud of her large brood, Marie shows off her grandchildren, and Leonard and Francis recount pride in their descendants. But their extended families don't extend as they once did. Allotment, and its system of inheritance, broke them up into nuclear families. Plural marriage was banned, and many members married non-Indians. Some of the Beard people go years without talking. While they guard their memories of Putinhin as precious, what their relatives say and do is far away. At times I feel like I'm passing messages between them.[16]

Evelyn says her grandpa comes back at funny times. A few years ago she got a check in the mail from the State of South Dakota for $545. She thinks it was an old-age payment for Dewey, which must have been compensation for the state funds he and Alice were forced to pay back after the gunnery-range sale. But there wasn't much in the way of explanation. "It was like my grandpa was saying, 'Here, you need this money.'"[17]

As her grandpa once told her cousin Celane about sharing, "It's not the same person that's going to pay you, but the Great Spirit will choose somebody to give you help." Evelyn says she really needed that money when it got there.[18]

The longer Dewey Beard lived, the more his past dogged him. One Little Bighorn battle reunion followed another, and each time the survivors were reminded of who was no longer with them. The public didn't want to let Putinhin forget where he happened to be one day in June, almost a lifetime before, even if the day had proved to be a false hope for the Lakotas.

The indefatigable Dave Miller organized a reunion of Little Bighorn survivors at Custer State Park in the Black Hills in 1948. A handful of Indian veterans of the battle were feted: Little Warrior, Pemmican, Little Soldier, John Sitting Bull, High Eagle, Iron Hawk, Comes Again, and Beard. Nicholas Black Elk, already celebrated as the author/narrator of *Black Elk Speaks*, was in a sanatorium, well into his nineties and unable to attend. The old clan was dwindling.[19]

On reunion day, the survivors did a wounded warrior dance in honor of Native men who fell in the two world wars, then a scalp dance to celebrate the victory of World War II. But the gathering was a bittersweet affair. The victory over Custer had got the Lakotas nothing except a long exile in Canada and the loss of the very hills where they were dancing. Beard refused to apologize to one reporter for "Custer's slaughter." Putinhin was testy, in fact, which was rarely the case (or rarely translated) in interviews. "Frankly, I would like to kick the whites out of here," he told the *Rapid City Journal*, "but I don't make trouble since I eat their white bread." He wasn't the only one. When John Sitting Bull pointed to the hills around them and said they still belonged to the Lakotas, many in the crowd yelled, "He's right. This is still their country!"[20]

Bill Groethe, a freelance newspaper photographer, covered the reunion. Only twenty-four, he had done an old-fashioned apprenticeship with a master of the black-and-white medium, Bert Hill of the Chicago and Northwestern Railroad. The former apprentice knew his craft well. After posing a couple survivors in front of a tipi, Groethe led a group of several others, dressed in war bonnets, fringed buckskin, and moccasins, up to the front of the Sylvan Lake Lodge, a majestic stone-and-timber hotel whose location was suggested by Frank Lloyd Wright in the 1930s.

"I got an apple crate out of the kitchen and set them on the south lawn and just had them look into the sky, into the sun," Groethe says of the individual portraits. He was shooting five-by-seven sheet film, and Beard was the last to sit. The sun was setting, and Groethe had only one sheet left. It was so dark by the time he got to Dewey, he took only two shots at short exposure on the same piece of film. He was running out of time and material.

But Groethe moved quickly in the shadow of Sylvan Lake Lodge. Beard budged too much on the first shot. On the next, he moved again. By day's end, Groethe didn't know if he had a keeper or not. When he developed the film, the first shot was wasted. But the second was a classic—a lean, chiseled Indian face that hovers somewhere between cliché and legend, the most elegant portrait we have of Beard, an image that seems anything but a last-minute prayer in fading light. It looks like the fruit of a long afternoon's work.

Leonard shows me a damaged print of that portrait at his place. It was hanging in his home when a tornado swept through Oglala in the late 1990s. Away on a trip when it happened, he came home to find his possessions scattered all over the yard. A neighbor who lived a half mile away came over and said, "Is this your picture? I found it in my back yard." Sure enough, it was the Groethe portrait, dented and dinged by the storm. "I always tell people," says Leonard, "This is my grandfather. He survived Little Bighorn. He survived Wounded Knee. And he survived the tornado, too, years after he passed away."

The Groethe reunion photos, piercing in their collective gaze, can still be seen in the Rapid City airport.

The further the battle receded in time, the more celebrated the survivors became. Thousands showed up at the battlefield in 1951 for the seventy-fifth anniversary, including a raft of high-ranking generals. After a wreath-laying ceremony, speeches about the need for a stronger military dominated the affair. Dancing and festivities proceeded, and when the band played "Taps" over the quiet battlefield at dusk, and then the national anthem, the day was over. Dewey Beard came with Joseph High Eagle from Pine Ridge, who carried the cartridge belt he took away from the battle. The agency paid them twenty-five dollars each to attend—though they believed they were owed twice as much, an amount they had difficulty obtaining. The Pine Ridge superintendent noted that "both are practically penniless."[21]

The fame of the survivors spread. An autograph hound from Virginia the same year was disappointed to learn that Beard couldn't write his name. So the superintendent got Dewey to stamp his thumbprint on a book about Little Bighorn and sent it to the collector. Though Alice could write in a rudimentary hand, Putinhin never bothered to learn. It was not the way of the Lakotas who raised him.[22]

When Iron Hail and his friends killed the miners in the Black Hills, at least the way Francis tells it, they couldn't have imagined what the old mining town of Deadwood, barely settled at the time, would look like a century later. A few years ago, Ernie and Sonja LaPointe used to go to a partners' slot-machine tournament twice a week in Deadwood at the Gold Dust Casino. Usually they would see an elderly white woman by herself, sometimes looking for a gaming partner. She'd say hi to the LaPointes, but Ernie didn't know her. Then she started talking to them one day over a cup of coffee, and Ernie mentioned his family. She brightened when he told the Sitting Bull story. "Oh I knew Johnny Sitting Bull!" she cried, "and Dewey Beard, too!" Ernie was stunned that this small, chatty senior citizen could have known any Lakota old-timers at all.

Corliss "Corky" Besselievre proceeded to give Ernie and his wife an ear-ful. It turns out that Dewey and Alice came to know a lot of white people their last few years. It was on a promotional trip to Denver for the premiere of *Calamity Jane*, starring Doris Day, that the Beards got to know Corky and her husband, Paul, in 1953. Paul was the new manager of the Black Hills, Badlands and Lakes Association, a civic outfit that promoted South Dakota sports and tourism. Dewey and Alice agreed to make the publicity trip to Denver with the Besselievres, but not before making some inquiries. "Old Dewey Beard had us checked out before he would ride with us," Corky says approvingly.

The last stage of Putinhin's life was a far cry from the first. He had hunted, he had fought, he had survived disaster, he had raised a family, he had ranched through the Great Depression, he had even watched as his *tiyospaye* was allotted and scattered. With the Besselievres he would find a way to make money and gain a friendly kind of notoriety, a local fame that must have been gratifying in the short run if not fully satisfying. In some ways he became a symbol of Lakota pride and history. In others, he was a sideshow, the aging shadow of a warrior, a man no one but Alice could understand on the road if ever he chose to speak.

The Beards traveled with the Besselievres as unofficial Indian "ambassadors" for the Black Hills, Badlands and Lakes Association during their last years. They did trade fairs in Kansas City, Chicago, Milwaukee, Minneapolis—any place the association could book. Touring might have reminded Beard of the old days with Buffalo Bill, minus the pomp and spectacle. He and Alice would schmooze with visitors and talk up South Dakota's Indian heritage. The Beards were paid handsomely for their efforts, she says—at least it was better than posing for quarters at Cedar Pass. Though communicating was tough, the four became friends. Alice would translate for Dewey because "she could get by" in English, says Corky. Like many people who function in a foreign culture without speaking the language well, he probably understood more than he let on.

The itinerary was less grueling than it had been with the Congress of Rough Riders. The trade fairs lasted about ten days. In the opening ceremony Dewey would stand on stage with Paul, dressed in war bonnet and buckskins, as they announced he was a Little Bighorn survivor. Putinhin stood at full attention when the national anthem was played. It must have been a moving sight for the audience, a once-hostile Lakota saluting Old Glory with the Cold War in full tilt. They stayed at big hotels, shopped in department stores, ate at good restaurants. On Fridays, the Beards would have fish at noon, as good Catholics might. But in the evening, Alice would ask for a steak. "Alice, this is Friday, don't you want fish?" Corky asked once. "No," she said, "we had fish this noon." The Beards adapted themselves creatively to the customs of an exotic culture.

Toward the end of the tour, Dewey and Alice would buy a suitcase for each branch of the family. (Their own belongings they kept in duffel bags, tied up with safety pins.) They would go to a dime store with Corky to buy the suitcases, then to a department store to fill them. They spreed on bargain items, and clerks extended sales on their behalf. And they ended up saving a lot of their earnings. When they came home from travel shows, Paul would try and get Dewey to take what he was owed in monthly installments, because Lakota people knew his pockets would be full. "The old way was, you share," Corky explains. "Immediately people would be at the doorstep. By the end of the week, Dewey and Alice had no money."

After Beard was appointed to lead the parade on All-American Indian Days in Sheridan, Wyoming, he and Alice came to Rapid City and told Paul they didn't have the money to go. So they borrowed it from the Besselievres, as they had many times before. Alice would ask for the money, and Dewey would handle it. It was like a rolling loan, says Corky. They'd come back, pay off the debt in its entirety, and then Alice would say, "Now broke." Paul would answer, "Alice, do you need some more money?" And she would say "Han," yes. There was a point of honor in paying it back each time. The Beards, like many on the reservation, would never have trusted their money to a banker.

Corky remained close to Alice until she died in 1960. After Dewey passed, Alice had to go for an examination at SiouxSan hospital in Rapid City one day. But she wouldn't take her clothes off until Corky came down from Sturgis to be with her. The Beards trusted the Besselievres implicitly, and with more than just money, a point that would be proven soon after Dewey passed.

Putinhin must have bridled, in some quiet way, at being paraded across the Midwest. Corky recalls one tourist pestering him about not speaking English, and other indignities must have occurred. But the money was too good to pass up. As he did at Cedar Pass, and long before with Cody, he became an entertainer to pay the bills. By the end of his life, just being there and saluting was the best he could do. Leonard bemoans his brush with tourism; Corky knows she wouldn't have known him otherwise. What must he have thought the time an inebriated Native from Wisconsin got on stage and started haranguing the crowd? Putinhin refused to even be seen on the same stage with him.

Corky is Presbyterian, finicky, and frugal. She grew up in South Shore, South Dakota, on Punished Woman's Lake, named for the legend of an Indian girl who fell in love with a white man. She met Paul Besselievre, whose father was a Congregational minister, when she was a high school cheerleader, and they married in 1940. Years later she lost him when he went under the knife for a prostate operation and the surgeon cut his colon. They were a strange pair to pal around with Dewey Beard.

Corky drives up to the casino in Deadwood on Sunday, the place where she met Ernie LaPointe. When she goes to gamble she brings a purse her grandmother made for her grandfather, complete with original stitching. She put her first twenty dollars of gambling profit in it, and she still uses it to pocket her winnings, which have been substantial. She does it through two-dollar blackjack bets and slots tournaments. "I'm way ahead of Deadwood," Corky says smartly to me one day. She even confides how much she's won—but not to repeat it.

I'll bet it's more than Dewey Beard ever saw, except for maybe that time they dumped out all the gold dust in the Hills.

Mario Gonzalez has a different tie to the Beard clan. His bond is blood and land. Rattling Hawk, his great-great-grandmother, was a first cousin to Putinhin, who was a good friend of her daughter, Anna Quiver Wilcox. Unlike the Black Hills, Badlands and Lakes Association, Mario's interest in the land has been getting it back, not bringing in tourists to enjoy it. Gonzalez is best known in Lakota country as the lead Oglala lawyer on the Black Hills restoration case, when he argued for the return of federally managed lands in lieu of accepting a court-ordered financial award from Washington.

Putinhin knew the Hills well. He also knew the story about how they came to have a red road around them. A long time ago there was a great race around the Hills, and all creation was there: the four-leggeds, like the buffalo, competed against the two-leggeds, like human beings and birds. The animals ran so hard they started to hemorrhage, and the blood came out of their mouths and stained the earth red forever. The two-leggeds won. Even today you can tell where they ran, because the dirt around the Hills is a deep shade of ochre. It was a Lakota just-so story, violent and beautiful in the same breath.[23]

The Hills were wrested from the Lakotas by a tribal "vote" in 1876 and a congressional act the following year, partly as revenge for the Custer battle. Gold had been discovered, and the area was ripe for economic development. But the government took the land without the necessary number of tribal signatures, a fact that would never be forgotten. Beard was on his way to Canada, or already there, when his people formally ceded the Hills. But the action, in absentia, would have embittered him, as it did many Lakotas, for a lifetime.

After the Hills passed out of Lakota control, a fight for compensation ensued. In 1920, following years of lobbying in which Joe Horn Cloud played a role, the Sioux were granted the right to make formal claims against the federal government—only to have their case dismissed in 1942. In 1950 they filed with the new Indian Claims Commission, and four years later they were dismissed again. They made jokes about it on Pine Ridge. Rex Herman said Wesley "Hot Shot" Jacobs used to ride out to visit neighbor Dewey on a Shetland pony, and Beard would tell him, "Hot Shot, when I get my Black Hills money, I'll buy you a big horse." But the horse never came. That couldn't have surprised Beard, who learned with his own land that the government could take what it wanted, decide what was fair, and pay out the balance as it pleased.[24]

The race around—and over—the Black Hills wasn't finished. The Sioux claim was revived in 1958, and in 1980, more than a century after the grab, the U.S. Supreme Court made a compensatory award to the tribe of $106 million. The various Sioux tribes, however, with Gonzalez leading the charge, have refused the money and insisted on getting the land back instead. The award has grown to $1 billion with interest in the meantime. It reminded me again of Francis's story about the Black Hills run-in with the miners. But this time the Lakotas weren't going to pour the gold dust on the ground, or even spend it.

Gonzalez practices Indian law in the historic Buell Building in downtown Rapid City, an office with high ceilings, stained-glass art deco windows, and the Book of Common Law and the Napoleonic Code perched on a shelf behind his desk. He sketches out a family tree on a sheet of note paper and takes me to meet his mother, then over eighty.

His strongest memory of Beard was at a Labor Day parade in Kadoka in 1955, he tells me. About ten at the time, he had a horse that was just broken, still a little wild, and he was afraid it would bolt that day in the festivities. In the afternoon, he went back to the poor part of Kadoka where his family lived in a house with no utilities or sewer. There was Beard, the last man standing from Little Bighorn, everyone said, getting ready to ride out of town.

"He was old and couldn't get his foot up to the stirrups," recalls Mario. "So my mother had me run out there with a chair and set it down so he could get on it and put his foot in the stirrup.

"I took a chair out there and set it up. Then he got on his horse and left. And that's the last time I ever saw him."

11

AMERICAN HORSE CREEK

Dewey Beard, if he was right, wasn't just the last survivor of Little Bighorn. He was the last of the Horn Cloud brothers left standing. And he suffered an even worse fate: he outlived all of his children, too. There were nine, by my reckoning, and he buried every last one of them, many in the St. Stephens cemetery. Some were infant deaths, common across America early in the last century. But it had to be a bitter blow to Iron Hail when his last son, Tommy, died in 1954 of renal failure, by which time his father was in his nineties. He was the second son named Tom, and left a wife and child and allotment behind. Reporter Bob Lee remembers seeing Beard crying when he visited him shortly after the death. Mourning the Lakota way—gouging flesh, cutting hair, giving away possessions—was a harsh but purgative process.[1]

After the 1955 Black Hills tour with the Besselievres, the old man took Paul aside one day. "Come down and bring an interpreter," he said through Alice. "I have many things I want to tell you." Dewey Beard was ready to recount the story of his life, Corky thinks. I know that tale by heart, because she tells it to me every year. But the next time Paul went down to Kyle, Dewey was dead.

Corky goes to what I call the "dreaded drawer" in the hall bureau off the bathroom in her tidy Sturgis home. The drawer is packed with bulging photo albums wedged so tight they're hard to pull out and even harder to stuff back in, especially in their original order, which she insists on. I gingerly remove one, and she has me spread it out on the kitchen table.

We leaf through the pages, filled with news clippings and photos, until we get to one that holds a piece of lined paper with a note scrawled in ink in a small, childlike hand:

"Kyle s D, November 1, 1955. I, Johnnie White Lance, I talked to Dewey Beard November 1 9 AM to 12 noon, and he said his son died. He want me to take care of him when he died. So I said all right uncle I take care of you so don't worry. He said he don't want tell his wife he's gone die.

"His wife really worry about him and he said Johnny your auntie got little money. If I die you try to help Alice. If you any expenses for me, any think on me, and tell my nephew Paul Boss, Sturgis, South Dakota, Johnny do all this for me. Please that all I want tell you, Mr. Dewey Beard, on November 1, 55."[2]

That was as close as Putinhin ever got to writing a will.

Dewey Beard died the next morning in his sleep in a cabin on American Horse Creek. He was a very old man indeed. He was older than the state of South Dakota, which had been born on the same month and day in 1889, by which time Beard had already witnessed an epic battle, endured years of exile, and started life over again as a farmer on Cheyenne River. November 2 was All Souls Day on the Catholic calendar, which marks the journey of the departed for purgatory, a fitting irony for a tough old convert like Beard. His death certificate doesn't give a cause of death, probably because the cause wasn't worth mentioning: he was just old. The elder from Red Water Creek had been alive, by most accounts, since before Abraham Lincoln was shot. "He went to sleep when he died," says Francis Apple. "That's the way I want to go."[3]

Birgil Kills Straight says they went to the house on Halloween. Beard was lying there, talking and chuckling, and seemed just fine. Those last days Marie would stay with Dewey and Alice as much as she could. On November 1, her parents came to pick her up at the cabin with the promise they'd be back the following day. Early the next morning, before they got back to Kyle, he died. "I thought to myself, if only I had stayed," Marie says. Only four when it happened, she somehow felt responsible for his death.

It has to be an early memory, I say to her. "I remember a lot of things," she replies. She adds, thinking of her mother, "We both remembered."

Marie went to the wake and didn't want to leave. She watched as they prepared her great-grandfather for burial. They washed him with herbs and ritually prepared his hair. The wooden casket, she recalls, was lined with a soft, velveteen gray cloth. The Catholic service and burial took place at St. Stephen's, the little building on the prairie north of Kyle that looks from a distance like a tugboat at sea. The Besselievres were running late, but Alice wouldn't let the priest start until they got there. When they did arrive, the widow came out to the car and shocked them with a few short words: Dewey told her he wanted "Paul Boss" to have his things, she said, all of them. Corky says they were "floored."

When the ceremony was done, they loaded the coffin on a pickup and drove to the open grave a hundred yards away. "As soon as that first shovel of dirt hit that coffin," said Bob Lee, a reporter and family friend, "women started wailing—keening." He was struck by the contrast between the silence of the church and the loud cries of the women. Lee, whom the Lakotas called Writes Straight for his even-handed reporting, said it was one of the strangest sounds he ever heard.

The Besselievres offered to come back the next week and pick up Dewey's items, but Alice said, "No, now," Corky remembers. Alice took them to the cabin where she lived with her husband. In a tent apart she had piled a stack of possessions a few feet high. "'If you don't take it," she warned them, "the Indians will take it, because when they lose a loved one, they're used to giving all their stuff away." She was worried the people would sell everything and drink up the money, Corky says. The good items were hidden at the bottom of the stack.

The cabin yard was a mess of wagons and horses, running dogs and kids. Alice was in humble mourning, dressed worse than Corky had ever seen, eating sage during the service to purify herself. At the funeral tent, they hung a cow next to a big cauldron where they would cut off pieces to cook as they needed them. Corky's daughter said, "Oh, I'm hungry," and Corky, not keen about the cloud of flies buzzing the makeshift potboiler, responded, "You are *not* hungry, Sharon."

Putinhin's passing made the papers. *Time* magazine reported that Dewey Beard died "in his tar-paper shack on the Pine Ridge Reservation" and called him one of the last of the Little Bighorn survivors. The obit appeared across from Dale Carnegie's in the week John Foster Dulles shared lobster and poularde with Generalissimo Francisco Franco in Madrid. The *Washington Post* hailed Beard as an "ancient Sioux who claimed to be a survivor of Custer's Last Stand" and whose true age was unknown. The *New York Times*, writing that Beard was "believed to be the last surviving Sioux Indian" of the battle, said that he lived on "charity" after losing his land to the gunnery range.[4]

Like many Indians, Iron Hail had no will. Wills are part of the written tradition—they cost money to draw up and execute. Many on the reservation consider them bad luck. Besides, he was landless, childless, and virtually penniless, his life shorn of entanglements. But between the time he passed on and when his estate was probated, Dewey Beard came into a small treasure. In 1956, Congress passed legislation compensating Pine Ridge gunnery-range landowners at the rate of $3,500 per family. It was finally recognized that the residents had been poorly handled and paid. The proceeds were divided between Putinhin's heirs: Alice, Celane, and Evelyn. But the money to buy more land came too late.[5]

Not sure what to do with Alice's treasure, the Besselievres stored all the items in a suitcase—for years. "But we weren't going to sell them," Corky says firmly. Eventually they loaned the collection to the Old Fort Meade Museum in Sturgis. There was the bear-claw necklace worn by Putinhin's grandfather, a beaded buckskin shirt with ermine skin tassels, deerskin leggings, moccasins, a war bonnet, an eagle-feather fan, and two medals, one from the St. Louis World's Fair. Today they're displayed in a glass case in Building 55, across the parade ground from Custer Avenue. The fort is where the Ghost Dancers, under Big Foot, were supposed to be confined before they slipped away to Wounded Knee. It's not a place where Lakota people venture often.

Soon after Beard's funeral, nephew Johnnie White Lance paid the Besselievres a visit. Tucked under his arm was a burnished, antique army bugle. Dewey had told Corky and Paul that he picked up a bugle at Little Bighorn, but he couldn't remember what happened to it. "You should have this to go with Dewey's things," Johnnie implored, explaining how the kids played with the bugle like a toy. He said he needed the money, so the Besselievres bought it. The bugle is also in the display case at Old Fort Meade, the name "White Lance" scratched on the stem.

"It's strange about that bugle," muses Marie. Putinhin, she says, used to dance with it at powwows. "He had it in his hand. He owned it. He even earned it. An article that would be sacred or very meaningful to our family and to the direct descendants of Dewey Beard is on display at Fort Meade." She thinks the family deserves better.

As an alternative, Marie offers Crazy Horse Memorial, the Black Hills site where the profile of the famous warrior is being blasted out of mountain rock by dynamite, a project that began more than a half century ago. Many family members agree that an Indian memorial seems a more fitting place for Beard's cherished things than a cavalry fort. "For those people," Marie says of Sturgis, "those are just objects. But they're more than that for the family." As the collection passes on to Corky's children, who didn't know Beard to speak of, the bond will fray. Marie says the Besselievres have the regalia "to keep, not to own."

Leonard has seen the bugle only once. "I seen it and left. It's the whole thought of the cavalry, what they did to my family. It's not a good feeling—this is what changed our whole way of life." He doesn't even want to take his children to Fort Meade, an admission he makes one day during a visit in Oglala with Corky, who sits on the museum's board of directors. Corky recoils at Leonard's suggestion that the bugle—or anything else—belongs elsewhere. "As long as I'm living—and I've lived in Sturgis for fifty some years—I'm not going to pull it out of the museum."

Alice and Dewey may have been right about giving things to *wasicu* like the Besselievres. Her heavy, deerskin beaded dress is also at the museum, but only by a stroke of luck. Before she died, in 1960, Alice told her family to make sure the Besselievres got the dress. But her relatives sold it instead. Corky and Marie think it was Martha Beard, Evelyn's mother, who peddled it to the owner of Reptile Gardens, a tourist attraction near Rapid City. Owner Earl Brockelsby offered it to Paul Besselievre for the same amount he paid—one hundred dollars, Corky recalls—and the dress went to the museum. Alice, who was born about 1880, told Corky that the dress belonged to her mother, which would make it close to 150 years old.

Little by little, the legacy of Dewey Beard was scattered, an ironic fate since *Oglala* means "to scatter one's own" in Lakota. Bob Lee, given the old man's ceremonial pipe at the funeral, donated it to Crazy Horse Memorial, where it's displayed in the main hall. The courting blanket Dewey and Alice gave Dave Miller on the occasion of his wedding has floated around for years from caretaker to caretaker. The University of Wisconsin and the Chippewa Valley Museum in Eau Claire have several items Putinhin sold or traded to collector Adin Newman, a Wisconsin banker who took a fancy to Ojibwa and Sioux art and crafts. Newman lobbied in Washington on behalf of tribes and took a number of car trips to the Badlands in the 1920s, when a five-hundred-mile drive was a big excursion. There he met Beard, probably at Johnson Brothers General Store in Interior, where Putinhin often traded.[6]

A friendship developed between the Midwest banker and the Lakota warrior. Beard would send craft items to Newman in exchange for money or presents. Adin's grandson Peter, one of the Newman Collection heirs who met Dewey at Cedar Pass, frames it formally: "They were exchanging gifts. And one of the gifts may have been money. But I don't think Dewey was interested in selling." Peter's wife, Kathy, believes Beard was too proud to accept charity, even if his people were starving, so he would offer items for money—or whatever he could get. "Many thanks for the grub," Beard chirped to Newman in 1929, in a ghostwritten letter from Kyle.[7]

In 1926 Newman paid Beard fifteen dollars for a beaded saddle blanket. And the Beards offered a beaded dress five years later—all fourteen pounds of it!—for eighty dollars to help Putinhin pay for his son Webster's funeral. Store owner L. A. Johnson advised Newman that "the best time to collect more Beard trinkets is when they have a celebration then they sell cheap." Given that some three hundred people showed for Webster's giveaway that year, his father wrote (or dictated) to Newman, "I am in debt greatly."[8]

Beard latched on to Adin Newman as he later did the Besselievres. He had found someone of means who valued Indian art and was willing to help him when times were tough. Finding a buyer for beadwork and tanned leather was a way to keep the family afloat, and some of those purchases, even from the Depression, are still in public view. Dewey was poor, and he sold what he had to, as Johnnie White Lance did, and Celane, and Martha Beard after him. He gave away even more when time ran out. It's a wonder that any of his legacy has survived at all. The irony is that Lakota people rarely see it.

I knew that Corky and Marie had to come together sooner or later. Corky hadn't been to the reservation since the funeral in 1955, and they remembered each other from the old days, when Marie visited Sturgis as a girl. But before I shuttled Corky down to Pine Ridge one summer, I wanted to see the Fourth of July parade in Kyle. Kyle is a small burg, not much bigger now than it was when Dewey and Alice used to walk along the road every day from American Horse Creek to buy food and collect their mail. Luther Standing Bear, who worked at the post office in the old days, claims he chose the name for the town because it was short and easy to spell.[9]

Kyle has about a thousand people today. A taco hut, a gas station, a few churches, a high school, and several tribal buildings are the main attractions. A Subway and a coffee shop have opened (and closed) in recent years, signs of a bigger world ebbing and flowing. At night from afar the town looks like a small metropolis sprawled along Medicine Root Creek, a host of glittering lights strewn along the road. But like many rez towns, it's over in less time than it takes to look over your shoulder at a gas pump or a stray dog.

The Independence Day parade is big. People came with deck chairs and blankets and huddled under what little shade borders the main drag through town, BIA Route 2. The participants marched and rode through town in every form of locomotion: kids on bikes and four-wheelers, riders on horseback, cars and pickups with proud, waving vets. There was a car wrapped in star quilts, an Obamamobile with an "Obama Rocks" banner, and a vehicle with a sign honoring "Lakota sovereignty," rather strange tonic for the Fourth of July.

Bringing up the rear was a red pickup with a young woman standing in the truck bed. She wore a striped Uncle Sam top hat with a feather in the band. Dressed in a red, white, and blue skirt and a T-shirt, she smiled and waved to the crowd lining the road. But there was a hand-lettered sign on the side of the car that had the words "Lady Poverty" scrawled on it. I didn't know what to make of that. It seemed like a Pine Ridge joke, patriotism with attitude. I thought of Rex Herman, who lost a brother and a home in World War II and later served in the First Marine Division in Korea; or Francis, whose grandfather limped for decades after Wounded Knee, who cleared mines for Uncle Sam. And I thought about Dewey Beard, a man who was on the winning side at Little Bighorn and survived Wounded Knee but scraped together the money to buy Liberty Bonds during World War I. They were a strange breed of patriots.

When I got Corky down to Wounded Knee a few days later, I was nervous. Would they dislike each other after all these years? Marie was there to give a tour to some state legislators who were an hour and a half late. So we killed time leaning against Marie's pickup and braving a stiff wind. There was Corky, clutching her blue scarf and swapping stories with Marie about "old Dewey" and the time he traded away his best eagle-feather headdress in Wisconsin. Or the time Celane came to Corky's place asking for money to buy a pair of matching suitcases for her daughter, probably Marie, who was going off to college. "My gosh, I didn't even have matched luggage myself," Corky said with a smile. They talked like people who suddenly remembered they hadn't seen each other for fifty years.

Then Marie told us about Wounded Knee, explaining the layout in the ravine below and how everything happened from the first shot. How Dewey escaped. How the young boy was thrown in the grave still alive. How she had more grandfathers than one hand could count, which she had to explain to Corky. I expected some friction between them, a sign their worlds could never meet. But for a couple hours on a windswept hill, stacks of baled hay on the horizon and not a cloud in the sky, they did. When they were done remembering, they embraced, and Corky put her hand on Marie's arm to steady herself. I couldn't take a picture of that. It felt too personal. And I didn't dare mention the bugle.

It was that same summer, and one night Marie did an oldies show on KILI for Vietnam vets. She started the evening with one of my favorites, an old Shirelles number. I remember listening to "Soldier Boy" waft out of the KILI studios on Porcupine Butte, just a few hundred yards from where Iron Hail shoved his fist down the mouth of an army cannon the day before Wounded Knee. It was a Pine Ridge kind of irony—the descendant of a family that was killed, even murdered, by the U.S. Army, spinning oldies for GIs from another controversial war a century later. Marie's voice was soft and lilting, buoyed by that Indian rez accent loaded with long, sliding vowels. When she purred, "Wooly Bully coming up next," it felt like a heady mist had descended, if only for an evening, over a haunted part of Pine Ridge.

A man who survived the Seventh Cavalry, camped with Crazy Horse, starved with Sitting Bull, and barnstormed with Buffalo Bill is still well remembered. The oft-claimed last survivor of the Custer battle seemed to take on a brighter glow the longer he lived—and, for some people, the longer he's been dead. Leonard reminds me his grandfather could outrun a horse in his bare feet in a hundred-yard sprint—and did so at many a Pine Ridge fair, a favorite story of his. Since that was a Bill Cody act, I'm inclined to believe it.

The family speaks of him with reverence. Evelyn Yankton calls him "a forever person." Marie is moved to tears by his memory. Leonard uses him as an inspiration, but even he allows for a patch of doubt. A stranger once told him, "I'm really tired hearing all this stuff about Dewey Beard. This Marie Fox Belly keeps talking about him and makes him into this almost superhuman being. I began to think that he doesn't even exist. Nobody's that perfect." He was more complicated than that, of course.

Marie, whose devotion to Putinhin is second to none, has a story about human frailty. She says one day, as casually as she would mention the weather, that Dewey had an illegitimate child before he married Alice. Marie went to school with one of his daughters, and didn't suspect they might be related. But her mother always told her that Dewey had a son in Porcupine. The man died in 1994, and Marie and her mother went to the wake. He looked like Dewey—had the same nose, wore a black hat like her grandpa, dressed like a cowboy. But the records show that he wasn't born until 1906, years after Dewey married Alice. If Marie is right, Putinhin had a child who survived him, but not one that can be verified in the records.

Many non-Indians who had experience on Pine Ridge trusted him completely. General Miles wrote him a warm recommendation. James McLaughlin, a hard-nosed and suspicious bureaucrat, was impressed by his integrity. Judge Eli Ricker thought him "honest." James Walker quoted Beard's Wounded Knee experience at length in his extensive research on Lakota culture.[10]

He was respected by his own people as well. Neighbors like the Hermans and Garnetts spoke highly of him—and still do. He avoided political feuds but took up larger causes for the community. In many ways, he epitomized the traditional Lakota concept of the *ikce wicasa*, or common man. He had a reluctance to lead, as Sitting Bull and Crazy Horse did, but a willingness to speak out and represent the *oyate*, the nation. He traveled on behalf of the Wounded Knee Survivors Association and, as a public witness, for the gunnery-range evacuees. He had more courage than ambition, more fortitude than drive. In the presidential campaign of 1952 he made cameo appearances for Eisenhower, mouthing the popular slogan "I Like Ike," but it seemed more like an old man's indulgence than a partisan habit or a need for the limelight.

There are parts of his life we know nothing about, a gap created by illiteracy, rural isolation, even modesty. But the day in Dewey Beard's life we know best is December 29, 1890. The most detailed account of what he did at Wounded Knee is in his own words. Lots of words, in fact, including an interview that lasted more than eleven hours over several days in 1907. His memory of the event (translated by brother Joe) is authentic and moving. There's next to nothing in the record about his personal role that day aside from what he tells us.

His parents, wife, and brothers were killed, a fact borne out by official and unofficial casualty lists. And Beard bore visible wounds of the encounter the rest of his life. His account of the massacre is riveting. He defended women and children. He fought with every bluecoat he met. He tells us that he killed at least seven soldiers—on a day when only twenty-five died. Putinhin gives a heroic account of himself. He was one of what the Lakotas call the *takini*, the survivors of Wounded Knee, those who had seen death but been resurrected.[11]

The Lakotas didn't admire modesty among warriors. They were expected to describe their exploits in graphic detail, called "kill talks," a popular form of entertainment and inspiration. Witnesses were expected to confirm heroic deeds, but witnesses weren't always present. A little boasting, then, could have been a good thing. Perhaps that is how Beard "knew" that a soldier he shot was killed, for example, among all the smoke and chaos that enveloped the action. At Little Bighorn, as he tells it, he had the luxury of seeing his handiwork at the end of the battle; at Wounded Knee he fled for his life and didn't return to the site for days.[12]

Dewey Beard remembered many things from that day. But memories are fallible. We don't have any record of what he recalled about Wounded Knee until many years after the fact, by which point his recollection must have already diminished. He said, in 1917, that recalling Wounded Knee was like remembering something that had happened just the day before. Such confidence might have been caused by the number of times he recalled the event—or the urgency with which he recounted it. But memories of trauma aren't any more reliable than other recollections. Time, urgency, repetition— all these may have led to confusing, inconsistent, or perhaps limited images to draw from as he grew older. The basic facts—the death of loved ones and his own scars—were undeniable. But sometimes his memory fooled him. He told one source he saw his wife killed in the battle; another time, it was his mother. For all we know, the translation was wrong.[13]

Wounded Knee wasn't a battle in the usual sense, either. It was a mass of confusion and terror for the Lakotas, even more than a typical military encounter, where the lines of battle would have been fairly clear and the combatants prepared. No one at Wounded Knee was paying much attention to what anyone else was doing, given the rain of bullets and the desperate flight of men, women, and children. The Lakotas were disoriented and dazed. Most of them were killed or badly wounded. The lack of witnesses isn't a surprise.

Joe Horn Cloud said that Dewey killed four soldiers. But Joe left the camp before the first shot was fired, and the best he could claim was to have watched the fight from afar. His statement seems based on what his oldest brother told him. A soldier's account of Wounded Knee verifies that the army met stiff resistance from Lakota people firing from a pocket in the ravine where Beard presumably hid, but no one can know who they were.[14]

One can only guess at the guilt he carried as a survivor—and how that shaped his memory. Did the death of loved ones lead him to inflate his own valor, if only as a defense against a crushing loss? The irony of Beard's heroism at Wounded Knee is that recalling it couldn't have given him much satisfaction; it yielded only the most bitter of memories, which one wouldn't expect from a show of extraordinary courage. If we believe his account, and we have good reason to, his finest hour as a warrior was his darkest one as a husband, son, and brother. On that worst of all possible days, he did what a warrior is trained to do and what his father had asked of him.[15]

When Cody came to film *The Indian Wars* in 1913, Beard was one of the few Lakotas to receive mention by name in the press accounts and publicity. At a time when many survivors of the fight were still alive, even if they weren't in the movie, it seems improbable that a poseur or braggart would have been allowed to steal the show. Cody and Miles, who both knew a good deal about Wounded Knee and the Lakotas, accorded Beard a privileged place in the film.

Nonetheless, myths still abound about Dewey Beard. It's said that Putinhin was also the last survivor of Wounded Knee—the perfect bookend for the Little Bighorn. It's true that he was one of the few to fight in and survive both engagements, to hear him tell it. By the 1930s, in fact, he seems to have been the only Lakota left who had been in both encounters. But he wasn't the last Wounded Knee survivor. Putinhin was nearly thirty when the massacre happened, and many of his fellow survivors, of course, were children. In 1938, when he testified on reparations in Washington, there were still forty-four living survivors. It only stands to reason that a young child in 1890 would have outlived him. In fact, Jennie (or Jessie) Running Horse, an infant at the massacre, was still alive in the 1970s and living in Pine Ridge.[16]

Others claim that Iron Hail's profile adorns the Indian-head nickel. The source for the claim may well have been Beard's "son," David Miller. "Every time I see a buffalo nickel," Miller wrote, "I remember Dewey Beard. The rugged Indian profile on the face of the five cent piece was patterned largely after the old warrior's craggy features." Miller was privileged to know a great deal about his adopted father, but he often confused the facts.[17]

He wrote that Beard posed for the nickel before the turn of the century, and Marie agrees. Her great-grandfather went east to be X-rayed for the bullet he took at Wounded Knee, she says (X-rays were discovered in 1895), and "he still had to carry that bullet until he died." While in Washington, the story goes, Beard met George Dewey, the hero of Manila Bay, whose name he adopted. That's when they did the profile, Marie thinks. Dewey said he posed with two other Indians whose portrait was supposed "to go on half a dime," she adds, using his own words. "He often wondered what part of that face on there was him."

James Earle Fraser, the designer of the nickel, confirmed that three Indians sat for him on the project. There was Iron Tail (Lakota)—not to be confused with Iron Hail—and Two Moons (Northern Cheyenne), he remembered. "And the third," he once admitted sheepishly to the commissioner of Indian Affairs, "I can not recall." Fraser, who had sculpted the famous Indian figure slumped over his horse, *The End of the Trail* (1894), when still a teenager, spent much of his boyhood in South Dakota and knew the Lakotas from personal experience.[18]

In fact, many Indians claimed the honor of being on the nickel, some of them in earnest. Native people sat for all kinds of paintings and photographs early in the century. And the nickel was even better than going on a postage stamp. The coin was minted from 1913 until 1938—and a nickel back then could get you a movie, a couple hot dogs, a good cigar, or a trip on the Staten Island Ferry. This nickel, in fact, was big news: it was a uniquely American design (with a buffalo on the obverse side), and the coin didn't have "In God We Trust" engraved on it, what would have been an ironic motto, to be sure, for a Wounded Knee survivor.[19]

Almost everyone agrees that Fraser had three models. But who was the third? Two Guns White Calf, a Blackfeet, claimed the honor, but Fraser said he never met him. "I can easily understand how he was mistaken in thinking that he posed for me," the sculptor wrote. "A great many artists have modeled and drawn him, and it was only natural for him to believe that one of them was the designer of the nickel."[20]

Fraser doesn't mention Beard in surviving correspondence. If he sat for one of the busts from which Fraser modeled the coin, the artist didn't remember him. It seems odd that Beard's translated name for Wasu Maza—Iron Hail—would resemble so closely that of Fraser's favorite Indian model, Iron Tail, who also lived on Pine Ridge, also was at Little Bighorn, also rode for Buffalo Bill—and must have known Beard personally. The potential for confusing the two in the historical record is great. Yet if Fraser could remember Iron Tail's name, one would think the closeness of the two men (much less the similarity of their translated names) made it unlikely he could forget the other.

Miller says Beard traveled with Iron Tail and Two Guns White Calf to Washington before the turn of the century for the sitting. But Fraser wasn't contacted to do the design until 1911. In the 1950s, the sculptor's widow, Laura Gardin Fraser, finally recovered the third name: the forgotten model was Big Tree, she said, a Kiowa who sat frequently for her husband. The third man on the nickel, said the widow Fraser, wasn't Dewey Beard.[21]

It's not too much to think that Iron Hail was under the honest impression he was part of the composite profile—he had the hard jawline and high cheekbones to prove it. He was widely photographed and painted during his lifetime, and he may well have met Fraser and posed for him during his travels. But with his limited grasp of English, misunderstandings were always possible. For my money, he had more important claims on history than being on a coin of the realm. And while Putinhin may not be stamped on the half dime, he outlived the much younger Fraser, just as he did so many others along the way.

The old places are gone now. The house and barn at Red Water. The Oshkosh camp in Rapid and the place on American Horse Creek. The old dance hall in Kyle and the Medicine Bow Day School, too. And that church in Pine Ridge where he was tended after Wounded Knee—the congregation got so big they needed another building and hauled the old one out to the prairie north of Oglala and set it down in the middle of an empty field, like a beached ship.

A lot of people like to say they knew Dewey Beard. Every time someone would tell me that, I would get in my car and drive half across the reservation to find a funny story or a lost photo. But "I knew Dewey Beard" doesn't mean much anymore. His peers are long gone. Most people old enough to have been adults when he was alive are either in the grave or live in a fog of old age where an anecdote might not readily come at the bidding of a white guy from Washington, DC, who doesn't speak Lakota.

"I seen him when I was a young kid at a sun dance," said Paul Little of Oglala, his voice edged with pride. Frosty Garnett brought out a check stub his father wrote Beard in 1910, holding it up like a family heirloom. Garnett paid Beard sixty dollars, on the First National Bank of Rapid City, for two cows and a calf. But Frosty, when he was young, was hustled out of the room whenever the old man came for a visit, so he doesn't remember much about him. Ellen Cuny told me her parents said Beard would cut a hole in the ice to go swimming in winter—but all she can remember is seeing him with her father. "I knew Dewey Beard," Lili Mae One Feather confessed one day in her living room, about a mile from Beard's last house, after an hour or so of searching her memory. "But I never talked with him."

Lakota children aren't supposed to bother their elders. Ernie LaPointe said he watched Beard's visits with John Sitting Bull from a distance, because his mother wouldn't let him get closer. Most people who remember Beard now were children at the time—their memories are passive, largely visual, most of them recollections of seeing or overhearing somebody but not talking with him. For those who didn't grow up understanding Lakota, Beard was even more remote.

Saying that you knew Dewey Beard, on Pine Ridge, is like saying you knew a war hero you saw march in the Memorial Day parade when you were in fifth grade. There's something unforgettable about that moment, but it passes out of sight quickly, gone before you can think of something to yell from the crowd or even remember to snap a picture.

Unlike Crazy Horse, we know for certain what Dewey Beard looked like. There are scores, if not hundreds, of photos of him, a rare thing for an Indian who wasn't a well-known chief. He posed often and gladly—for professionals like Groethe, for grainy wire photo shots on his tourist jaunts, for hundreds of tourist snaps and Polaroids that evoke little more than a feather-bonneted and wrinkled old man in front of a tipi. And like his many names, Beard's countenance shifts with the frame and the season.

We have no likenesses from childhood, and I'm not even sure I would recognize Dewey Beard as a boy. By his forties he was lean and handsome, a wiry and straight-shouldered Indian rancher. This is the public Beard. He looks dutifully into the distance or gazes straight at the camera, a Native with no visible fear of anything like losing his soul. But a candid image of Putinhin is rare. He usually gave himself up in guarded moments. A smile or a shrug or a wince, anything that would put him in the moment, is hard to find until the last years. He was, even in his photos, classic and unyielding, as worthy of an Indian coin or stamp as Geronimo or Red Cloud.

People lose their physical distinctiveness with age. As I page through the photos of an aging warrior, he changes as much as the clouds over Kyle on a lazy afternoon. In profile his rugged jawline and leathery wrinkles command respect. The skin is deep and burnished, even in a two-tone photo. But the old man named Iron Hail takes a different cast looking straight on, gaunt and tired at times, the glimmer of a scowl about to surface. In street clothes he looks older and fatigued. Posed with a tomahawk, he looks stiff and unbending—but who wouldn't? And in some photos his hair is cropped short. That was the most humiliating concession Lakota men made to the modern world. In their way of thinking, you cut your hair when someone close to you died.

It was with short hair that the Horn Cloud brothers sat for a pair of formal portraits in Kyle in 1907. The sitting echoed a popular convention of the day, the Indian boarding school photo. Native students of the era would sit for a camera before they started school, clad in traditional dress and long hair—then they would pose later after their conversion was complete, dressed in school uniform and wearing shorn locks. In the first of the Kyle photos the brothers, except Joe, are regal and imposing in their regalia, what must have been a grand dress-up occasion at the time.

In the "after" photo, White Lance sits to the left and Dewey to the right, a stern-looking Joseph behind them with his chin raised defiantly. Beard is perched on a chair with his hands curled in fists and wears a fur-lined overcoat, work pants, and scarf. His angular face and grim mouth give him a determined, even fearless gaze. The brothers look fiercely resolved, but wary. When you look at both photos, the conversion seems magical and convincing, a sleight-of-hand done through a mere change of garb. But there is no sense of the terrible leap they made.

Written documents also strain to capture the truth of Iron Hail. The simplest fact-gathering mission for a census list or ration roll encountered in Dewey Beard a slippery subject. He was a foe of the modern bureaucratic credo. Precision, efficiency, promptness—at least in the modern record-keeping sense—were foreign virtues to Putinhin. He lacked a birth certificate, of course. His writing skills were limited to scratching an X on a ration roll. His age seemed to waver with every census and interview. His name had as many phases as the moon, waxing from Putinhin to Wasu Maza to Horn Cloud to Dewey Beard.

He wasn't the only one, of course. Dates and names, translated by harried and careless officials, make Indian census material fickle. And the many mistakes that crop up are magnified by the extensive record keeping on reservations. No people in our country are better enumerated than American Indians, mistakes and all. Native people were entered on the government grid long before any American received a Social Security number, much less thought to question the provisions of watershed legislation like the Patriot Act.

So Dewey Beard's documented life is full of "half-facts," information that may be partly true, but misleading or even false in other ways. His state death certificate, witnessed by Johnnie White Lance, is no exception. File number 287990 gives Beard's residence as being in Shannon County, Township 39, four and a half miles southwest of Kyle, the house that Marie remembers. His "Length of Stay" is given as "Life," what amounts to a bureaucratic nicety, since Beard never lived there on a permanent basis. His date of birth is given as "3-1858," presumably March 1858, a date the BIA contests on its censuses.[22]

Under "Usual Occupation," the clerk typed "None." That may have been true for an old man at the end of his life, but Beard had done so much in a century that the answer falls just short of dereliction of duty. (In a similar certificate for the BIA, his wife gave his occupation as "Showman.") His birthplace is listed as "Pine Ridge Reservation," a location that didn't exist when he was born and geographically inaccurate according to family lore. He's identified as a U.S. citizen, what would have been true only after the Indian Citizenship Act of 1924. Born as close to the heartland as any bull-dogging cowboy, Beard was near sixty before he was eligible to vote for the likes of a presidential candidate like Calvin Coolidge or Robert La Follette.

The form gives a "yes" under U.S. Armed Forces, but then a line of X's is typed over the answer, as though nephew Johnnie had second thoughts. And why wouldn't he? Beard was a battle-tested veteran, having driven a steel-tipped arrow through a Seventh Cavalry trooper at Little Bighorn and killed soldiers at Wounded Knee, by his own telling. He was a veteran, all right, but a partisan of the wrong side. With barely more than fifty words typed in its pre-drawn blanks, Beard's death certificate has more half-truths in it than a tabloid gossip column.

The bureaucracy had its revenge on Dewey Beard, and his people, in the random and impersonal ways bureaucracies do. It never compensated the Horn Clouds for Wounded Knee. It took allotment 1775 from Beard for a bombing range, then dragged its feet for over a decade before offering payment that arbiters considered fair. It offered money for the Black Hills (after he was long gone), but never returned any of the land. Even if Beard became a practicing Catholic, a member of the PTA, and carried around an "I Like Ike" poster, it didn't matter. The Interior and Defense Departments seemed to toy with him like a tired spider, a brave and wily Iktomi who couldn't get away.

It was strange I ever came across his story. Beard had no knowledge of letters, unfathomable for someone like me whose life has been devoted to writing. The alphabet, under his gaze, would have been a row of slashes and squiggles. The English Bible would have been a cache of exotic stories in a language as remote as Latin. No wonder he didn't sign a treaty. It would have been like blindfolding me and telling me to walk across a mile of open prairie with the faith that I wouldn't stumble.

We do share this much: his spoken English probably wasn't much better than my Lakota. When you don't know a language, the spoken words you hear come like a rush of water, and you stick your hand in to cup a mouthful, only to have them slither down your hands and drip away. So you begin to think that maybe some words are just not that useful. Maybe that's what Dewey and John Sitting Bull used to laugh about, surrounded by all that silence at Ernie's place.

12

THE SONG OF DEWEY BEARD

The more I visited St. Stephens, the more it bothered me that Beard's grave was unmarked. I'd seen horses walking in the cemetery, tattered American flags flying, grave stones overgrown with weeds. One summer I found Marie and Luke tending the family plots by mowing grass and leaving plastic lilies on the sod. Another year, on Memorial Day, Francis and I waited for a color guard that never arrived. The day I took Corky to visit, she was shaken by the absence of any stone. Dewey Beard deserved more than that, she said, as angry as I've ever seen her.

Ernie LaPointe says marking a grave is part of the written tradition. In an oral culture you remember someone by the stories people tell, he says, stories preserved in the mind and heart. John Sitting Bull, his relative, is buried west of Oglala in an unmarked grave, much like Dewey. But leaving a grave untouched is a hard thing for someone like me who learned how to read before I could ride a bike. I ask Marie to show me the exact spot where they buried her great-grandfather. "I pretty much know where everybody is," she says, pointing to an overgrown swath of grass near the marker for Thomas Beard. But she won't always be here. Sooner or later, the place will be forgotten.

In pre-reservation days, corpses were often draped in a buffalo hide and left on a scaffold on a tree limb, open to the elements. Tools and weapons might be left with them, even a favorite horse to accompany the deceased to the resting place of the dead. Once the body had decomposed, the bones of the deceased would be buried.[1]

But the government and the church changed all that. Most Oglalas were converted by heavy Catholic and Episcopalian efforts—Francis, after all, is known as "Father Apple," and St. Stephens cemetery has a whole neighborhood devoted to his family. In the old days, the body might have been put in a place only the family knew. That's how they buried Crazy Horse. But Leonard thinks the reason for an unmarked grave today is more mundane: "I don't even have headstones for my parents," he says. "And they've been dead for twenty years. But it's always my intention that sometime when I get enough money, I'll do it." I don't think Marie has enough money to buy a stone for Putinhin.

Ernie knows about family burials. Sitting Bull was interred in a concrete-covered grave in 1890 at Fort Yates cemetery in North Dakota, he tells me, following the gun battle that cost him his life. When the post was abandoned and other graves were moved in 1903, his plot remained in a lonely, secluded place.

In the 1950s the Sitting Bull family decided it was time to move their ancestor back to South Dakota. When North Dakota refused, they secretly secured permission from the Standing Rock Indian agent. Under cover of night in April 1953, Ernie's mother, Angelique, and her sisters, with help from activist Clarence Grey Eagle, arrived at Fort Yates before dawn. They removed the concrete slab with the help of a truck and dug six feet into the earth until they found and removed the remains. The wooden coffin had deteriorated badly, and though some of the bones were still intact, almost nothing was left of the skull.[2]

The group backfilled the hole and drove to South Dakota, then reburied the remains near Mobridge in a site above the Missouri River. North Dakota screamed and howled, but the family had the new site filled with twenty tons of steel and concrete, making sure no one would ever unearth it again. You might say that Ernie's mother, Sitting Bull's granddaughter, was a grave robber.

Some officials put up big bright lights on the monument, Ernie explains. And a few months later they unveiled a six-ton granite bust of Sitting Bull sculpted by the famed Korczak Ziolkowski. But family history had it that Sitting Bull shied away from the limelight. Buffalo Bill made him a spectacle in the Wild West show one year, Ernie acknowledges, but he didn't like it. "He was kind of like Atlas holding the world. He was a humble guy who cared for his people. He wanted to uphold them. When they put that monument over him, my mother didn't like it. It elevated him to a position he wouldn't want to be in."

Beard's feelings about the reburial aren't recorded. But he wasn't impressed with how the man he once followed into Canada was remembered. In 1954 they started filming *Sitting Bull*, a biopic starring J. Carrol Naish in the title role. When Hollywood decided to film in Mexico instead of South Dakota, Beard recommended a nationwide boycott. Rapid City hosted the premiere that summer and invited Beard, now one of the few Little Bighorn survivors, to attend. Iron Hail wore a headdress and full regalia to the premiere at the Elks Theater, where the governor showed for a photo op with Angelique and her sisters. Once in the darkened theater, Putinhin nodded off and slept through the Custer battle scene.[3]

Angelique LaPointe had her own three minutes of fame soon after. In 1958 she turned up on *I've Got a Secret* with Betsy Palmer—dressed like a blond cowgirl/Indian princess—and Henry Morgan, attired in gunslinger black. Roy Rogers crooned "Oh Carry Me Back," and host Garry Moore strutted around in an oversized Stetson. Ernie's mother, garbed in a beaded hair band, beaded earrings, bone breastplate, and deerskin dress, hardly says a word. It takes Bill Cullen all of thirty seconds to guess who her ancestor was. "Chief Sitting Bull is my grandfather," she admits, only one tooth visible. Angelique looks down at her hands, nervous and embarrassed. She speaks softly and looks a little glum. "My grandfather got killed before I was born."[4]

Sitting Bull's bones may not have found their final resting place yet. Ernie and his family are considering moving the remains once again. His older sister decided he's just another tourist attraction near Mobridge, and they don't like the way the site is maintained. The state is resisting their requests for disinterment, knowing a good tourist draw when they see one. "South Dakota thinks he's property, like a piece of land," Ernie says. Some have proposed moving the remains to the Little Bighorn, and the battlefield has welcomed the idea. But Ernie won't have it. "I don't want no Crow talking over my great-grandfather's grave."

Now the family is inclined to bury the remains in a secret place. That's how they buried Crazy Horse. After his death at Camp Robinson in 1877, his family interred the body in an unnamed location—but where, exactly, has been the subject of more debate than the infamous Crazy Horse photo. Some say he's buried near Manderson, on Pine Ridge. Others believe he's buried in Beaver Valley, Nebraska, where Dave Kadlecek is a fourth-generation rancher on land his great-grandparents homesteaded. His own parents talked with a lot of traditional Lakotas in the 1960s who pointed out Beaver Valley as the likely burial spot. Crazy Horse camped there just before his final surrender, and Beard mentions the place when recalling Crazy Horse's last days.[5]

Dave took me down to the creek where an old elm tree had been brought down in a recent flood. It was near a dam his family built to keep water for livestock. His parents interviewed many elders before deciding that Beaver Creek was the place. The tree, they think, was where the body was originally put. The trunk has been cut up in sections and lies there, wired together, dead but not gone. The burial site, some think, is nearby.

Kadlecek, a friend of Leonard's, respects the mystery of Crazy Horse. He allows tribal and non-tribal people to camp on the land for religious purposes, as long as they respect the property. The antithesis of his vision is the great Crazy Horse carving by Ziolkowski in the Black Hills—much larger than Mount Rushmore—where Beard occasionally appeared as a tourist draw. The same man who sculpted the Sitting Bull bust near Mobridge set out to carve the face of a whole mountain, a task never finished in his lifetime that his children are pledged to complete. That mountain got me to thinking.

Sitting Bull's grave is a tourist attraction. Crazy Horse was laid to rest in a place no one knows. As I traveled to Pine Ridge every summer, I began to hope there could be a place for Beard between those extremes: just a modest cut stone with life dates and a name set in the earth at St. Stephens. Francis told me he wants a marker for Beard, and Evelyn talked about putting up a bust. But Marie is different. "He was born free," she says one day, and I think she wants her memory of him to be that way, too. She looks after the grave, tidying the plot, but has done little to commemorate it. I urge her to put up a stone, even offer to raise money, but nothing happens. Maybe she plans to do it on her own, or maybe she likes the idea of no one else knowing where he's buried.

There's another possibility. And maybe it has nothing to do with Marie. Maybe that patch of overgrown grass represents something bigger—just the revenge of an illiterate man on history, the only peace Putinhin found in a life of roaming and fighting and trying to keep his family alive. But I am where I come from. Every time I go to the cemetery, I want to see a piece of rock with his name carved on it. At least his father, and his last surviving son, got that much.

One day Francis said he wanted to go to St. Stephens. We took a drive north from Kyle along a gravel road lined with sunflowers. We passed his house with the little corral out front, the rocky badlands to the north within view. We drive up to the little white clapboard church, one room and shingled, with a concrete-block addition out back. The building, crowned with a pitched roof and a cross at the top, has a big metal bell in the front yard. Around all of it a fence of barbed wire is strung.

There's always an American flag, sometimes tattered, flying in the cemetery. The weeds and sunflowers have grown higher than a lot of the crosses. Grasshoppers flit through the high grass. We walk over to the spot where Putinhin is buried, and Francis gets quiet all of a sudden.

"I can't sing it just like him, but I know the words," he says. "I could never sing it like him, he's the only one that can. But I'll try." By then I remembered the promise he made years before out at the Lakota Prairie Ranch—about the song of Putinhin that lies buried in the Library of Congress. Francis sang the song once at a wake for Norman Jennings, a war hero in Merrill's Marauders who shot three Japanese in one day. "I tried to sing it as best I can. They said I was pretty good. Made a lot of people cry."

The old people "have a special way of singing it," he goes on. "They don't sing like we do." He leans up against Tommy Beard's tombstone. "So—" he begins hesitantly. "Are you ready?" He asks me to turn off the tape recorder while he does a dry run. He leans over and bows his head, looking down at Dewey Beard's grave. He's dressed in tennis shoes and jeans and his crumpled Obama hat, a defrocked Episcopalian priest about to let go in an empty graveyard.

He calls it a warrior song. "We don't come from a land of chiefs. They were made chiefs after they went to Washington. They gave 'em a big old medal and put a war bonnet on them."

Francis cries out a few vocables—sounds with no meaning—and then I pick out a couple words in Lakota. "Something like that," he says, finishing his warm-up. Sometimes he sings the song at football games, he says, but just a single stanza, a faint battle cry from the past. "The people don't know it. No one questions me. But traditionally, you have to do four stanzas, two push-ups they call it."

He asks me again if I'm ready. He says something in Lakota about his grandfathers. Then he starts. His voice, already old, sounds ancient as he sings out the first verse, and older still as he descends the steep scale of notes. His voice starts to weaken at the end of a phrase, curls down, falters and breaks for a moment, but he takes a deep breath and finishes strong and resonant, doing each of the four stanzas in turn. "Oglala warriors, tell about me in a good way: I am a warrior." He recites the lyrics clearly in English at the end, so a visitor from afar doesn't miss it. With a little luck, maybe even Whiskers can hear him.

Francis seems sheepish. "I tried, anyway," he says. I've never heard him apologize before. Then he decides before we leave that I need an Indian name. Francis can never remember my real one. He calls me Waste (WASH-tay) Chicago—the old Lakota barnstorming phrase—since I come from the Chicago area. He looks down at the ground and thinks about it. "Comes from the East," he says finally, repeating it in Lakota. I write down the Lakota words, somehow both honored and embarrassed. The name never sticks. I'm not even sure he remembered it. It was just what felt right for an old Lakota man to do with a nosy wasicu who'd been badgering him with questions for years.

So there we stood at St. Stephens, where all the roads in this story end up. Putinhin, marked or not, is in company he would like. There's his brother

Joe Horn Cloud, children Tommie and Webster and Carrie, granddaughter Celane and her husband Jonas Fox Belly, the pair who ran away to get married. There's old man White Lance who limped after Wounded Knee, and there's all of the Apples—Francis's wife Freda, his mother Susie who was White Lance's daughter, Kenneth, and Eugene, who died young. There's Dewey's interpreter Jake Herman, and Jake's wife, and his grandsons, Rex's sons. Even half of Dave Miller's ashes are there. Most of the people I still know on Pine Ridge are destined for this place, an island of cut stones and plastic flowers anchored to the Dakota prairie.

I take Francis home, about a mile down the gravel road. We talk about dying on the way back. He jokes that he doesn't believe in hell because he might have to go there someday. Then he tells me another story about Beard. In the old days he would take Francis and the young ones by wagon down to the annual fair in Pine Ridge. They would stop over at Wounded Knee en route, and he would point out to them what happened that day long ago. But they didn't listen much—they were just kids. When it got dark, before they continued their journey the next day, Putinhin would climb the hill, curl up on top of the mass grave, and fall asleep. Francis said the kids were too scared to go up there, so they would pitch a tent in the valley and wait for him to come down in the morning. He always did.

We sit in his driveway for a time. I'm thinking that I've heard how songs can become personal possessions of people in Indian country, almost like property. When Francis gets out, I ask him if anyone owns the song of Dewey Beard, the way they own his army bugle or the bear-claw necklace from Wyoming or his ceremonial pipe.

He just shakes his head.

I think it must belong to everyone.

When a story comes to an end in Lakota country, the teller usually says "Hechetu yelo," which means "That's all there is," or "There's no more to say."

But there is more.

Francis died of cancer in the summer of 2013. So did Albert White Hat Sr., the man who told the story of the Little Bighorn witness, one of my favorite teachers. Leonard developed diabetic ulcers and has lost some of his toes. Marie had been fighting cancer and was hard to find sometimes—one night she was at a wake, the next a funeral for her sister-in-law, the next, her grandson was bitten by a spider and rushed to the emergency room. They have their own lives to lead, and some have already finished. I'm sure they got tired of a city boy writing a book that never seemed to finish, the fate of many a good idea on Pine Ridge.

Things get lost on the reservation. Money disappears. Plans go stale. People die young and violent. They raised Leonard's school building seven years ago, and there it stands on the east side of Oglala, its first class a group of two-year-old toddlers. Francis always talked about his many books in the works. Marie pondered a gravestone for Grandpa Beard, and the folks at Crazy Horse Mountain have promised her a cut-stone marker, though nothing ever happens.

One of the last times we talked, Marie was in a hospital bed in Rapid, summoning all her grit to say she was due to go home soon in spite of a bad prognosis. Her cancer was declared terminal in January 2014, and she passed away in April. Leonard, who lost his eldest daughter a few years back, was walking with braces. Corky says she isn't meant long for this world, though she seems tough as leather. And Rex Herman, who won two Purple Hearts in Korea, never fails to say "I'm still above ground" whenever I call. They're approaching an age when they can understand what it must have felt like to live as long as Putinhin did. Their memories fade, concentration flags, they repeat stories they told me years ago. Sometimes I'm tempted to tell them they're the last ones standing.

But they're not. Evelyn's granddaughter is headed to Black Hills State College, and Rex's, a scholarship student and valedictorian, graduated from Duke. One of Leonard's daughters just got married. And Chaz Thompson, Marie's only grandson, was studying nursing at the reservation college before he lit out for Idaho. He's the fourth generation in the family to play music on KILI. Chaz is six foot four, weighs 250, and has episodes of asthma and allergies. He's a self-taught guitarist and versatile musician. The first time he touched a cello, he says, they asked him if he'd had lessons. He even learned how to play "Taps" on the trombone.

His family named him Wasu Maza, grandmother Marie says proudly, after Putinhin.[6]

I thought of Chaz one night back in Washington. In 2010, Dewey's brother, the fallen tribal policeman Frank Horn Cloud, got his name engraved, with many others, on the National Policeman's Memorial, one hundred years after he fell in the line of duty. They handed out thousands of candles for the evening ceremony downtown, and when darkness fell, volunteers came around and lit them. Everyone in the plaza seemed to be holding up a small cup of light. They read the list of new memorial induct-ees, hundreds long, and Frank's name didn't come until almost the end. As we were working our way through the crowd to get home, a military bugle struck up the lonely call of "Taps," and it occurred to me, a world away from Pine Ridge, that the new Wasu Maza, aka Chaz Thompson, the great-great-great-grandson of Dewey Beard, could have played right along with them on the old slide trombone.

NOTES

Abbreviations

BBHC: Buffalo Bill Historical Center, McCracken Library, Cody, Wyoming

BIA-PR: Bureau of Indian Affairs, Pine Ridge, South Dakota

CCF: Central Classified Files

DBI: "Dewey Beard Interview," AFC 1958/017, American Folklife Center of the Library of Congress

DHME: David Humphreys Miller Estate, Battle of the Little Bighorn and Beyond Collection, Great Falls, Montana

DWU: Dakota Wesleyan University, McGovern Library and Archive, Mitchell, South Dakota

NARA-KC: National Archives and Records Administration, Kansas City, Missouri

NARA-W: National Archives and Records Administration, Washington, DC

NSHS: Nebraska State Historical Society, Special Collections, Lincoln, Nebraska

OLCA: Oglala Lakota College Archives, Kyle, South Dakota

RG: Record Group

SDSA: South Dakota State Archives, Pierre, South Dakota

SUL: Syracuse University Library, Syracuse, New York

UWEC: University of Wisconsin Eau Claire, Eau Claire, Wisconsin

Introduction

1. For the history of the Alex Johnson, I relied on a CD, *The History of the Hotel Alex Johnson: Showplace of the West*, and other publicity materials available from the hotel. I have previously sketched the details of Beard's life in "The True Legend of Dewey Beard" (three-part series) and "Last Man Standing."

2. The tape recording of the Beard interview is cataloged in the American Folklife Center of the Library of Congress as "Dewey Beard Interview," AFC 1958/017 [hereafter DBI]. The interviewer was Leland Case, and the recordist was Bates Littlehales. A transcript of the recording is held at Black Hills State University, the Case Library for Western Historical Studies, in Spearfish, South Dakota. The transcript records what was said in English but not the original Lakota. Corliss "Corky" Besselievre, who was present at the interview, recalled a number of background details.

1. Origins and Family

1. Indian Office, Office of Indian Affairs, and Indian Bureau are previous names for the Bureau of Indian Affairs, so named in 1947. My usage of these names in the text follows that chronology as much as possible, though one should note that it is the same government agency referred to throughout. My source for most, though not all, of the census information on Beard is www.ancestry.com, U.S. Indian Census Schedules, which provides photographic pages of annual Indian censuses performed by the BIA. I've provided microfilm equivalents for these pages wherever possible. For Beard's birth year, see, for example, 1920 Pine Ridge census, M595, roll 371, p. 125; or 1928 Pine Ridge census, M595, roll 374, p. 13; or 1932 Pine Ridge census, M595, roll 378, p. 30. In earlier censuses, before the BIA simply noted the year of birth, Beard's age, counting backward, more closely aligns with a birth year of 1864. See, for example, 1899 Pine Ridge census, M595, roll 367, p. 119. The 1907 interview refers to Ricker, *Indian Interviews*, 209.

2. Beard's obituary appeared in *Time* on November 14, 1955.

3. U.S. House of Representatives, *Sioux Indian Tribes, North and South Dakota*, 86.

4. For Many Wounded Holes, see Special Indian Census of 1880, Standing Rock Reservation, Volume III, M1791, roll 4, sheet 359, District 2, Schedule 1. Many Wounded Holes is listed as Horn Cloud's eldest son, age fifteen in 1880. In the 1886 census, M595, roll 33, p. 89, Horn Cloud's eldest is listed as twenty years old, under the name Whiskers. Most of the family names correspond between the two censuses. But whether Many Wounded Holes was the later Dewey Beard, or perhaps his brother, is not known. In subsequent Cheyenne River censuses, the name Whiskers came to stick: see M595, roll 33, Cheyenne River, p. 113, frame 0151 (1887). In the 1890 census, Whiskers is domiciled apart from his birth family, with a wife, Eagle, and a younger male: see M595, roll 33, Cheyenne River, p. 71, frame 0240. He is listed in the 1890 census as twenty-four years old.

5. The source of the Iron Hail name is DBI. Beard gave his birthplace as Nebraska in the 1920 federal census: T625, roll 1726, sheet 58.

6. For the Horn Cloud genealogy, see Joe Horn Cloud to Secretary of Interior Lane, May 8, 1915, CCF 1907–1939, Pine Ridge, 61226-1915-175.5 PI163-E121, RG 75, NARA-W. Celane Beard, Dewey's granddaughter, claims relation to Big Foot, Crazy Horse, and Sitting Bull in Penman, *Honor the Grandmothers*, 31.

7. Much of my research was done through in-person and telephone interviews conducted between 2005 and 2012. In the text I attribute information gained from these interviews to my sources. Since the reporting is a cumulative result of many conversations over the years, dates are largely superfluous. Tapes and notes of all interviews are in possession of the author.

8. See Fuller, "Life after Wounded Knee," 48, for life-expectancy statistics.

9. For Webster Beard's death, I rely on South Dakota certificate of death 137449-5931. See Penman, *Honor the Grandmothers*, 28, for Celane and Dewey.

10. On the subject of Indian naming, see Littlefield and Underhill, "Renaming the American Indian." A good account of the arbitrariness of Indian names is in Lame Deer, *Lame Deer, Seeker of Visions*, 22.

11. For a recent survey of Lakota speakers, see *Lakota Country Times*, June 21–27, 2007, A2.

12. For incorrigibles, see M 1011, roll 106, Annual Narrative Statistical Reports (Pine Ridge, 1910–1929), 1911, frames 0054–0056.

2. Growing Up

1. I rely on several standard sources for most of the ethnographic information in this chapter: Hassrick, *The Sioux*, is the classic academic study of the Sioux, an invaluable though dated source; Mails, *Mystic Warriors of the Plains*, is a sweeping, informed, and sympathetic account of Plains Indians; and Walker, *Lakota Society*, is a classic and reliable ethnographic source on the Oglalas and the larger Lakota tribe.

2. For the Lakota names of months, which vary according to the translation and source, see Hassrick, *The Sioux*, 174.

3. For Minneconjou etymology, see DeMallie, "Sioux until 1850," 757.

4. See Price, *The Oglala People*, 5–7, for the organization of the Lakotas.

5. For Iron Shell's winter count, see Hassrick, *The Sioux*, 346–51. For general descriptions of winter counts, see Hassrick, *The Sioux*, 8–11; and Walker, *Lakota Society*, 87–89. Luther Standing Bear, in *My People the Sioux*, 3, reflects on how he was raised on the traditional calendar but later had to "count back" to find his real age according to white chronology. Walker, *Lakota Society*, 87, says older Oglala knew when they were born, but not their age.

6. For Lakota census figures, I use DeMallie, "Sioux until 1850," 748; for language, see 718.

7. The essential book on Indian sign is Clark, *The Indian Sign Language*. Clark, a cavalry officer who participated in many key Indian campaigns, was a fluent signer. On "white man" sign, see 402; for "Sioux" sign, see 341–48. On "Sioux" sign, see also DeMallie, "Sioux until 1850," 751; and Mails, *Mystic Warriors of the Plains*, 5. For scalping and mutilation, see Hassrick, *The Sioux*, 90, 99, 109. Fools Crow says his grandfather cut off the head of a Crow enemy—see Mails, *Fools Crow*, 37. A more modern publication on sign is Tomkins, *Indian Sign Language*.

8. Mails, *Mystic Warriors of the Plains*, 85–86. Also see Hassrick, *The Sioux*, 315–16.

9. Hassrick, *The Sioux*, 12, 109; and Walker, *Lakota Society*, 57. For kinship etiquette, see DeMallie, "Teton," 808–9.

10. Hassrick, *The Sioux*, 352.

11. Walker, *Lakota Society*, 57–58.

12. For the *tiyospaye*, see Walker, *Lakota Society*, 5–6; Hassrick, *The Sioux*, 11–14; and White Hat, *Life's Journey—Zuya*, 37–44. For Beard's relation to Crazy Horse, I rely on DBI. Some circumstantial references to their relationship were reported in the press. For example, "Nephew of Crazy Horse Recalls Custer's Last Stand," *Jackson (MI) Citizen Patriot*, March 27, 1955, in 1993, file 23, box 4, folder 32, Jeanne Smith Collection, OLCA. See also Ruby, *A Doctor among the Oglala Sioux Tribe*, 221. It's not clear what Beard meant by "uncle"—whether a blood connection or acknowledgment of a close relationship—but he affirmed their closeness on a number of occasions. See Price, *The Oglala People*, 2, on sacred hoop.

13. On the council, see Price, *The Oglala People*, 7–9.

14. On camp mobility, see Hassrick, *The Sioux*, 172–73.

15. See winter counts in Walker, *Lakota Society*, 140–41; and Hassrick, *The Sioux*, 347, 349. The Iron Shell count (Hassrick), for example, lists 1818, 1845, and 1850 as epidemic years. On disease, see Gibbon, *The Sioux*, 89.

16. On parents and children, see Walker, *Lakota Society*, 57. On games, see Hassrick, *The Sioux*, 143–47; and Mails, *Mystic Warriors of the Plains*, 516. A good primary-source description of games is in Standing Bear, *Land of the Spotted Eagle*, 35. For Beard's own recollection of games, see Starita, *The Dull Knifes of Pine Ridge*, 251.

17. On the hunt, see Standing Bear, *Land of the Spotted Eagle*, 33–34; and Mails, *Mystic Warriors of the Plains*, 516. On praying for a buffalo hunt, see Hassrick, *The Sioux*, 194.

18. On claims to body parts of the buffalo, see Walker, *Lakota Society*, 40; and Mails, *Mystic Warriors of the Plains*, 209.

19. On training for hunt, see Mails, *Mystic Warriors of the Plains*, 209 and 514. Standing Bear confirms much of Leonard's story about Beard in recounting his own experience; see *Land of the Spotted Eagle*, 21, and *My People the Sioux*, 60–66.

20. Beard mentions counting in Miller, "Echoes of the Little Bighorn," 37.

21. For horsemanship skills, see Mails, *Mystic Warriors of the Plains*, 226, 516, 519. Standing Bear says he used to crawl up his horse's leg before he was old enough to jump on it; see *Land of the Spotted Eagle*, 21. Hassrick describes how horses were broken; *The Sioux*, 185–86.

22. See Hassrick, *The Sioux*, 230, on making bows. For tracking and reading signs, I rely on Mails, *Mystic Warriors of the Plains*, 523–27, and for water and fire, 531 and 536.

23. Many Native American combat veterans tell the same story as Francis for experiences during World War II, the Korean War, and the Vietnam War. In Indian country one hears the story so often it almost has the status of an urban legend.

24. Walker discusses bear medicine in *Lakota Belief and Ritual*, 91–93, and 157–59. I also rely on DBI for bear references. For war medicine, see Hassrick, *The Sioux*, 98. For general Plains spiritual beliefs, see Mails, *Mystic Warriors of the Plains*, 87–107; for Lakotas specifically, see Hassrick, *The Sioux*, 245–65.

25. Hassrick, *The Sioux*, 257–261.

26. Hassrick puts the Lakotas on horseback before the 1740s; see *The Sioux*, 69–70. DeMallie, in "Sioux until 1850," 727, says they had plenty of mounts by the 1770s. See Gibbon, *The Sioux*, 87, on guns and 91 on buffalo hunting.

27. Standing Bear reports going on a war party at the age of nine in *My People the Sioux*, 75–77. Starita says Beard rode in his first war party two years before Custer in *The Dull Knifes of Pine Ridge*, 251. See Mails, *Mystic Warriors of the Plains*, 520, on typical age of warriors. On fraternal societies, see Wissler, "Societies and Ceremonial Associations."

28. On the "language" of feathers, see Mails, *Mystic Warriors of the Plains*, 300–302. For counting coup, see Hassrick, *The Sioux*, 96–98.

29. On the psychology and ideology of war among the Lakota, see Hassrick, *The Sioux*, 76–100. Also see Mails, *Mystic Warriors of the Plains*, 73–74. For role of migrating herds in shaping territory, see DeMallie, "Teton," 797. On eastern tribes, see Gibbon, *The Sioux*, 77–78; and for various effects of the horse culture, see Hämäläinen, "Rise and Fall of Plains Indian Horse Cultures," and White, "The Winning of the West."

30. An excellent analysis of an Indian tribe with imperial ambitions is Hämäläinen, *The Comanche Empire*, 1–17.

31. There are numerous proposed etymologies for *wasicu*. See DeMallie, "Teton," 799, for what seems the most likely; Lame Deer translates it as "fat takers," an etymology Francis agrees with, in *Lame Deer, Seeker of Visions*, 44. Also, see Daniels, "Cultural Identities among the Oglala Sioux," 218, and Walker, *Lakota Belief and Ritual*, 72–74.

32. Standing Bear, in *My People the Sioux*, 6, calls it a disgrace to kill a white man.

3. Little Bighorn

1. The literature on the battle is enormous, but here are a few sources I found particularly helpful. Michno, *Lakota Noon*, offers an extraordinary array of Indian eyewitness perspectives on the battle. Fox, *Archaeology, History, and Custer's Last Battle*, is a valuable account of troop movements during the battle. Any of the various eyewitness volumes compiled by Hardorff are excellent primary sources, including *Cheyenne Memories of the Custer Fight* and *Indian Views of the Custer Fight*. For basic information about the battle, I relied on Gardner, *Little Bighorn Battlefield National Monument*. The bibliography on the battle, beyond that, is

almost too large to imagine. For the last veteran, see "Briton Was Last-Known Veteran of World War I," *Washington Post*, February 8, 2012, B6.

2. The Sotheby's announcement is in *Washington Post*, December 11, 2010, A3.

3. John Koster and others claim to have unearthed the story of a white soldier, Frank Finkel, who survived the actual fighting with the Custer contingent and lived until 1930; see Koster, *Custer Survivor*. According to Michno, Charles Windolph, a member of the Reno-Benteen command, survived until 1950 (*Lakota Noon*, 313). Also see *Deadwood Magazine*, http://www.deadwoodmagazine.com/archivedsite /Archives/Windolph.htm. As for Indian survivors, some non-combatants outlived Beard, including "Grandma" Dirt Kettle, noted below.

4. "75th Anniversary Observance, Battle of the Little Bighorn, June 24, 25, 1951," Robert M. Utley MS 62, box 4, folder 12, and unaddressed letter dated June 26, 1951 MS 62, box 4, folder 1, BBHC. A man claiming to be Sitting Bull's son—and a veteran of the battle—was said to have celebrated his 121st birthday in 1978, which seems highly unlikely; see *Sturgis Tribune*, April 8, 1978.

5. There are numerous accounts of the Rosebud campaign. See, for example, Utley, *The Lance and the Shield*, 140–42; and Powers, *The Killing of Crazy Horse*, 182–91. Beard apparently told some reporters that he was at the Rosebud. See, for example, *Omaha Evening World Herald*, November 2, 1955.

6. The quotation on numbers is from Miller, "Echoes of the Little Bighorn," 37. My recounting of Beard's experience of the battle relies on the Miller article, but more on DBI. The Miller source is questionable in places for reasons explained later in the chapter. The Library of Congress interview, on the other hand, has Beard speaking directly on tape and is the best source on the battle from his point of view. Beard's account is rendered into rough English by the translator, but his words were translated more carefully by Leonard Little Finger over the course of several hours of patient listening. I use Michno, *Lakota Noon*, to estimate the chronology of the battle.

7. The grandma story was told to me by Little Finger—Beard told Leonard it was his first battle, which is contradicted by some sources.

8. The quote is from DBI.

9. The story of Walks Under the Ground is told in Miller, but more convincingly in DBI.

10. Beard tells about counting coup in DBI. For additional extended Indian accounts of the battle, see Marquis, *Wooden Leg*, 217–57; and Neihardt, *Black Elk Speaks*, 80–99.

11. The story of the bugle is well attested to in lore of family and friends—Marie Fox Belly and Corliss Besselievre both confirm it. The bugle isn't mentioned in DBI, but it's referred to by the translator, Johnny Bruguier, as though noted in an earlier

conversation. Starita, *The Dull Knifes of Pine Ridge*, 250, says Beard used to show off a cavalry jacket and gun belt, but he doesn't mention a bugle. There was a bugle in the family for years, with the name "White Lance" scratched on the stem, now on display at Fort Meade in Sturgis, South Dakota. Corliss and Paul Besselievre had the piece authenticated by the Smithsonian after Beard died—the museum could only say that it matched what would have been used during the period. The horse story is told by Jake Herman in "Dewey Beard," from "Oglala Sioux Sun Dance, August 1–4, 1968," unpaginated photocopy owned by Rex Herman.

12. For axes, see Hardorff, *Indian Views*, 91, and for boys, 189; for maggots, see Hardorff, *Cheyenne Memories*, 162, and for dogs, 111. At all three battles cited, Indian women and children were killed indiscriminately. For other accounts of the campaign, see Greene, *Lakota and Cheyenne: Indian Views of the Great Sioux War, 1876–1877*.

13. For background on Miller, see Dial, "Survivors Portraits"; and Holtzmann, "A Brush with History." For much of my information on Miller I rely on his own files, DHME. I consulted the files in 2007 when they were stored near Great Falls, Montana, at the home of Brad Hamlett. The Afraid of Enemy story is told in Christopher Knopf, "Tribute to David Humphreys Miller," DHME. Miller wrote his own popular history about Little Bighorn, *Custer's Fall*.

14. I rely on Miller's South Dakota Hall of Fame Nomination Form, submitted posthumously by his second wife, for his career details, DHME.

15. Miller's wife claims fourteen languages in the Nomination Form, p. 11, DHME; Holtzmann says the same in "A Brush with History." For the Navajo claim, see "It's a Good Day to Die," DHME.

16. "Traveling Salesman Happy Only When Painting Sioux," *Rapid City Journal*, May 21, 1950, 21.

17. For Beard's age, see Miller, "Echoes of the Little Bighorn," 37, which is contradicted by Beard's remarks in DBI; for Wounded Knee story, see Miller, "John Sitting Bull, Left-on-the-Battlefield," DHME. Beard, in his many accounts of the massacre, never mentions John Sitting Bull. For name of Dewey, see Miller, "Echoes of the Little Bighorn," 39. Censuses make clear that he was officially known as Dewey Beard as early as 1899; see M595, roll 367, Pine Ridge, p. 119. Other scholars have expressed similar concerns about Miller. See Michno, *Lakota Noon*, 34, 51, 223, 292–93; Hardorff, *Hokahey*, 144–45; and Dippie, "Drawn to the West," 17–18.

18. Though some scholars doubt that Miller painted his subjects directly, rather than from photographs, the photo of Miller as a young man painting survivor Joseph White Cow Bull, included in this book, suggests otherwise, and other photos exist. And Miller's closeness to the Beards is indubitable: there is a photo of him with Celane at Wounded Knee in DHME, and he was photographed with Beard in Rapid City (see below).

19. The quote is from "The Most Unforgettable Character I've Met," p. 2, DHME.

20. The wedding reception is described and pictured in "Indian Expert and TV Specialist Married," *Rapid City Journal*, July 25, 1954, 13.

21. Putt told me it was Mount Roosevelt, but Miller's nomination for the South Dakota Hall of Fame, submitted by his widow, says different. Marie thinks it was Harney Peak.

22. Crazy Horse has inspired a deep and varied literature. The classic is Sandoz, *Crazy Horse*. A respected recent life is Bray, *Crazy Horse*. A fine account of his last campaigns is Powers, *The Killing of Crazy Horse*.

23. The quote and Beard's account of Crazy Horse is from DBI.

24. The Dirt Kettle story is told in Jake Herman to J. W. Vaughan, October 24, 1956, box 1, folder 1956, Jesse Wendell Vaughn Papers, American Heritage Center, University of Wyoming, Laramie, courtesy of Putt Thompson. The PBS "History Detectives" tried to authenticate a different Crazy Horse photo in 2009 (season 7, episode 5) and found it was of someone else. The show also purported to have a letter written by Beard on the subject, which isn't possible unless it was dictated by him.

25. The Comes Out Holy story is from DBI.

26. Beard told the *Jackson (MI) Citizen Patriot*, March 27, 1955, that he killed Custer's bugler and later went back for the bugle and firearm.

27. Will G. Robinson to Byron Painter, November 14, 1955, "Dewey Beard" biography file, SDSA.

28. Indian reticence to talk about the battle was widely reported. See, for example, Marquis, *Wooden Leg*, 348–49; Standing Bear, *My People the Sioux*, 83; and Hardorff, *Indian Views*, 55–56.

29. The tales were taped by James Emery and are held in the Emery Collection at OLCA, James E. Emery Tapes, disc 1, track 3, and disc 2, track 2. The English translation is by Leonard Little Finger.

30. For the English translation of Beard's testimony in Lakota on DBI, I am indebted, as noted above, to Leonard Little Finger.

31. For firing arrows, see Mails, *Mystic Warriors of the Plains*, 401.

32. Beard told Miller there was a scalp dance after the battle; see Miller, "Echoes of the Little Bighorn," 38. Others, like Wooden Leg, said there was no celebrating, at least on the evening after the fight; see Marquis, *Wooden Leg*, 256.

4. Canada

1. The Smithsonian report on the repatriation of Sitting Bull's hair is Billeck and Bruemmer, "Assessment of a Lock of Hair and Leggings Attributed to Sitting Bull."

2. Miller writes about John Sitting Bull in "John Sitting Bull, Left-on-the-Battlefield," DHME.

3. *Rapid City Journal*, July 12, 1954, 3, and July 13, 1954, 3.

4. As many times as Ernie has told me the story about the silver dollars, he's never entirely sure that the sleeper was Beard. But each time he tells it, he seems more confident.

5. The Slim Buttes battle is recounted in Utley, *The Lance and the Shield*, 166–67, and Wolf Mountain is described on 180. A more detailed description of Slim Buttes is in Powers, *Killing of Crazy Horse*, 207–16; for Wolf Mountain see 248–49.

6. The stories of the thundercloud and Crazy Horse's death are recounted in DBI. For the families that surrendered with Crazy Horse, see Buecker and Paul, *The Crazy Horse Surrender Ledger*.

7. Beard's account of Canada, unfortunately brief, is in Herman's "Dewey Beard."

8. Sitting Bull has had many biographers. The earliest classic was *Sitting Bull: Champion of the Sioux*, Stanley Vestal (Norman: University of Oklahoma Press,1989, 1932 reprint). An authentic Indian perspective written by a descendant is LaPointe, *Sitting Bull*. See also Utley's *The Lance and the Shield*.

9. My basic understanding of the years in Canada was gained from Manzione, *I Am Looking to the North*; and MacEwan, *Sitting Bull*.

10. For the quote, see Finerty, *War-Path and Bivouac*, 269; for horses, see 284.

11. Phillips is quoted in MacEwan, *Sitting Bull*, 109.

12. For the differences between Mounties and U.S. Army, see Manzione, *I Am Looking to the North*, 6–7.

13. Ottawa's dilemma is well described in Manzione, *I Am Looking to the North*, 51 and 70–71; the 1877 commission is described on 100–107.

14. For Black Elk, see Black Elk, *The Sixth Grandfather*, 209. For horseflesh, see Pennanen, "Sitting Bull," 135. The Beard quote is from Herman, "Dewey Beard."

15. Bull Horn Country is from Herman, "Dewey Beard"; Fort Yates is from DBI.

16. An account of the Lakotas who remained in Canada is Papandrea, *They Never Surrendered*.

17. The 1880 census is in M1791, roll 4, "Schedules of Special Census of Indians," Standing Rock Reservation, Sheet 359, District 2, Schedule 1. See also Dickson, *The Sitting Bull Surrender Census*, 104, 294. Though the census reflects families as of 1880, it was compiled in late 1881. Horn Cloud's family was also included on the Standing Rock annuity list compiled in December 1881.

18. The Horn Cloud family is listed as engaged in farming in the 1886 census supplement, M595, roll 33, 168.

5. *Wounded Knee*

1. Odgers is quoted in Heidi Bell Gease, "Lakota Protestors Chase Off Military Helicopters at Wounded Knee," *Rapid City Journal*, May 3, 2010. Other accounts

I used were Steve Young, "Protesters Keep Guard Aircraft Out of Wounded Knee Event," *USA Today*, May 3, 2010; and Roseanna Renaud, "Two Bulls Apologizes for Wounded Knee Incident," *Lakota Country Times*, May 4, 2010, 1.

2. A brief sketch of the years at Cheyenne River and Joe's schooling can be found in Ricker, *Indian Interviews*, 191. Marie says they belonged to the Congregational Church.

3. Joe Horn Cloud to James McLaughlin, July 23, 1920, SC11, box 1, folder 4, OLCA.

4. Daniel Horn Cloud, biography file, SDSA.

5. A good secondary account of the 1889 commission can be found in Hyde, *A Sioux Chronicle*, 202–28. As for the Black Hills, the George Manypenny Commission obtained a signed agreement ceding the Hills in 1876, which was ratified by Congress the following year.

6. See Biolsi, *Organizing the Lakota*, 39–45, on how the individual vote undermined traditional politics.

7. My source for the transcript of commission proceedings is Senate Executive Document No. 51, "Sioux Reservation," 51st Congress, 1st session; for Hump, see 172–75, and for roster of signees at Cheyenne River, see 288–96.

8. Hyde, *A Sioux Chronicle*, 225. The agreement was not, strictly speaking, a treaty, since Congress abrogated the formal treaty process in 1871. Such covenants with tribes were subsequently known by terms like "agreements" and folded into legislative acts.

9. The best contemporary source on Wovoka and his followers is Mooney, *The Ghost Dance Religion*. See page 821 on Wovoka's powers.

10. See Mooney, *The Ghost Dance Religion*, 822–24, for a brief description of dance preparations, and 915–27 on the dance itself.

11. Mooney, *The Ghost Dance Religion*, 916–17, provides a contemporary eyewitness account by Mrs. Z. A. Parker.

12. The description of the Beards and their relationship with the Ghost Dance is from Ricker's interviews with Joseph Horn Cloud and Beard. Ricker, *Indian Interviews*, 192.

13. On the newspaper war, see Coleman, *Voices of Wounded Knee*, 58, 167.

14. Coleman, *Voices of Wounded Knee*, 93. For the Eastman quote see *From the Deep Woods*, 218–19.

15. Walker, *Lakota Society*, 157.

16. Walker, *Lakota Society*, 158.

17. My account of the trek to Wounded Knee largely relies on the testimony of Beard and Joseph Horn Cloud in Ricker, *Indian Interviews*, 191–226. To align the chronology of the move, I also use Coleman, *Voices of Wounded Knee*; and Utley, *Last Days of the Sioux Nation*, 167–86.

18. See http://digital.library.okstate.edu/kappler/Vol2/treaties/sio0998.htm#mn50 for signers of 1868 treaty. Big Foot in Washington is mentioned in McGregor, *The Wounded Knee Massacre*, 17.

19. For the cattle detail, I rely on a translation from the Lakota, by Leonard Little Finger, of an account Beard gave of Wounded Knee in the 1950s. See Emery Tapes, disc 1, track 2, OLCA.

20. The quote is from Emery Tapes, disc 1, track 2, OLCA.

21. The story of the Hotchkiss gun is from Ricker, *Indian Interviews*, 216. Beard gave several accounts of Wounded Knee that I rely on to different degrees. Beach's "Wounded Knee" provides an extended account of Beard's experience. Beach's account, with some embellishment, was based on the work of Dr. James Walker, a physician who gathered ethnographic information on Pine Ridge around the turn of the twentieth century and interviewed Beard about Wounded Knee. That interview can be found in Walker, *Lakota Society*, 157–68. The longest and most detailed interview with Beard about Wounded Knee was done by Ricker in 1907. See Ricker, *Indian Interviews*, 208–26, which was simultaneously translated by Joe Horn Cloud. The account in Ricker provides the bulk of the Wounded Knee narrative in this biography. In 1913 Beard gave an abbreviated account to Melvin Gilmore; see Gilmore, "The Truth of the Wounded Knee Massacre." In 1917 he gave a notarized account of the massacre in Washington, DC, cited below. Beard later told his story in McGregor, *The Wounded Knee Massacre*, 95–98.

22. The gun quote is from Ricker, *Indian Interviews*, 216.

23. The fear quote appears in Ricker, *Indian Interviews*, 217.

24. Horn Cloud's talk is in Ricker, *Indian Interviews*, 217.

25. The story of the mock execution is told in Ricker, *Indian Interviews*, 218–19. But Beard doesn't offer this detail in all his Wounded Knee accounts—it's given a different spin in Walker, *Lakota Society*, 164, for example, and McGregor doesn't mention it at all. That raises a larger question about the overlap of the Beard narratives, of which Ricker is by far the longest. Many details coincide in the different sources, while others do not. Part of that is no doubt due to the length of the Ricker interview, done over the course of six sittings. Certain disparities also result from Beard's memory of the massacre, which no doubt grew hazier with time. None of the interviews appears to have been given before the turn of the twentieth century, with the possible exception of Walker, which means that the events Beard is narrating were over a decade old (in the case of McGregor, much older than that). There are many inconsistencies, some of the significant ones noted below, and they are likely due to a faltering memory, an imprecise translation, or even embellishment, unconscious or otherwise.

26. The shooting soldier is from Walker, *Lakota Society*, 165.

27. Beard identified this deaf man as Black Coyote in Ricker, *Indian Interviews*, 219. In Walker, two men are the catalyst for the first shot, Black Fox and Yellow Turtle, neither of them deaf; see *Lakota Society*, 164–65. In McGregor, this figure is neither deaf nor given a name; see *The Wounded Knee Massacre*, 97. Oddly, Miller says the trigger man was John Sitting Bull; see *Ghost Dance*, 229–30. So far as I know, Beard never identified his friend John as the man in question.

28. Rough Feather is from McGregor, *The Wounded Knee Massacre*, 100, and Afraid of the Enemy is in 118; Beard is in Walker, *Lakota Society*, 165.

29. The firecrackers are from Ricker, *Indian Interviews*, 220.

30. The breathing is from Walker, *Lakota Society*, 166. The lap is from Ricker, *Indian Interviews*, 220.

31. Marie says Beard was wounded several times; Celane, in Penman, *Honor the Grandmothers*, 18–19, says four. Beard's own accounts are inconsistent, but given different entry and exit points for a bullet, he no doubt had more than two wounds. One doctor said he had wounds in his chest, back, and left thigh; see Ruby, *A Doctor among the Oglala Sioux Tribe*, 222. In 1938 testimony before Congress, he notes being shot twice. See U.S. House of Representatives, *Sioux Indians: Wounded Knee Massacre*, 22–23.

32. The women in the ravine are from Ricker, *Indian Interviews*, 221.

33. This account of Beard's mother is from Ricker, *Indian Interviews*, 221. A strange inconsistency in his several accounts is that he told Walker he saw his wife killed, not his mother; see Walker, *Lakota Society*, 166–67. He told Walker her name was Yellow Leaf. It's hard to know which is right, or whether they both are—both women perished in the fight.

34. The prairie fire is from Ricker, *Indian Interviews*, 222.

35. Horn Cloud's quote is from Ricker, *Indian Interviews*, 217.

36. For Beard's feeling sick, see Walker, *Lakota Society*, 167.

37. For Joe's words, see Ricker, *Indian Interviews*, 225.

38. For description of camp, see Dewey Beard notarized statement, March 12, 1917, CCF 1907–1939, General Service, 70018-1917-054, Part 1 (2 of 3) PI163-E121, RG 75, NARA-W. For quote on singing, see Emery Tapes, disc 1, track 2, OLCA. The lyrics of the song are translated by Leonard Little Finger from DBI.

39. His reminiscence of the camp is from a conversation he had with Melvin Gilmore on October 27, 1913. The interview is from the Melvin Randolph Gilmore Papers, Series 3, Miscellany, NSHS—I am indebted to David Grua for providing me with a copy of this letter. For a published version, very close to the manuscript, see Gilmore, "The Truth of the Wounded Knee Massacre," 251.

40. The baby's fate is recalled by Beard in Ricker, *Indian Interviews*, 226. There may have been a surviving sister, Alice, but I was unable to follow the course of her

descendants on Pine Ridge. Leonard, Marie, and Francis were all vague about Alice and her progeny.

41. The memories here are from McGregor, *The Wounded Knee Massacre*: for Weasel Bear, 101; Rough Feather's wife, 120; Pipe on Head, 99; Kills White Man, 111; Stand, 117.

42. Beard's sad conclusion is rendered in DBI.

43. Benét's poem is "American Names," with the famous last line that inspired Dee Brown's *Bury My Heart at Wounded Knee*. See Moses, *Wild West Shows*, 228.

44. John Little Finger told McGregor that he was Big Foot's grandson; see *The Wounded Knee Massacre*, 17. In 1920 he told James McLaughlin the same thing; see James McLaughlin to Cato Sells, January 12, 1921, CCF 1907–1939, General Service, 70018-1917-054, Part I (1 of 3) PI163-E121, RG 75, NARA-W. See Little Finger, *Lightning and Thunder Spoke to Me*, for an account of the hair lock and his relationship with his grandfather John.

45. The most comprehensive discussion of the Indian casualty list for Wounded Knee is Jensen, "Big Foot's Followers at Wounded Knee"; for specific burials, see 198. For Horn Cloud, see Ricker, *Indian Interviews*, 204–6; for Beard, see Miller, "Echoes of the Little Bighorn," 39; for army totals, see Utley, *Last Days of the Sioux Nation*, 228.

46. For Weasel Bear, see McGregor, *The Wounded Knee Massacre*, 101; for Medicine Woman, see Coleman, *Voices of Wounded Knee*, 315–16; for White Lance, see McLaughlin to Sells, January 12, 1921 (cited in note 44 above).

47. Eastman, *From the Deep Woods*, 218. Beard mentions seeing Dr. Eastman after Wounded Knee in DBI. A good biography of Eastman is Wilson, *Ohiyesa: Charles Eastman: Santee Sioux*.

48. Joe told Gilmore about the aftermath of Wounded Knee; see Gilmore, "The Truth of the Wounded Knee Massacre," 248.

49. Beard mentions horse burials in DBI. The boy's burial story is in Penman, *Honor the Grandmothers*, 20. The contractor's fee is in Coleman, *Voices of Wounded Knee*, 352.

50. The quote is from "Report of the part taken by the troops of the Department of Dakota in the Sioux Indian campaign during the latter part of 1890 and the early part of the present year," Thomas Howard Ruger, 1891, p. 96, copy in University of South Dakota Archives and Special Collections, Vermillion. For the findings of the Court of Inquiry, see Coleman, *Voices of Wounded Knee*, 360–64.

51. For quotes, see Cozzens, *Eyewitness to the Indian Wars*, 577. For medals, see Coleman, *Voices of Wounded Knee*, 364.

52. See Coleman, *Voices of Wounded Knee*, 310, on the duration of the encounter, and 316–17 for civilian accounts.

53. For Mooney's assessment, see *The Ghost Dance Religion*, 870.

54. Mooney, *The Ghost Dance Religion*, 881.

55. Coleman, *Voices of Wounded Knee*, 373–75; and DeMontravel, *A Hero to His Fighting Men*, 210–11.

56. Leonard Little Finger told me the story of Beard in the agency office, and it's corroborated, with some variation, in Jake Herman, "Oglala Sioux Sun Dance," 1968, courtesy of Rex Herman.

57. For the Craven story, see Hank, "Gus and Jessie McGaa Craven," 537. The story is also told by Craven's granddaughter in F. Y. Peterson, "Dewey Iron Hail," 37. There's some confusion over whether this event took place before or after Wounded Knee, but the latter seems more likely.

6. Cody

1. The death certificate for Beard held by the BIA is similar, but not identical, to the one filed with the state. See "Beard" file, BIA-PR. See Cody, *Memories of Buffalo Bill*, and Muller, *My Life with Buffalo Bill*, for personal reminiscences of William Cody.

2. Maddra, *Hostiles*, 136–37 and 57–62.

3. Maddra, *Hostiles*, 152.

4. My account of the 1895 tour is partly based on the 1895 newspaper scrapbook and brochures held on microfilm at the Buffalo Bill Historical Center in Cody, Wyoming. Some of these articles lack dates or even names of newspapers. For general information on tour, see MS6, roll 4, BBHC. Tour accounts below that are undated or unpaginated are from MS6, roll 2, "Buffalo Bill Cody Scrapbooks: 1883–1895," BBHC. Confirmation of Beard's appearance on the tour is in M1282, roll 24, "Letters Sent to the Office of Indian Affairs," Charles G. Penney to Commissioner of Indian Affairs, April 11, 1895, frame 263, NARA-W. Beard's name also appears on the 1895 company roll, General Records, Main Decimal Files, 047—Buffalo Bill's Wild West Show Contracts, 1891–95, Pine Ridge, RG 75, NARA-KC.

5. For Cody and tableaux, see *Washington Post*, September 22, 1895, 16; see *Daily Gazette*, May 15, 1895, for performers; for Oakley, see *Haverhill Gazette*, undated; for Arabs, see *Boston Globe*, June 14, 1895, 3; for Cossacks and cowboys, see *Washington Post*, October 3, 1895, 4.

6. For show setup, see the *Daily Argus*, May 8, 1895; for Cody details, see *Atlanta Constitution*, July 28, 1895, 8, and October 29, 1895, 9, and *Washington Post*, October 3, 1895, 4.

7. For Indians and parade, see *Atlanta Constitution*, October 29, 1895, 9; for music, see "Red Horsemen on Parade," undated, unidentified.

8. For price, see *Washington Post*, September 22, 1895, 16. The quote is from the *Springfield (MA) Homestead*, June 1, 1895.

9. For arena and lighting, see *Boston Daily Globe*, June 12, 1895, 2, and June 10, 1895, 2; *Reading Eagle*, May 7, 1895, and *Birmingham Daily Post*, November 16, 1887; for attendance, see *Hartford Post*, June 4, 1895.

10. For clothing, see *Washington Post*, October 3, 1895, 4, and "The Wild West Show," undated; for rain, "Wild West Defies the Rain," undated; for Cooper, *Boston Daily Globe*, June 20, 1895, 4; for racing, see Moses, *Wild West Shows*, 22.

11. Living conditions are described in a variety of partly identified articles from BBHC: *Springfield Homestead*, June 1, 1895; *Rochester Post Express*, August 12, 1895; *Pittsburg Post*, September 2, 1895.

12. For the Indian camp, see *Boston Journal*, June 10, 1895, *Rochester Post Express*, August 12, 1895, and *Syracuse Standard*, August 5, 1895; on smallpox, see *Lowell Morning Citizen*, July 2, 1895; on chairs, see *Springfield Homestead*, June 1, 1895.

13. For cameras, see *Syracuse Standard*, August 5, 1895; for payday, see *Brooklyn Standard Union*, June 24, 1894; for clothing, see Moses, *Wild West Shows*, 116; monthly pay is mentioned in many places, including *Springfield Homestead*, June 1, 1895, and is confirmed in Pine Ridge General Records, Main Decimal Files, 047, "Buffalo Bill's Wild West Show Contracts, 1891–95," RG 75, NARA-KC.

14. The Cape Cod ceremony is described in an unidentified Gloucester paper in "They Offered Thanks," July 10, 1895; for the visit to the commissioner, see *New York Times*, October 4, 1895, 9.

15. The Oswego story is recounted in *New York Times*, August 7, 1895, 1; the Salem weather is described in "They Offered Thanks."

16. The dragoon is reported in *Boston Daily Globe*, May 24, 1895, 1; the Cossack is noted in *New York Times*, September 24, 1895, 10; the elopement is reported in *Washington Post*, October 7, 1895, 2.

17. *Atlanta Constitution*, October 31, 1895, 9, notes how Crazy Bull got his name and the history of the case; details of the investigation are provided in the October 30 edition of the *Constitution*. The *Washington Post* reports on posting bond and the eventual settlement on November 1, 1895, 1, and November 27, 1895, 1.

18. For the European tour, see *Washington Post*, October 2, 1895, 10; the display ad is from *Boston Daily Globe*, June 9, 1895, 18; the *Post* detailed the matinee performance on October 3, 1895, 4.

19. For the sometimes confused strategy behind taking the Lakotas eastward, see Maddra, *Hostiles*, 54–62.

20. The 1895 schedule is included in MS6, roll 2, BBHC.

21. See Moses, *Wild West Shows*, 62–79, for criticism of Cody and other shows, and 74 for the Morgan reference.

22. Moses, *Wild West Shows*, 122, 127.

23. For later shows like the Miller Brothers, see Moses, *Wild West Shows*, 174–85.

24. For the Ghost Dance, see *Philadelphia Times*, April, 28, 1895; for soldiers, see *Cleveland Evening Post*, undated.

25. *Syracuse Standard*, August 5, 1895.

26. See Moses, *Wild West Shows*, 171, on Cody changing riders; the newspaper article is "Chief Fought in Real Battle Now Seen on Movie Screen," undated and unidentified, though likely from Adrian, Michigan, courtesy of Corliss Besselievre.

27. The information on Chief Woman is from Eva Beard probate hearing, December 19, 1914, CCF 1907–1939, Pine Ridge, 2483-15-350 PI163-E121, RG 75, NARA-W; and Alice Beard's testimony, May 28, 1957, from Dewey Beard's probate hearing, "Dewey Beard," BIA-PR. Chief Woman is listed as Mary Beard on the 1899 census, forty-five years old—M595, roll 367, p. 119.

28. For the naming process in Lakota country and its rationale, see Littlefield and Underhill, "Renaming the American Indian."

29. The first Pine Ridge census that denotes Beard as "Dewey" is 1899, M595, roll 367, p. 119. The George Dewey derivation, as sound as it seems, may not be right, though Marie and Dave Miller were convinced of it. In 1898 Dewey won the battle of Manila Bay and was lionized in the press, so the appearance of his name Dewey in the following year's Indian census makes sense. But a document in the "Daniel Horn Cloud" file at SDSA, in Lakota, notes Beard's name as Dewey Horn Cloud Beard—and is dated two years earlier, 1896. Alas, the copy is an early photostat, and most of it is impossible to read. George Dewey was living in Washington in 1895 when Cody's show visited, and since the military brass attended one of the Wild West performances, it's possible Dewey and Beard became acquainted there. Everything else is conjecture. Beard's son Webster was christened George Webster in 1917, according to records from Holy Rosary Church, Pine Ridge, South Dakota, which suggests that George was considered a special name in the family.

30. Pine Ridge 1900 census, M595, roll 368, p. 117.

31. My information about Alice comes from Marie, the Pine Ridge Indian censuses, and recollections of Celane in Penman, *Honor the Grandmothers*, 23.

32. The story of the film is well told in Paul, "Buffalo Bill and Wounded Knee." Other sources on the movie include Brownlow, *The War, the West, and the Wilderness*, 224–35; N. M. Peterson, "Buffalo Bill's Lost Legacy"; Bob Lee, "The Little Known Bill Cody: Scout Turned Film Producer," *Rapid City Journal*, in a weekly series that began on June 15, 1969, 11; and Moses, *Wild West Shows*, 228–48.

33. Edison's twenty-second short on the dance can be viewed through the Library of Congress website.

34. Miles is quoted in *Moving Picture World*, October 25, 1913, 362.

35. For Brennan's figures, see *Moving Picture World*, August 15, 1914, 899; and "Great

Audience Is Held in Tense Wonder by the Buffalo Bill Indian War Pictures," unidentified article, BBHC.

36. The soldier ruse is noted in Brownlow, *The War, the West, and the Wilderness*, 230.

37. The quote is from *Moving Picture World*, March 14, 1914, 1370. The shooting platform is noted in Ryley Cooper, "Great Moving Pictures Camp Leaves Today for Badlands Battleground," *Denver Post*, October 21, 1913, 2. Cooper wrote a series of articles for the *Post* on the making of the film. The carousel reference is in Moses, *Wild West Shows*, 235.

38. *Chadron (NE) Journal*, October 17, 1913, 8; Ryley Cooper, "Circles of Indians Fire Forth Death as Redmen Battle Whites before Lens," *Denver Post*, October 17, 1913, in John Brennan Papers, Scrapbook 1, p. 258, SDSA.

39. John Brennan to William McCune, November 25, 1913, M1229, roll 70, frame 378, Miscellaneous Letters Sent by the Agent at Pine Ridge Agency, 1876–1914, NARA-W; Cody's boast is in "Great Audience Is Held in Tense Wonder."

40. Brennan's wife is quoted in Paul, "Buffalo Bill and Wounded Knee," 185.

41. The Miles testimonial is quoted in McGregor, *The Wounded Knee Massacre*, 98.

42. Garrison and Lane's reaction is in "Officials Thrilled by Realistic Films of Indian Battles," unidentified clipping, BBHC; Denver reference is to Frances Wayne, "Real Soldiers, Real Indians, Real Heroes March, Fight, Die, in Great War Films," undated clipping, BBHC; for hype, see *Moving Picture World*, September 12, 1914, 1500, and August 15, 1914, 899.

43. Gilmore's quote is in "White Man Suggests Indian Version," November 30, 1913, unidentified newspaper, p. 307, in John Brennan Papers, Scrapbook 1, SDSA; for Owl King and Afraid of the Enemy, see McGregor, *The Wounded Knee Massacre*, 108–9 and 119, respectively.

44. Yellow Robe is quoted in *Rapid City Journal*, October 21, 1913, 1.

45. The Horn Clouds' reaction is noted in an undated article from the *Omaha Daily News*, "Indians Say Buffalo Bill Pictures Mislead," Pine Ridge, Main Decimal Files, 047, "Fairs and Expositions: Buffalo Bill's Wild West Show, 1912–1915," RG 75, NARA-KC.

46. The monument dedication ceremony is described in "Red Men Erect Monument to Fallen Warriors," *Omaha World Herald*, June 7, 1903, p. 24.

47. Beard is named in "Thrill of Actual Battle Leaps Forth from Indian War Films," *Denver Post*, undated, in John Brennan Papers, Scrapbook 1, p. 306, SDSA; also see *Duluth News Tribune*, May 14, 1914, 6. See Brownlow, *The War, the West, and the Wilderness*, 232, for Ghost Dance quote—unfortunately, Brownlow cites the wrong source for the quote, and I've never found its origin; for scouts, see *Emporia (KS) Gazette*, November 30, 1914, 5.

48. The fourteen hours is cited in Brownlow, *The War, the West, and the Wilderness*, 232; for boast, see *Emporia Gazette*, November 30, 1914, 5.

49. John Brennan to General Baldwin, December 10, 1913, in John Brennan Papers, Scrapbook 1, p. 313, SDSA; for Wells, see *Rapid City Daily Journal*, January 10, 1914, John Brennan Papers, Scrapbook 1, p. 309, SDSA.

50. The bullet story is recounted in Walsh, *The Making of Buffalo Bill*, 346.

51. See Paul, "Buffalo Bill and Wounded Knee," 188–90, for a discussion of theories regarding disappearance of the film.

7. *Fox Belly*

1. The Fox Belly probate and will documents, including some family history, are in CCF 1907–1939, Pine Ridge, 69805-1923-350 PI 163-E 121, RG 75, NARA-W. Fox Belly also goes by the name Coyote (or Coyotte) Belly in official correspondence.

2. A fine overview of Indian scouting is Dunlay, *Wolves for the Blue Soldiers*.

3. For the sparse details on Fox Belly's life, I rely mostly on the "Coyote Belly" file, Leavenworth Penitentiary Records, RG 129, NARA-KC: see Henry Tidwell to Leavenworth Warden, September 30, 1921, and Trusty Prisoner's Agreement, 7203. See also "Declaration for Survivor's Pension-Indian Wars" and "Statement of William Garnett," CCF 1907–1939, Pine Ridge, 86777-1921-725 PI 163-E 121, RG 75, NARA-W.

4. The details of the marital dispute are from Fox Belly family statements in Pine Ridge, General Records, "General Correspondence, Alphabetical, E–F," RG 75, NARA-KC.

5. The account of the Frank Horn Cloud incident is based on several sources, including the Fox Belly family statements cited in the previous note. I've also relied on agency correspondence, including the following letters: John Brennan to Commissioner of Indian Affairs, August 9, 1915, Henry Tidwell to E. E. Wagner, August 5, 1920, and E. B. Merrit to George Running Horse, undated, all from CCF 1907–1939, Pine Ridge, 61226-1915-175.5 PI 163-E 121, RG 75, NARA-W.

6. Joe's remark is in "Statement of Joe Horn Cloud, March 8, 1910, Pine Ridge, General Correspondence, Alphabetical, E–F," RG 75, NARA-KC.

7. For quote from Joe see "Statement of Joe Horn Cloud, March 8, 1910."

8. For Frank Horn Cloud's legacy, see statement of Dolly Horn Cloud, CCF 1907–1939, Pine Ridge, 47616-1914-350 PI 163-E 121, RG 75, NARA-W.

9. The trial is noted in *Rapid City Daily Journal*, September 11, 1910, 1, and *Sunday State Journal*, Lincoln NE, September 11, 1910, 3; *Daily Huronite*, March 25, 1910, also discusses the case.

10. Details of Fox Belly's life are from probate records, CCF 1907–1939, Pine Ridge, 69805-1923-350 PI 163-E 121, RG 75, NARA-W.

11. The physical description is from hospital and physician's records, "Coyote Belly" file, RG 129, NARA-KC.

12. His occupations are documented in daily labor records, RG 129, NARA-KC; his record is confirmed in Warden to H. M. Tidwell, April 4, 1921, RG 129, NARA-KC.

13. For Fox Belly's words, see Trusty Prisoner's Agreement, 7203; for pardon request, see Warden to Tidwell, April 4, 1921, both in RG 129, NARA-KC; for divorce, see probate records, family history card, 698-1923-350, NARA-W.

14. Joe Horn Cloud's objection to the pardon is in Joe Horn Cloud to Interior Secretary Lane, May 8, 1915, NARA-W. Fox Belly's economic situation and scout pension are in "Coyote Belly," RG 129, NARA-KC.

15. Fox Belly's cause of death and funeral are described in physician's notes in "Coyote Belly," NARA-KC.

16. The wedding is described in Penman, *Honor the Grandmothers*, 43.

17. Fuller, "Life after Wounded Knee," 48.

8. Pine Ridge

1. Pine Ridge and its environs have a rich literature, most of it written by outsiders. Starita's *The Dull Knifes of Pine Ridge* is a generational saga. A recent account is Frazier's *On the Rez*, a thoughtful and entertaining journey through Oglala country. A more spiritual travel account is Nerburn's *Neither Wolf nor Dog*, while Matthiessen's *In the Spirit of Crazy Horse* is an investigation of Wounded Knee II. My personal favorite is Glover, *Keeping Heart on Pine Ridge*, written by a local resident.

2. The description of Pine Ridge that follows derives, in large part, from the superintendents' reports, M 1011, roll 106, Annual Narrative and Statistical Reports, Pine Ridge, 1910–1929. See 1910 report, frame 04. See Robertson, *The Power of the Land*, 64, on Bennett County.

3. See 1927 report, frame 0843; 1934 report, frame 0317; 1930, frame 0024; and 1935 report, frame 0361.

4. By 1918 there were more than eight thousand Pine Ridge allottees; see 1918 report, frame 0219. And see Lawson, "The Fractionated Estate," 71. For allotment and the Dawes Act, see Hertzberg, "Indian Rights Movement," 305–8; and Prucha, *The Great Father*, 224–32.

5. For the 1889 act, see Lawson, "The Fractionated Estate," 49. Also see 1911 report, frame 0060; 1912 report, frame 0085; and 1918 report, frames 0219 and 0220. See also Robertson, *The Power of the Land*, 78.

6. The transcript of Joe Horn Cloud's appearance before the committee is in U.S. House of Representatives, *Complaint of the Pine Ridge Sioux*, 5.

7. U.S. House of Representatives, *Complaint of the Pine Ridge Sioux*, 26.

8. Robertson, *The Power of the Land*, 105–7, 128, 154.

9. For rules, see 1915 report, frame 0158; for hair, see DeMallie, "Teton," 816; on the Standing Bear decision, see Moses, *Wild West Shows*, 63, 76, and 294. By 1925,

Indians were full citizens and possessed freedom of movement; see 1925 report, frame 0736.

10. For population figures, see 1912 report, frame 0078; 1930 report, frame 0036; and W. O. Roberts to Cliff Schlegel, August 12, 1941, Pine Ridge Decimal Files, 124.9-143, "127 Roll of Honor Men," Pine Ridge, RG 75, NARA-KC.

11. The allotment tracts are found in MS 2, U.S. Government Record Books Collection, box 5, Office of Indian Affairs Tract Book, Pine Ridge Reservation, 3 of 7, 1906–1918, p. 66, OLCA; for allotment details and Roosevelt, see allotment certificate, vol. 661, page 223, "Dewey Beard," BIA-PR.

12. "Petition for the Sale of Land by Original Allottees" and "Industrial Status Report," 5-372, "Dewey Beard," BIA-PR.

13. John S. Lindley to John R. Brennan, May 25, 1915, BIA-PR; undated report, 1775, "Dewey Beard," BIA-PR; and "Industrial Status Report," "Dewey Beard," BIA-PR; For walking, see Penman, *Honor the Grandmothers*, 19.

14. See Biolsi, *Organizing the Lakota*, 16–17, on Individual Indian Money accounts. See Robertson, *The Power of the Land*, on purchase orders, 134. For Beard's withdrawal, see Henry Tidwell to Indian Commissioner, April 28 and May 12, 1920, Pine Ridge, 34218-20-225, CCF 1907–1939, RG 75, NARA-W.

15. On rolls, see Biolsi, *Organizing the Lakota*, 17–19 and 25–27. Beard is noted in 1939 in Pine Ridge, Health and Welfare Records, Economic Survey and Related Records, 1940–41, "Rations, Social Security," RG 75, NARA-KC. For turn-of-the-century rations, see MS 2, U.S. Government Record Books Collection, box 17, Annuity Payroll, Pine Ridge Reservation, 1892–1899, OLCA, p. 132 (1899), and box 18, p. 159 (1902).

16. The undated "Industrial Status Report" (see note 12 above) makes clear that Beard was not a citizen in about 1914. For competency, see "List of Indians of the Medicine Root District," General Records, General Correspondence, Alphabetical, "Name List of Indians of Competency," Pine Ridge, RG 75, NARA-KC.

17. For allotment sales, see Annual Narrative and Statistical Reports, 1921 report, frame 0420; for quote, see 1916 report, frame 0208.

18. For land patents, see 1922 report, frame 0515; for Beard land sale, see "Form of Affidavit of Vendee," January 14, 1919, and "Report on Cash Sale of Allotted Indian Land," "Dewey Beard," BIA-PR.

19. For ponies, see 1922 report, frame 0510, and 1924 report, frame 0696; for the Beard ranch, see Dewey Beard, no. 12, Pine Ridge Industrial Survey, Medicine Root District, March 21, 1925, Report of Industrial Surveys, 1922–1929, Pine Ridge PI 163-E762, RG 75, NARA-W.

20. The story about jumping on a pony is told by Jim Tidball, whose family leased land on the reservation in the mid-1930s near the Beard ranch.

21. See Pine Ridge Industrial Survey, Medicine Root District, Reports of Industrial

Surveys, 1922–1929, Pine Ridge P163-E762, RG 75. Fools Crow puts the best years of reservation life on Pine Ridge as 1895 to 1920 and suggests that World War I—both in casualties and the worldly attitudes of returning veterans—accounted for a big change; see Mails, *Fools Crow*, 109–11.

22. Annual Narrative and Statistical Reports, 1927 report, frame 0856.

23. For Day School 29, see Education Records, School Histories, 1934–1942, "School Histories," Pine Ridge, RG 75, NARA-KC; for Day School 23, see Report of Attendance, December 31, 1931, Education Records, School Reports, 1920, 1931–1934, "Semi Annual Reports," Pine Ridge, RG 75, NARA-KC.

24. Will H. Spindler, "History of Potato Creek Day School," and No. 23 Day School, both from Education Records, School Histories, 1934–1942, "School Histories," Pine Ridge, RG 75, NARA-KC.

25. Beard's connection to the PTA is noted in "The Potato Creek News," March 1939, 21–22, Decimal Files, "041—School Publications Bulletins, 1939," Pine Ridge, RG 75, NARA-KC. For a published account that discusses Pine Ridge day schools in the 1920s and 1930s, see Red Shirt, *Turtle Lung Woman's Granddaughter*, 135–38.

26. Annual Narrative and Statistical Reports, 1930 report, frame 0041, and 1924 report, frames 0694–96; for quote, see 1926 report, frame 0807.

27. A detailed discussion of the IRA on Pine Ridge can be found in Reinhardt, *Ruling Pine Ridge*, 19–41; for general voting numbers, see 35; for referendum numbers, see Main Decimal Files, "065—Wheeler-Howard Act 1934," Pine Ridge, RG 75, NARA-KC.

28. Clow, "Tribal Populations in Transition," 183. On IRA voting, see Biolsi, *Organizing the Lakota*, 80–83.

29. Price, *The Oglala People*, 172–73.

30. The events of that February are recounted in "The Potato Creek News," February 1939, Decimal Files, "041—School Publications Bulletins, 1939," Pine Ridge, RG 75, NARA-KC.

31. Annual Narrative and Statistical Reports, 1919 report, frame 0248, 1910 report, frame 0022, and 1931 report, frame 0089. Also see Southerton, "James R. Walker's Campaign," 146.

32. The Beard children and their life dates are listed in "Summary of Family History and Inventory," "Dewey Beard," BIA-PR. Fools Crow says much the same about the loss of children in the 1920s in Mails, *Fools Crow*, 90, 117.

33. South Dakota certificate of death, 137449-5931. Also see L. A. Johnson to Adin Newman, March 19, 1931, Adin T. Newman Collection, UWEC.

34. Dewey Beard to Adin Newman, May 9, 1931, Adin T. Newman Collection, UWEC.

35. See Annual Narrative and Statistical Reports, 1920 report, frame 0290; for Horn Cloud, see *New York Times*, August 19, 1912, 9, and *Boston Daily Globe*, August

24, 1911, 2. Also see *Indian Sentinel*, Summer 1921, 332. For Catholicism on the reservation, see Vecsey, "A Century of Lakota Sioux Catholicism at Pine Ridge."

36. See Penman, *Honor the Grandmothers*, 40–41, for Beard's beliefs. For sun dance, see "Dakota Indians' Sun Dance Recalls Spirit of Old West," file 67, "Sundance— Pine Ridge," box 5, folder 32, Jeanne Smith Collection, OLCA. Fools Crow says that sun dances with piercing were practiced even after the ban in 1881, but not until 1952 did dancers publicly pierce; see Mails, *Fools Crow*, 43, 119.

37. Industrial Status Report, 5-372, "Dewey Beard," BIA-PR. For alcohol on Pine Ridge during the Depression, see Annual Narrative and Statistical Reports, 1935, frame 0364, and Lenard Young, "Life on the Pine Ridge Reservation, 1930–1937," p. 14, box 3748A, SDSA. "Survey of Indian Reservations, 1935, Pine Ridge Agency," Series 152, "Survey of Needy Indians," RG 75, Pine Ridge, NARA-KC, doesn't mention alcohol as a major health problem. But in "The Sioux," in the September 1948 issue of *Holiday* (140–41), Donald Wayne describes it as a major issue. Fools Crow suggests that the problem deepened during the 1930s; see Mails, *Fools Crow*, 147. For a general study of the Lakotas and drinking, see Medicine, *Drinking and Sobriety*, 24, 37, 46, 56.

38. South Dakota certificate of death, 195388.

39. The story of Francis and the Paoli church is recounted in *Philadelphia Inquirer*, September 2, 1985, M10, May 1, 1989, A1, and May 11, 1990, B1.

40. Statement of Dewey Beard, March 12, 1917.

41. Joe Horn Cloud to James McLaughlin, July 23, 1920, enclosed in letter from McLaughlin to Cato Sells, January 12, 1921, CCF 1907–1939, General Service, 70018-1917-054, Part I (1 of 3) PI163-E121, RG 75, NARA-W.

42. McLaughlin to Sells, January 12, 1921. For correspondence regarding Sioux Depredations Act and list of claimants, see Gonzalez and Cook-Lynn, *Politics of Hallowed Ground*, 316–30.

43. For bill, see Wounded Knee Massacre, folder 13, drawer 125, Francis Case Collection, DWU.

44. For scale of payments, see July 19, 1939, statement from Francis Case, Wounded Knee Compensation Bill, folder 4, drawer 125, Francis Case Collection, DWU; for Indian demands, see Leo Iron Hawk to Francis Case, undated, Wounded Knee Compensation Bill, folder 5, drawer 125, Francis Case Collection, DWU.

45. Telegram, February 26, 1938, Wounded Knee Compensation Bill, folder 6, drawer 125, Francis Case Collection, DWU; and *Washington Post*, March 7, 1938, X8. Photo with Collier, undated, is from Adin Newman Scrapbook, McIntyre Library, UWEC.

46. U.S. House of Representatives, *Sioux Indians: Wounded Knee Massacre Hearings*, 22.

47. U.S. House of Representatives, *Sioux Indians: Wounded Knee Massacre Hearings*, 24.

48. Francis Case to James Pipe on Head, May 8, 1941, Wounded Knee Compensation Bill, folder 2, drawer 125, Francis Case Collection, DWU.

49. U.S. House of Representatives, *Sioux Indians: Wounded Knee Massacre Hearings*, 41.

50. Dewey Beard to Francis Case, March 27, 1940, and letter from Dewey Beard, December 22, 1941, both in Wounded Knee Compensation, folder 2, drawer 125, Francis Case Collection, D W U; and Dewey Beard to Francis Case, November 23, 1944, Wounded Knee Massacre—Indian Files, drawer 125, box 1, Francis Case Collection, D W U.

51. Gonzalez and Cook-Lynn, *Politics of Hallowed Ground*, 65–66.

9. *Gunnery Range*

1. U.S. House of Representatives, *Sioux Indian Tribes, North and South Dakota*, 86.

2. U.S. House of Representatives, *Sioux Indian Tribes, North and South Dakota*, 86; and *Rapid City Journal*, September 13, 1955, 1.

3. U.S. House of Representatives, *Sioux Indian Tribes, North and South Dakota*, 85; and *Rapid City Journal*, September 13, 1955, 1.

4. For general figures, see Holiday et al., *American Indian and Alaska Native Veterans*, 4.

5. "Memorandum for Use of Indian Lands for Military Purposes during World War II," C C F 1940–1943, "Aerial Gunnery Range, Pt. 2," 53A-367, R G 75, N A R A-W. For Pine Ridge, see Clow, *Aerial Gunnery Range*, 103, which is the best secondary source on the gunnery range taking.

6. I have written at length about seizures of Indian land during World War II for *Indian Country Today*. See October 11, October 18, October 25, November 1, and November 8, 2006, issues. Also see Hooks and Smith, "The Treadmill of Destruction."

7. Francis Case to the President, March 15, 1945, and The Black Hills of South Dakota as a Home for the United Nations, "128—United Nations Correspondence File," Francis Case Collection, D W U.

8. For background on the bombing range, see Burnham, *Indian Country, God's Country*, 123–26.

9. For labor quote, see undated memorandum, Francis Case; for Rapid City quote, see Francis Case to A. S. Holm, December 11, 1941; also see Francis Case to Colonel Kennedy, November 10, 1941, all in "Gunnery Range," Francis Case Collection, D W U.

10. Francis Case to David Kennicott, December 22, 1941, Francis Case to W. P. Mollers, December 16, 1941, and A. S. Holm to Francis Case, January 24, 1942, all in "Gunnery Range," Francis Case Collection, D W U.

11. Boyd Leedom to Francis Case, February 26, 1942, and Francis Case to A. S. Holm, December 9, 1941, in "Gunnery Range," Francis Case Collection, D W U.

12. Francis Case to General H. H. Arnold, November 14, 1941, "Gunnery Range," Francis Case Collection, DWU.

13. Francis Case to A. S. Holm, November 28, 1941, "Gunnery Range," Francis Case Collection, DWU.

14. Louis Mousseau to Francis Case, June 17, 1942, and Francis Case to Louis Mousseau, July 7, 1942, "Gunnery Range," Francis Case Collection, DWU.

15. W. O. Roberts to the Commissioner of Indian Affairs, October 12, 1942, Series 210—Records of Aerial Gunnery Range, "Correspondence Regarding Relocation," Pine Ridge, RG 75, NARA-KC.

16. Most of the Jake Herman account comes from an unpublished curriculum from the Rapid City schools, courtesy of Rex Herman, called "Lakota Indian Values," edited by Barbara Walch, which includes an autobiographical article written by Jake called "Broncs, Bulls, and Baggy Pants" on pages 105–9.

17. The quote is from Jake's son Paul Herman. Much of the anecdotal information about Jake is from Paul and his brother Rex.

18. Interview with Jake Herman, American Indian Research Project, file 72, MSI, Group 1, box 2, folder 21, Jeanne Smith Collection, OLCA. Quote is from "Broncs, Bulls, and Baggy Pants," 107.

19. From Jake Herman, "My Brother," by Jake Herman, courtesy Rex Herman.

20. From Jake Herman, "Ta-Tanka, or Buffalo," Wa Ho Si, Oglala Sioux Sun Dance program, August 6–9, 1964, Pine Ridge Agency, courtesy Rex Herman.

21. For Beard income, see Health and Welfare Records, "Economic Survey and Related Records—Economic Survey 1937, B," Pine Ridge, RG 75, NARA-KC; for general numbers, see "Report on Hearings before the U.S. Senate Committee," 1940, p. 11, Pine Ridge, RG 75, NARA-KC.

22. Clow, *Aerial Gunnery Range*, 13–15.

23. Series 210, Records of Aerial Gunnery Range, "Report on Bombing Families Evacuated, July 1942–September 1942," Pine Ridge, RG 75, NARA-KC.

24. For house and possessions, see "Report on Bombing Families Evacuated." Appraisals are discussed in Clow, *Aerial Gunnery Range*, 23–30, 215–16.

25. "Program for Investment of Funds," Records of the Aerial Gunnery Range, Series 210, "AGR Budgets MR District 1943," Pine Ridge, RG 75, NARA-KC.

26. Frey, "Legislative History." For payments, see Social Security documents, June 16 and August 8, 1943, "Dewey Beard," BIA-PR.

27. "Program for Investment of Funds," NARA-KC.

28. Clow, *Aerial Gunnery Range*, 58, 67; and Ralph Bristol to Assistant Commissioner Zimmerman, September 5, 1942, "Aerial Gunnery Range, Pt. 1," CCF 1940–1943, 53 A-367, box 143, Pine Ridge, RG 75, NARA-W.

29. Clow, *Aerial Gunnery Range*, 55.

30. Clow, *Aerial Gunnery Range*, 108.

31. Public Law 769 (70 Stat. 625); see Clow, *Aerial Gunnery Range*, 126, for details on the law's passage.

32. Clow, *Aerial Gunnery Range*, 72.

10. Last Man Standing

1. Health and Welfare Records, "Economic Survey and Related Records—Economic Survey, 1937, B," Pine Ridge, RG 75, NARA-KC.

2. The Beards were featured in the May 1955 issue of *Friends* magazine, a Chevrolet publication, p. 30.

3. *New York Times*, August 7, 1955, 2.

4. The White Lance probate records are in CCF 1907–1939, PI 163-E121 HM 1998, File 86582-36, Pine Ridge, RG 75, NARA-W.

5. Clow, "Tribal Populations in Transition," 181–95.

6. For the *hunka*, see Hassrick, *The Sioux*, 297–98.

7. *Tomahawk*, 1951, dir. George Sherman, Universal Pictures.

8. *Battles of Chief Pontiac*, 1952, dir. Felix Feist, Jack Broder Productions.

9. Beard's interview about the movie *Crazy Horse* appeared in the *Jackson (MI) Citizen Patriot*, March 27, 1955.

10. *The Last Hunt*, 1956, dir. Richard Brooks, Metro-Goldwyn-Mayer.

11. Penman, *Honor the Grandmothers*, 33–34.

12. Penman, *Honor the Grandmothers*, 23.

13. Penman, *Honor the Grandmothers*, 45.

14. Penman, *Honor the Grandmothers*, 42.

15. For Celane's time at Holy Rosary, see Penman, *Honor the Grandmothers*, 40–41.

16. On the crumbling of *tiyospaye*, see Gibbon, *The Sioux*, 103.

17. Evelyn's probably right about the check. Public Law 89-505 (1966) permitted Washington to bring suit on behalf of, among others, Indian allottees like Beard whose estates had been tagged with state liens. These so-called "2415 claims" weren't fully settled for decades, at which point Beard's only remaining granddaughter, when she received the check, was about sixty years old.

18. Penman, *Honor the Grandmothers*, 30.

19. There seems to be some dispute over whether Pemmican was actually at the battle. But he appears in the group pictures. Also, some claim Little Soldier was also absent; see "Little Big Horn Survivors Dwindle," *Rapid City Journal*, September 24, 1950. Ernie LaPointe believes that Little Soldier was at the battle.

20. My main sources for the reunion are "Custer Massacre Survivors to Stage Pow-Wow," August 30, 1948, 2, and "Sioux Would Fight Custer Battle Again for Freedom," September 2, 1948, 1, both in the *Rapid City Daily Journal*.

21. O. R. Sande to Kenneth Crouch, August 30, 1951, Decimal Files, 047, "Fairs and Expositions—1951–1953," Pine Ridge, RG 75, NARA-KC. For anniversary celebration, see "75th Anniversary Observance, Battle of the Little Bighorn, June 24, 25, 1951," Robert M. Utley MS 62, box 4, folder 12, and unaddressed letter dated June 26, 1951, MS 62, box 4, folder 1, BBHC.

22. O. R. Sande to Kenneth Crouch, November 9, 1951, "Fairs and Expositions, 1951–53," NARA-KC.

23. Beard tells this story about the Hills in Emery Tapes, disc 2, track 2, OLCA.

24. For background on the Black Hills case, see Lazarus, *Black Hills, White Justice*; and Gonzalez and Cook-Lynn, *Politics of Hallowed Ground*.

11. American Horse Creek

1. Thomas Beard certificate of death, Washington State, December 4, 1954, "Tommy Beard," and Summary of Family History and Inventory, "Dewey Beard," both in BIA-PR. The Beard family history lists seven children with Alice, and Dewey lost two others in his first marriage.

2. The note from Johnnie White Lance is quoted courtesy of Corliss Besselievre.

3. The South Dakota certificate, 287990, gives no cause of death; a different certificate in his tribal file gives "senility" as a cause, BIA-PR.

4. *Time*, November 14, 1955, 114; *Washington Post*, November 4, 1955, 40; *New York Times*, November 4, 1955, 29. More extensive obits can be found in the *Rapid City Journal*, November 2, 1955, 1, *Omaha Evening World Herald*, November 2, 1955, and *Sioux Falls Daily Argus Leader*, November 2, 1955, 1.

5. Public Law 769 (70 Stat. 625). See Clow, *Aerial Gunnery Range*, 126, for details of the law.

6. For etymology of *Oglala*, see DeMallie, "Sioux until 1850," 757.

7. Dewey Beard to Adin Newman, March 26, 1929, Adin T. Newman Collection, UWEC.

8. L. A. Johnson to Adin Newman, June 9, 1931, and Dewey Beard to Adin Newman, May 9, 1931, Adin T. Newman Collection, UWEC. For saddle blanket and dress, see L. A. Johnson to A.T. Newman, July 9, 1926, and L. A. Johnson to A.T. Newman, April 18, 1931, from Adin T. Newman Collection, UWEC. All transcripts from Newman Collection courtesy of Nichole Ray.

9. Standing Bear, *My People the Sioux*, 234.

10. Ricker's comment is from a notecard that historian Mari Sandoz made in her research on Pine Ridge; see box 7, folder 6, MS1, Jeanne Smith Collection, OLCA. Also see Ricker, *Indian Interviews*, 208; and McGregor, *The Wounded Knee Massacre*, 94.

11. Dewey Beard interview, pp. 5–7, October 27, 1913, Melvin Randolph Gilmore Collection, Series 3, Miscellany, Notebook, NSHS, courtesy David Grua.

12. Hassrick, *The Sioux*, 99.

13. On memory and its shortcomings, see Schulz, *Being Wrong*, 71–75. Beard's remark about Wounded Knee is from his notarized statement on March 12, 1917. Beard says he saw his wife killed in Walker, *Lakota Society*, 166–67; in Ricker, *Indian Interviews*, 222, he says it was his mother.

14. See Ricker, *Indian Interviews*, 201, for Joe's account; see Utley, *Last Days of the Sioux Nation*, 221, for the soldier's account. Ricker regarded Beard as "honest"— see MS 66, Mari Sandoz Collection, roll 42, frame 212, NSHS; but his opinion of Joe Horn Cloud was that he was unreliable at best, and maybe even a liar—see MS 66, Mari Sandoz Collection, roll 42, frames 806 and 808, NSHS.

15. Boyd Bosma interviewed Mesteth, a man who didn't experience the massacre but who helped bury the dead and knew many of the survivors. Mesteth says that White Lance, not Beard, was known for his bravery during the encounter—but he seems to confuse the brothers on other points, and at one point he says of Beard that "he was the only brave man that lived out of that Wounded Knee battle." Bosma, "An Interview with Jim Mestech [*sic*]."

16. See U.S. House of Representatives, *Sioux Indians: Wounded Knee Massacre*, 21, for survivors in 1938. McGregor, *The Wounded Knee Massacre*, 94, claims that in the mid-1930s Beard was the only survivor of both encounters. Wooden Leg, a Cheyenne, was still alive in the 1930s—see Marquis, *Wooden Leg*, 336—though he may have passed by the time McGregor wrote. For long-lived survivors, see Flood, *Lost Bird of Wounded Knee*, 45. Running Horse was profiled in an undated article found in the John Brennan Papers, Scrapbook 1, p. 242, SDSA, and a relative confirmed this in a letter to the *Rapid City Journal*, October 14, 2007, A5, about her grandmother Jessie Sword Running Horse.

17. "The Most Unforgettable Character I've Met," p. 1, DHME.

18. U.S. Department of Interior statement, June 12, 1931, box 13, "Buffalo Nickel," James Earle and Laura Gardin Fraser Papers, SUL.

19. For the story of the nickel, see "Buffalo Nickel: The Most American Coin," box 22, "Buffalo Nickel," SUL. The article first appeared in the spring 1957 issue of *News from Home* and was reprinted by *Coin World* on December 23, 1964.

20. Department of Interior Statement, June 12, 1931, SUL.

21. "Buffalo Nickel, the Most American Coin," 6.

22. See South Dakota certificate of death 287990 for details.

12. The Song of Dewey Beard

1. Hassrick, *The Sioux*, 333–38.

2. The details of Sitting Bull's burial are taken from DeWall, *The Saga of Sitting Bull's Bones*, which includes copies of many contemporary news clippings that detail the reburial.

3. Sioux Falls *Argus Leader*, February 18, 1954, Sitting Bull Memorial, Indian Files, 82nd and 83rd Congress, Clippings file 4, DWU; and *Rapid City Daily Journal*, August 20, 1954, 1.

4. "I've Got an Adult Western Secret," episode of *I've Got a Secret*, Mark Goodson/Bill Todman, CBS, October 1, 1958.

5. For the Kadlecek family's version of the burial see Kadlecek and Kadlecek, *To Kill an Eagle*.

6. For more about Chaz, see *Rapid City Journal*, "Lakota Students Document Life on Reservation," July 13, 2008, 1.

BIBLIOGRAPHY

Archives

Black Hills State University, Leland D. Case Library for Western Historical Studies, Spearfish, South Dakota

Buffalo Bill Historical Center, McCracken Library, Cody, Wyoming

Bureau of Indian Affairs, Pine Ridge, South Dakota

Dakota Wesleyan University Archives, McGovern Library, Dakota Wesleyan University, Mitchell, South Dakota

      Senator Francis H. Case Collection

David Humphreys Miller Estate, Battle of the Little Bighorn and Beyond Collection, Great Falls, Montana

Library of Congress, The American Folklife Center, Washington DC

Montana Historical Society, Helena, Montana

National Archives and Records Administration, Kansas City, Missouri

National Archives and Records Administration, Washington DC

Nebraska State Historical Society, Special Collections, Lincoln, Nebraska

Oglala Lakota College Archives, Kyle, South Dakota

      James Emery Collection

      Jeanne Smith Collection

South Dakota Historical Society, Pierre, South Dakota

      John Brennan Collection

Syracuse University Library, Special Collections Research Center, Syracuse, New York

      James Earle and Laura Gardin Fraser Papers

University of South Dakota Archives and Special Collections, Vermillion, South Dakota

University of Wisconsin Eau Claire, Eau Claire, Wisconsin

      Adin T. Newman Collection of Historical Indian Artifacts and Memorabilia

University of Wyoming, American Heritage Center, Laramie, Wyoming

Wyoming State Archives, Cheyenne, Wyoming

Published Sources

Beach, Rex E. "Wounded Knee." *Appleton's Booklovers Magazine* 7, no. 6 (June 1906): 731–36.

Billeck, William T., and Betsy Bruemmer. "Assessment of a Lock of Hair and Leggings Attributed to Sitting Bull, a Hunkpapa Sioux, in the National Museum of Natural History, Smithsonian Institution." Repatriation Office, National Museum of Natural History. 2007.

Biolsi, Thomas. *Organizing the Lakota: The Political Economy of the New Deal on the Pine Ridge and Rosebud Reservations.* Tucson: University of Arizona Press, 1992.

Black Elk. *The Sixth Grandfather: Black Elk's Teachings Given to John G. Neihardt.* Ed. Raymond J. DeMallie. Lincoln: University of Nebraska Press, 1984.

Bosma, Boyd. "An Interview with Jim Mestech." *Indian Historian* 11, no. 2 (Spring 1978): 18–21.

Bray, Kingsley M. *Crazy Horse: A Lakota Life.* Norman: University of Oklahoma Press, 2006.

Brownlow, Kevin. *The War, the West, and the Wilderness.* New York: Knopf, 1979.

Buecker, Thomas R., and R. Eli Paul, eds. *The Crazy Horse Surrender Ledger.* Lincoln: Nebraska State Historical Society, 1994.

Burnham, Philip. *Indian Country, God's Country: Native Americans and the National Parks.* Washington DC: Island Press, 2000.

———. "Last Man Standing." *South Dakota Magazine* 22, no. 2 (July–August 2006): 34–39.

———. "The True Legend of Dewey Beard." *Indian Country Today*, September 12, 19, and 26, 2005.

Clark, William Philo. *The Indian Sign Language.* Philadelphia: L. R. Hamersly, 1885.

Clow, Richmond. *The Aerial Gunnery Range, Pine Ridge Reservation, 1942–1983.* Institute of American Indian Studies. University of South Dakota. N.d.

———. "Tribal Populations in Transition." In *The Sioux in South Dakota History: A Twentieth Century Reader*, ed. Richmond Clow, 179–203. Pierre: South Dakota State Historical Society Press, 2007.

Cody, Louisa Frederici. *Memories of Buffalo Bill.* New York: Appleton, 1919.

Coleman, William S. E. *Voices of Wounded Knee.* Lincoln: University of Nebraska Press, 2000.

Cozzens, Peter, ed. *Eyewitness to the Indian Wars, 1865–1890.* Vol. 4. Mechanicsburg PA: Stackpole Books, 2004.

Daniels, Robert E. "Cultural Identities among the Oglala Sioux." In *The Modern Sioux: Social Systems and Reservation Cultures*, ed. Ethel Nurge, 198–245. Lincoln: University of Nebraska Press, 1997.

DeMallie, Raymond J. "The Sioux until 1850." In *Handbook of North American Indians*, 13, part 2:718–60. Washington DC: Smithsonian Institution, 2001.

———. "Teton." In *Handbook of North American Indians*, 13, part 2:794–820. Washington DC: Smithsonian Institution, 2001.

DeMontravel, Peter R. *A Hero to His Fighting Men: Nelson A. Miles, 1839–1925*. Kent OH: Kent State University Press, 1978.

DeWall, Rob. *The Saga of Sitting Bull's Bones*. 1984. Crazy Horse SD: Korczak's Heritage, 2006.

Dial, Scott. "Survivors Portraits." *Southwest Art* 4, no. 9 (March 1975): 64–67.

Dickson, Ephraim D., III, ed. *The Sitting Bull Surrender Census*. Pierre: South Dakota State Historical Society Press, 2010.

Dippie, Brian. "Drawn to the West." *Western Historical Quarterly* 35, no. 1 (Spring 2004): 4–26.

Dunlay, Thomas W. *Wolves for the Blue Soldiers: Indian Scouts and Auxiliaries with the United States Army, 1860–90*. 1982. Lincoln: University of Nebraska Press, 1987.

Eastman, Charles Alexander. *From the Deep Woods to Civilization*. 1916. Chicago: Lakeside Press, 2001.

"Famous Buffalo Nickel Only One of James E. Fraser's Great Works." *Coin World*, December 23, 1964, 48+.

Finerty, John F. *War-Path and Bivouac, or The Conquest of the Sioux*. 1890. Norman: University of Oklahoma Press, 1994.

Flood, Renee Sansom. *Lost Bird of Wounded Knee: Spirit of the Lakota*. New York: Scribner, 1995.

Fox, Richard Allan, Jr. *Archaeology, History, and Custer's Last Battle: The Little Bighorn Reexamined*. Norman: University of Oklahoma Press, 1993.

Frazier, Ian. *On the Rez*. New York: Farrar, Strauss, Giroux, 2010.

Frey, Rosemary L. "The Legislative History and Implementation of the Statute of Limitations 2415 Indian Claims." Master's thesis, University of South Dakota, 1986.

Fuller, Alexandra. "Life after Wounded Knee. *National Geographic* 222, no. 2 (August 2012): 30–67.

Gardner, Mark L. *Little Bighorn Battlefield National Monument*. Western National Parks Association, 2005.

Gibbon, Guy. *The Sioux: The Dakota and Lakota Nations*. Oxford: Blackwell, 2003.

Gilmore, Melvin R. "The Truth of the Wounded Knee Massacre." *American Indian Magazine* 5, no. 4 (Winter 1917): 240–52.

Glover, Vic. *Keeping Heart on Pine Ridge: Family Ties, Warrior Culture, Commodity Foods, Rez Dogs, and the Sacred*. Summertown TN: Native Voices, 2004.

Gonzalez, Mario, and Elizabeth Cook-Lynn. *The Politics of Hallowed Ground: Wounded Knee and the Struggle for Indian Sovereignty*. Urbana: University of Illinois Press, 1999.

Greene, Jerome A., ed. *Lakota and Cheyenne: Indian Views of the Great Sioux War, 1876–1877*. Norman: University of Oklahoma Press, 1994.

Hämäläinen, Pekka. *The Comanche Empire*. New Haven: Yale University Press, 2008.

———. "The Rise and Fall of Plains Indian Horse Cultures." *Journal of American History* 90, no. 3 (December 2003): 833–62.

Hank, Joy Keve. "The Story of Gus and Jessie McGaa Craven." *South Dakota Historical Collections and Report* 27 (1954).

Hardorff, Richard G., ed. *Cheyenne Memories of the Custer Fight*. 1995. Lincoln: University of Nebraska Press, 1998.

———, ed. *Hokahey! A Good Day to Die! The Indian Casualties of the Custer Fight*. 1993. Lincoln: University of Nebraska Press, 1999.

———, ed. *Indian Views of the Custer Fight: A Source Book*. Norman: University of Oklahoma Press, 2004.

Hassrick, Royal B. *The Sioux*. 1964. Norman: University of Oklahoma Press, 1977.

Hertzberg, Hazel Whitman. "Indian Rights Movement, 1887–1973." In *Handbook of North American Indians*, 4:305–23. Washington DC: Smithsonian Institution, 1988.

Holiday, Lindsay, Gabriel Bell, Robert Klein, and Michael Wells. *American Indian and Alaska Native Veterans: Lasting Contributions*. Washington DC: U.S. Department of Veterans Affairs, 2006.

Holtzmann, Roger. "A Brush with History." *South Dakota Magazine* 13, no. 6 (March/April 1998): 10–17.

Hooks, Gregory, and Chad L. Smith. "The Treadmill of Destruction: National Sacrifice Areas and Native Americans." *American Sociological Review* 69 (August 2004): 558–75.

Hyde, George E. *A Sioux Chronicle*. 1956. Norman: University of Oklahoma Press, 1980.

Jensen, Richard E. "Big Foot's Followers at Wounded Knee." *Nebraska History* 71, no. 4 (Fall 1990): 194–212.

Kadlecek, Edward, and Mabel Kadlecek. *To Kill an Eagle: Indian Views of the Last Days of Crazy Horse*. 1981. Boulder CO: Johnson Books, 2003.

Koster, John. *Custer Survivor: The End of a Myth, the Beginning of a Legend*. Palisades NY: History Publishing Company, 2010.

Lame Deer, John (Fire), and Richard Erdoes. *Lame Deer, Seeker of Visions: The Life of a Sioux Medicine Man*. New York: Simon and Schuster, 1972.

LaPointe, Ernie. *Sitting Bull: His Life and Legacy*. Salt Lake City: Gibbs Smith, 2009.

Lawrence-Lightfoot, Sara, and Jessica Hoffman Davis. *The Art and Science of Portraiture*. San Francisco: Jossey-Bass, 1997.

Lawson, Michael. "The Fractionated Estate: The Problem of American Indian Heirship." In *The Sioux in South Dakota History: A Twentieth Century Reader*, ed. Richmond Clow, 45–84. Pierre: South Dakota State Historical Society Press, 2007.

Lazarus, Edward. *Black Hills, White Justice: The Sioux Nation versus the United States, 1775 to Present*. New York: HarperCollins, 1991.

Littlefield, Daniel F., and Lonnie E. Underhill. "Renaming the American Indian: 1890–1913." *American Studies* 12, no. 2 (Fall 1971): 33–45.

Little Finger, Leonard. *Lightning and Thunder Spoke to Me*. Counting Winters Press, 2005.

MacEwan, Grant. *Sitting Bull: The Years in Canada*. Edmonton, Alberta: Hurtig, 1973.

Maddra, Sam A. *Hostiles? The Lakota Ghost Dance and Buffalo Bill's Wild West*. Norman: University of Oklahoma Press, 2006.

Mails, Thomas E. *Fools Crow*. 1979. Lincoln: University of Nebraska Press, 1990.

———. *The Mystic Warriors of the Plains*. 1972. New York: Marlowe, 1996.

Manzione, Joseph. *I Am Looking to the North for My Life: Sitting Bull, 1876–1881*. 1991. Salt Lake City: University of Utah Press, 1994.

Marquis, Thomas B., interpreter. *Wooden Leg: A Warrior Who Fought Custer*. 1931. Lincoln: University of Nebraska Press, 1957.

McGregor, James. *The Wounded Knee Massacre from the Viewpoint of the Sioux*. 1940. Rapid City S D: Fenske, 1997.

Medicine, Beatrice. *Drinking and Sobriety among the Lakota Sioux*. New York: AltaMira, 2007.

Michno, Gregory F. *Lakota Noon: The Indian Narratives of Custer's Defeat*. Missoula M T: Mountain Press, 1997.

Miller, David Humphreys. *Custer's Fall: The Native American Side of the Story*. 1957. New York: Penguin Putnam, 1992.

———. "Echoes of the Little Bighorn." *American Heritage* 22, no. 4 (June 1971): 28–39.

———. *Ghost Dance*. New York: Duell, Sloan and Pearce, 1959.

Mooney, James. *The Ghost-Dance Religion and the Sioux Outbreak of 1890*. 1896. Lincoln: University of Nebraska Press, 1991.

Moses, L. G. *Wild West Shows and the Images of American Indians, 1883–1933*. Albuquerque: University of New Mexico Press, 1996.

Muller, Dan. *My Life with Buffalo Bill*. Chicago: Reilly and Lee, 1948.

Neihardt, John G. *Black Elk Speaks: Being a Life Story of a Holy Man of the Oglala Sioux*. 1932. Lincoln: University of Nebraska Press, 2004.

Nerburn, Kent. *Neither Wolf nor Dog: On Forgotten Roads with an Indian Elder*. New World Library, 2002.

Papandrea, Ron. *They Never Surrendered: The Lakota Sioux Band That Stayed in Canada*. LaVergne T N: Lightning Source, 2009.

Paul, Andrea I. "Buffalo Bill and Wounded Knee: The Movie." *Nebraska History* 71, no. 4 (Fall 1990): 182–90.

Penman, Sarah, ed. *Honor the Grandmothers: Dakota and Lakota Women Tell Their Stories*. St. Paul: Minnesota Historical Society Press, 2000.

Pennanen, Gary. "Sitting Bull: Indian without a Country." *Canadian Historical Review* 51, no. 2 (June 1970): 123–40.

Peterson, Frances Y. "Dewey Iron Hail." *Frontier Times* 35, no. 4 (Fall 1961): 37–38.

Peterson, Nancy M. "Buffalo Bill's Lost Legacy." *American History*, October 2003, 51–80.

Powers, Thomas. *The Killing of Crazy Horse*. New York: Knopf, 2010.

Price, Catherine. *The Oglala People, 1841–1879: A Political History*. Lincoln: University of Nebraska Press, 1996.

Prucha, Francis Paul. *The Great Father: The United States Government and the American Indians*. Abridged ed. Lincoln: University of Nebraska Press, 1986.

Red Shirt, Delphine. *Turtle Lung Woman's Granddaughter*. Lincoln: University of Nebraska Press, 2002.

Reinhardt, Akim D. *Ruling Pine Ridge: Oglala Lakota Politics from the IRA to Wounded Knee*. Lubbock: Texas Tech Press, 2007.

Ricker, Eli S. *The Indian Interviews of Eli Ricker, 1903–1919: Voices of the American West*. Vol. 1. Ed. Richard Jensen. Lincoln: University of Nebraska Press, 2005.

Robertson, Paul. *The Power of the Land: Identity, Ethnicity, and Class among the Oglala Lakota*. New York: Routledge, 2002.

Rollyson, Carl. *Biography: A User's Guide*. Chicago: Ivan Dee, 2008.

Ruby, Robert H. *A Doctor among the Oglala Sioux Tribe: The Letters of Robert H. Ruby, 1953–1954*. Lincoln: University of Nebraska Press, 2010.

Sandoz, Marie. *Crazy Horse: The Strange Man of the Oglalas*. 1942. Lincoln: University of Nebraska Press, 2004.

Schulz, Kathryn. *Being Wrong: Adventures in the Margin of Error*. New York: Harper Collins, 2010.

Southerton, Don. "James R. Walker's Campaign against Tuberculosis on the Pine Ridge Reservation." In *The Sioux in South Dakota History: A Twentieth-Century Reader*, ed. Richmond Clow, 141–56. Pierre: South Dakota State Historical Society Press, 2007.

Standing Bear, Luther. *Land of the Spotted Eagle*. 1933. Lincoln: University of Nebraska Press, 1978.

———. *My People the Sioux*. 1928. Lincoln: University of Nebraska Press, 1975.

Starita, Joe. *The Dull Knifes of Pine Ridge: A Lakota Odyssey*. 1995. Lincoln: University of Nebraska Press, 2002.

Tomkins, William. *Indian Sign Language*. New York: Dover, 1969.

U.S. House of Representatives. *Complaint of the Pine Ridge Sioux. Hearings before the Committee on Indian Affairs*. 66th Congress, 2nd session. April 6, 1920.

———. *Sioux Indians: Wounded Knee Massacre. Hearings before the Subcommittee on Indian Affairs*. 75th Congress, 3rd session. H.R. 2535. March 7 and May 12, 1938.

———. *Sioux Indian Tribes: North and South Dakota. Hearings before the Subcommittee on Indian Affairs of the Committee on Interior and Insular Affairs*. 84th Congress, 1st session. H.R. 30. September 9, 10, and 12, 1955.

Utley, Robert M. *The Lance and the Shield: The Life and Times of Sitting Bull*. 1993. New York: Ballantine, 1994.

———. *The Last Days of the Sioux Nation*. New Haven: Yale University Press, 1963.

———. "Wounded Knee and Other Dark Images: The West of Dewey Horn Cloud." *The American West: The Magazine of Western History* 16, no. 3 (May/June, 1979): 4–11.

Vecsey, Christopher. "A Century of Lakota Sioux Catholicism at Pine Ridge." In *Religious Diversity and American History: Studies in Traditions and Cultures*, ed. Walter H. Conser Jr. and Sumner B. Twiss, 262–95. Athens: University of Georgia Press, 1997.

Walker, James R. *Lakota Belief and Ritual*. Ed. Raymond J. DeMallie. 1980. Lincoln: University of Nebraska Press, 1991.

———. *Lakota Society*. Ed. Raymond J. DeMallie. 1982. Lincoln: University of Nebraska Press, 1992.

Walsh, Richard J. *The Making of Buffalo Bill: A Study in Heroics*. Indianapolis: Bobbs-Merrill, 1928.

Wayne, Donald. "The Sioux." *Holiday*, September 1948, 99+.

White, Richard. "The Winning of the West: The Expansion of the Western Sioux in the Eighteenth and Nineteenth Centuries." *Journal of American History* 65, no. 2 (September 1978): 319–43.

White Hat, Albert, Sr. *Life's Journey—Zuya: Oral Teachings from the Rosebud*. Salt Lake City: University of Utah Press, 2012.

Wilson, Raymond. *Ohiyesa: Charles Eastman, Santee Sioux*. Urbana: University of Illinois Press, 1983.

Wissler, Clark. "Societies and Ceremonial Associations in the Oglala Division of the Teton Dakota." *Anthropological Papers of the American Museum of Natural History*. New York, 1912.

INDEX

Afraid of Enemy, Silas, 34

Afraid of the Enemy, 73, 104

akicita (Lakota police), 109

Aplan, Jim, 40

Apple, Francis, Sr.: author's first meeting with, 9–12; and Black Hills story, 126–28; censure of, 138; death of, 200; and Dewey Beard's advice for survival, 130; and Dewey Beard's death, 176; as grandson of Daniel White Lance, 9; and Grey Horse Society dance, 159–60; and Korean War, 22; military service of, 129–30; and Paoli church controversy, 138, 224n39; religious background of, 10; and song of Dewey Beard, 198–200; and songs, 11; and St. Stephens, 195; surname of, 126; on Wounded Knee, 129, 200

Apple, Freda, 131, 200

Arnold, H. H., 148

Bailey, James, 89

Baldwin, Frank, 82, 100

Ball, Suzan, 48, 162

Battles of Chief Pontiac (movie), 161–62

Beard, Alice Lone Bear, xvi, 88, 137, 218n31; allotment of, 122; dress of, 179–80; and English language, 170; and granddaughter's elopement, 114; and gunnery range compensation,

178; and hospital, 171; and husband's funeral, 176, 177; and loans, 171; marriage of, 98, 183; and movies, 162; teaching of, 164, 165; traveling with, 171; writing of, 169

Beard, Carrie, 124, 132, 137, 153, 200

Beard, Dewey: account of Little Bighorn battle by, 31–34; account of Wounded Knee by, 72–78, 213n21, 214n31, 214n33; and adoption of David Miller, 37; age of, 1; and allotment, 121–22, 128, 222n11; birth of, 2, 4; and Black Hills, 43; and censuses, 211n17; children of, 175, 223n32, 228n1; and churches, 135–36; and citizenship, 192; and common-law marriage to Chief Woman, 97, 98; and compensation for gunnery range allotment, 155, 156, 178; and confusion with Iron Tail, 187–88; on Crazy Horse and Sitting Bull, 39; criticism of *Indian Wars* by, 104, 219n45; death certificate of, 191–92, 216n1, 228n3; and death of Custer, 32, 41; and elopement of granddaughter, 114; and enrollment at Pine Ridge, 117; and filming of *Sitting Bull*, 196; genealogy of, 3, 7, 55; as Ghost Dancer, 64; grave of, 197–98; health of, 122; and Hollywood, 160–63; and horses, 10, 11, 21, 33, 52, 124–25, 152, 222n19; and Hotchkiss